MW01379440

E$caping Oz

Protecting your wealth during the financial crisis

JIM MOSQUERA

Mosquera, Jaime (Jim) Jr.
Escaping Oz: Protecting your wealth during the financial crisis
ISBN 1453891218
EAN-13 9781453891216

This publication intends to provide accurate and authoritative information in regard to the subject matter covered. If professional advice is needed to execute the strategies detailed, the services of a competent professional should be sought.

This book has been composed in Palatino Linotype and Bookman Old Style for the main text, and Tahoma for headings.

Printed in the United States of America

For my son and all our children.

Contents

Prologue		ix
Introduction		3
PART I	THE JOURNEY	
Chapter 1	Origin of Our Problem	15
Chapter 2	Inflation	47
Chapter 3	Deflation	55
Chapter 4	Human Behavior	79
PART II	THE CRISIS	
Chapter 5	How did we get into the crisis?	123
Chapter 6	Government Action	137
Chapter 7	Is Government a Good Borrower?	155
Chapter 8	Speculative Bubbles	169

Continued on next page

PART III	PREPARING OUR ESCAPE	
Chapter 9	Investor Psychology	187
Chapter 10	Bank Investing	201
Chapter 11	Real Estate Investing	217
Chapter 12	Bond Investing	233
Chapter 13	Stock Investing	251
Chapter 14	Retirement Accounts	269
Chapter 15	Money Investing	277
Chapter 16	Alternative Investments	287
Chapter 17	Investor Types & Model Portfolios	293
Chapter 18	Planning for the Future	303
	Epilogue	313
Appendix A	Inflation Example	321
Appendix B	Bubble Dramatization	329
Appendix C	Understanding Bonds	331
Appendix D	Economic & Investment Laws	335
	List of Figures & Credits	339
	References	349
	Acknowledgement	363

Prologue

For years, I sensed that things did not feel quite right. I remember my cousin entertaining employment at a company called Household Finance Corporation (HFC) in the late 1980s. HFC was probably one of the first companies to provide consumer loans under an installment plan – the borrower could pay the loan in monthly installments rather than a future lump sum. It was the epitome of credit creation. Someone needed money for consumption loans and this company was eager to offer them at high rates of interest. The lending tactics seemed predatory to me and to attorneys general in the U.S. causing the company to settle a suit for millions in 2002. I coined the expression "The Wonderful World of Credit".

Credit seemed like magic to me. I was not raised to embrace credit. I don't recall my family having anything other than a house payment. If you could not afford something, you saved for it and then you bought it. Not many of my relatives in Panama owned a dwelling, they rented. They could not make a large down payment and there were not as many lenders willing to extend credit for 30 years, something we take for granted today. I remember a next-door neighbor who was from South

Korea telling me that her family did not believe in credit even for a house. This is quite different from today where our culture steers people towards home ownership. Money is not a problem for us since there is always a lender eager for you to sign on the dotted line.

When I left graduate school and became a working stiff, I remember how enthusiastic I was to purchase my first car. It was a blue Toyota Supra, with 200 horsepower and sleek lines - the sports car of my dreams. Granted, I was single and had no obligations or debt but my dad questioned me about how much I spent on that car. After discount, the car cost $16,000. My starting salary in my new job was $33,150. My dad asked me how I felt about spending nearly half my salary on a car. I really did not think twice about it since I had no debt and I was sharing a townhouse with two other guys, making my car payment quite manageable. My dad also reminded me that I really was not making $33,150 but something far less thanks to taxes. Heck, I spent more than half my annual salary on that car!

Today, I cannot imagine spending half my annual salary on a car even if I were in the same circumstance. Though I was raised to think about saving money, the allure of that brand new sports car was too much to resist. I could buy the car only because a lender was willing to give me money. The lender had <u>confidence</u> that I would pay off the loan in three years and I had the <u>confidence</u> that I could as well. Three years later, I owned the car outright but was shocked to learn the vehicle was worth about 55% of its original value.

Why did I underline the word "confidence" in the previous paragraph? Confidence was a feature of our economy allowing lenders to lend and borrowers to borrow. The lending is credit and the borrowing is debt. In my example, I wanted the car and a bank lent me the money. I had no other financial obligations and made a good salary. It really was a slam-dunk decision for the bank's lending officer.

Our economy became overly dependent on lending and borrowing. When that was insufficient, our financial system devised new ways of lending more. Politicians, of course, had to get involved and they did what they could to facilitate more borrowing and lending. The public could not get enough, so they became more risky in their borrowing practices.

We find ourselves, not just as a nation, but also as a world economy in truly uncharted waters. Christopher Columbus had nothing on us. One of my favorite subjects in college was money and banking. I learned about both but had no idea of the destructive capability of excessive credit creation. Fortunately, I became acquainted with the Austrian economists. They conclude that when an economy creates excessive credit, it deflates like a balloon. The more credit the bigger the balloon, the bigger the balloon the more air that can come out. I don't think any economist, government official or financial analyst can argue that the amount of credit generated in our world economy is beyond imagination. An Austrian economist would expect a whole lot of air to come out of that balloon.

Letting air out of the balloon is the only way to keep it from popping. The market let some of the air out but governments put more air in. If the balloon pops, then we face something for which we have no manual. If we let the air out, it will be painful but at least we will still have a balloon.

The deflating balloon is a metaphor for the credit deflation that I anticipate in our economy. Signs are already evident in the housing market. Society has grown so accustomed to having a large balloon that we really don't have a plan for living with a smaller one. Not only can we live with a smaller one, we have done so before.

Most of what I will propose will be contrary to what you have heard or read. I realize that going against conventional wisdom is a risky approach. I can see what's going to happen to the balloon and it's not pretty. That does not mean my forecast is a 100% guarantee. I *can* guarantee the balloon has never been anywhere close to this size – this is a problem on an unimaginable scale. While the things may not unfold as I describe them, the economy <u>will</u> deal with the size of the balloon. Even if I am 100% wrong, you are unlikely to get hurt financially. The worse case scenario is that you earn less on your investments and wealth plan than otherwise. The best-case scenario allows you to preserve your family's wealth and positions you to survive and perhaps prosper.

While I no doubt have a strong interest in selling copies of this book, there are also broader goals at hand. The direction of our country's future lies in the balance. Please consider how your financial health will affect the nation as a whole.

Jim Mosquera, November 2010

E$caping Oz

Introduction

Financial Land of Oz

In the movie *The Wizard of Oz*, twelve-year-old Dorothy Gale sees her new landscape and remarks to her dog Toto, "We're not in Kansas anymore." Our economy is nowhere near Kansas either. We didn't get to Oz suddenly in a tornado – we got here on a burro. The yellow brick road to the Emerald City will lead us to the Wizard who will help us get home. The Wizard is supposed to be a supernatural being standing tall and strong capable of giving us what we wanted. When Toto pulls back the curtain, the Wizard we will ultimately find is someone insignificant who created this false image of omnipotence. All along, we felt we had to trust the Wizard, but the Wizard will ultimately not have the answer. We will have to be resourceful and find our own way home. Lucky for us, we can find our way home but it will require considerable work on our part. The Wicked Witch of the West will be plotting to steal our ruby slippers and setting other traps so we have to keep an eye out. We can melt this Wicked Witch with our economic fountain of knowledge. Our journey will have us questioning our minds, our hearts, and our courage but we will realize that we have what it takes to leave Oz and get back home.

In order to leave the Land of Oz, we need to figure out how

we arrived. Retracing our steps will not be easy. It will be much more painful returning home than it was getting to Oz.

Our journey to Oz began long ago when we started manipulating the most important economic good, money. Yes, money is an economic good though society has forgotten. The definition of money changed. We forgot how to produce and save. We became addicted to credit. The wealth that so many thought they had was illusory. For many people that realization began in 2007 when the stock and real estate markets were crushed like the Wicked Witch of the East. Investors found out that wealth was not the perceived equity in a home nor was it the paper gains in the stock market.

Many feel, and simply are, poorer. Here are ten sobering statistics about the Financial Land of Oz:

1. 61% of Americans live paycheck-to-paycheck.

2. 36% save nothing for retirement.

3. 43% have less than $10,000 saved for retirement.

4. In the last year ¼ of American workers postponed retirement.

5. Personal bankruptcy filings have been over 1 million for 11 of the last 15 years despite statistics like GDP indicating the economy grew for all but 2-3 of those years.

6. Only the top 5% of households earned enough income to match housing price increases since 1975.

7. Banks own a greater share of residential housing net worth than all Americans put together. Mortgage debt exceeds home equity by multiple trillions of dollars.

8. The bottom 50 percent of income earners in the United States now collectively own less than 1 percent of the nation's wealth.

9. The average Federal worker earns 60% more than his counterpart in the private sector.

10. 40 million Americans rely on food stamps and 21% of children in the U.S. live below the poverty line.

For many Americans, the feeling of being poorer began with the roof over their head. As one of the statistics indicated, banks own a greater share of housing net worth than homeowners themselves do. While the residential real estate market has experienced pronounced declines, greater declines lie ahead. The sub-prime market was the first catalyst for this decline and the wave of resetting - less than prime - Alt-A loans will provide fuel for the next price collapse. This decline should push more banks to the brink of insolvency.

The stock market made its high in 2007 before experiencing a dramatic fall. Investors could not get over the shock of a market that was supposed to head to Dow 40,000. The rally beginning in March 2009 reignited hope. Hope is all this market has.

Government came to the rescue by trying to spend money the public was otherwise saving. Spending reached such a level that in fiscal 2009, expenditures in Medicare, Medicaid, Social Security, and other mandatory programs were *greater* than Federal receipts. Government had to borrow just to cover the mandatory spending deficit! Deficits ballooned to the point where discussion of a trillion plus dollar shortfall rolled off the tongue with ease. The current administration has no qualms about maintaining this rate of spending in the near future. Such spending has no historical precedent. It is ironic that the United States used to chastise other countries for reckless spending.

The Federal Reserve came to the rescue as well by taking on assets dragging down the banking system. Their action increased the amount of money banks had in their coffers. The money made available in the economy, by this action alone, increased by well over a trillion dollars. However, the money has not found its way into the economy since banks have not lent it.

With trillion dollar government deficits and trillion plus injections of money in the economy, we should be in the middle of a massive hyperinflation, right? That is conventional wisdom; add money to the economy and you should have inflation. Despite government and Fed action, there is no massive inflation. In fact, we have many signs of deflation.

Most of us have no idea what deflation is – do you? Deflation is a reduction in the amount of outstanding money and credit. In a credit-based society, the reduction of credit is fatal to expansion and the continuing rise of prices. Banks become more hesitant to lend. Consumers saturated with debt are unwilling to assume any more. The deflation seen thus far in our economy is a sign of things to come.

Unfortunately, economic realities cannot be repealed. Economies in our time expand and contract resulting from credit cycles and social mood. Attempting to fight these cycles only prolongs the eventual outcome.

Future America

America, your future is threatened. These are not words I say lightly. The nation's deteriorating financial condition, both public and private places its welfare in great peril. I am talking about our standard of living, our way of life. You picked up this book for a reason. Maybe you feel nothing can be done and simply want a way to protect your family's wealth. Maybe you want to be part of a solution. Both are necessary for financial health and security.

INTRODUCTION

Before we try to lay the finger on any one thing that got us in this financial mess, we need to understand how we got here. Trust me; this understanding is of the utmost importance. You wouldn't want your doctor operating on you unless he understood the human body. You don't learn calculus before algebra. The approaches presented will make little sense without this understanding.

The human condition includes emotion. Emotion permeates our society and our economy. That emotion leads to trends and sometimes those trends are quite pronounced. Pronounced trends lead to speculative bubbles. Show me a financial panic and I will show you a speculative bubble preceding it. Not just individuals but governments play into the speculation.

When you speculate, it is with your own or family's money. When governments speculate it is also with your family's money. This is something people overlook. Government produces nothing and has no money of its own; they are custodians for our money. Government is only what the people allow it to be. Unfortunately, we the people allowed government to become an unrecognizable leviathan. Politicians aided the growth of the leviathan by pandering to *we the people*.

I constantly hear politicians boast about how they create jobs. Let me say this very clearly. Politicians do not create jobs. The only things politicians can do is take money and spend it, also known as fiscal spending. The word "fiscal" comes from the Latin "fiscus" which described a basket used to collect revenues for the Roman emperor. Our politicians demanded a larger basket so they could spend more and we gave it to them. When the basket was still not large enough, they added more baskets. The next time you hear a politician claiming they created a job, roll your eyes.

I don't want to diminish the role of government in our society. We need government but we don't need them to do so much. Government has two important roles in our society and we will discuss those roles. We the people also need to quit asking government to do so much. Our government's fiscal policy is a reflection of our own financial habits. We asked government to do more but we were unwilling to give them the money to do it. In the 1980s, the matter of cutting taxes while increasing spending became political dogma. Government got so good at spending that we are in a long-term trend where personal income comes less from private sources and more from government transfer programs or government salaries. Individually we did the same as government; we spent more but only through debt. The culture of debt replaced the culture of thrift. Why save money for something you really wanted when you could borrow.

We lived in self-indulgent times. Remember Gordon Gekko in the movie *Wall Street*? "Greed is good." Marketing slogans in the early 1980s said, "You can have it all." Consumerism emerged with its own doctrines like "bigger is better", "faster is better", "more is better". Consumerism by itself is not a bad thing. Economically we should strive for a better outcome. If we produce more we can consume more. Our problem emerged when we began to consume more without producing more. The only way to make that happen was to borrow from the future to consume now.

All of this borrowing made the economy and our financial system more complex. Imagine a group of people sitting in a circle throwing a ball of yarn back and forth. When the yarn ball is completely unwound, you end up with a complex pattern of threads spanning the diameter of the circle. If I asked you to pull up on a single thread, could you do it without moving another thread? Not likely. This is our economy. Each of those threads affects us personally. Pull on the retirement thread and you move health care. Pull on the vacation spending thread and you move the one sending your kids to summer camp. Pull on the tax thread and you move spending on highways and bridges.

We will no longer have the ability to make single-threaded decisions. One decision will at least affect another.

Those decisions are already raising questions about how you might fare economically in the future. If you are in your 20s, you are probably concerned about the debt you accumulated going to the university that was supposed to give you that choice job. If you don't have a job, you were reacquainted with family and are living in your old room. If you are in your 30s, you might be thinking about how you are spending money on your kids. Will they go to private school? Can they go to sports camps? People in their 40s are worried about having to pay for their kids' higher education. Have I saved enough for retirement? People in their 50s and 60s may be postponing retirement since they have nary enough saved.

You will have to be personally responsible for your economic recovery. There is a television commercial where a restaurant patron asks a bunch of questions about things on the menu and then segues to something completely unrelated to dinner. The commercial continues with the person in front of their doctor. After explaining a few things, the doctor asks if there are any questions. You can hear a pin drop. You cannot be silent in pursuing your economic recovery. Ask questions. Ask your financial planner. Ask your elected officials. Ask your school. Ask your banker. If you are not satisfied with an answer, ask more questions.

Economic problems, if severe enough, can also bring social upheaval. This could be a good thing or a bad thing. Some of the worst demagogues in recent memory preyed on the ignorance of the masses. Don't let a demagogue prey on ignorance. These demagogues may pretend to be the Wizard but we know there is no such thing. In the worst case, they may be nothing more than the Wicked Witch of the West posing as a friend. At best, they are just someone pulling levers behind a curtain making the problem worse.

Even if no demagogue appears, you will have a government navigating unchartered waters. Under these conditions, governments can become more draconian. They can enact new rules and regulations. They may have to quell civil unrest. You need to understand why these issues are so important or you will face a more strict government.

We can return home to Kansas. Kansas will be a different place than it was before but it will still be home. If we sharpen our minds, strengthen our hearts, and build our courage we can get back home without the Wizard's help.

Layout of Book

Part I of this book gives you a background on our crisis – why we have a financial balloon in the first place. I realize not everyone may have an interest in reading the whys behind our crisis but I implore you to read Part I anyway. Consider Part I to be all about the fundamentals. Part I will allow you to gather the necessary tools in order to learn to think for yourself. You will need that skill in the days ahead particularly in regards to your money. For too long our society has been on autopilot and we did not take notice of what was happening.

Part II discusses our economic crisis. The fundamentals we learned about in Part I led to the decisions that ultimately led to the crisis. After we got into the crisis, our Wizards tried to figure out how to get out of it. Can the Wizards really help?

Part III uses the information from Parts I and II to suggest a course of action for investments and wealth preservation. Part III also explores how most investors make decisions and who you are as an investor. Now more than ever, it is important to preserve your wealth rather than swinging for the fences and hitting a home run. This is your path to Kansas.

I provide a summary of the important points explored at the end of most chapters. For those with an interest in chapter skimming this is an alternate approach to understanding the book's content.

PART I

THE JOURNEY

Part I provides the foundational knowledge needed to understand our economic and financial problems. Many of our problems came because we allowed profound changes to occur without fully understanding their implications.

What is the one thing that makes economic and financial transactions possible? It's money. Discussing money is crucial if you are to build a foundation of wealth preservation for your family. We can talk about money all we want but we also need to understand how everyone's behavior contributes to economic decisions. A human behavior pattern ultimately affects how our economic and financial trends develop. You will need the foundation of Part I to have meaningful dialogue with others on how to shape this country's future, a future that hinges so much on economic and financial health.

Chapter 1
Origin of Our Problems

How do you figure out the source of our problems when there are so many contributors? Even though we got to Oz very slowly, what fueled our arrival? Good detectives look for the source through a root cause analysis (RCA). RCA is a formal term used to describe a process to arrive at the source of a problem with the intent of eliminating the cause or at least mitigating the chances of it occurring. RCA tells the tale of how and why a problem occurred. The missteps leading to our current economic problems were numerous and have a checkered history. Some of the missteps resulted from treating symptoms rather than addressing the problem.

Have you ever tried to play home repair technician? Jeff fancies himself as being handy around the house. He has a toilet that flushes inadequately. At times, it seems there is not enough water to do the job. Jeff gets lazy at first and has a gallon container next to the sink that he uses to pour water in the tank or the bowl to complete the job manually. He then decides it must be something with the floater ball and replaces it. That does not work. Jeff then thinks it must be the toilet itself and replaces it. Finally, he becomes convinced it is the valve providing the feed to the toilet tank and replaces it. Nothing seems to work.

Jeff's friend, Kristen, comes over and asks a few questions. Kristen wonders if there is a particular time of the day when the toilet seems to have this problem. Jeff says that it occurs in the morning after he wakes up. Kristen notices his in-ground sprinkler system and asks when it was installed. The problems with the toilet started around the same time. After heading to the basement, Kristen determines that for whatever reason, the company installing the sprinkler system tapped into the same water feed as that for the culprit toilet. When the sprinkler system came on in the morning it reduced the flow to the toilet, so after the first person used it, it became a problem for the next person. The next day Jeff calls a plumber to tap a different feed for the sprinkler.

Kristen teases Jeff for the next week. For all his supposed mastery of home repair, he was unable to diagnose the toilet problem. All Jeff did was work around the problem until Kristen identified what was wrong. The story of our problems is one fraught with missteps and symptom treating. We can find the root cause if we go back in time and go back to the basics.

Why Do We Need Money?

Without money, people satisfy themselves through direct exchange, or bartering. You have something I want and I have something you want. These mutual desires are the double coincidence of wants. Double coincidence of wants means that in any barter transaction two parties must have coincident desires for what the other has. In order for bartering to work, you must be able to exchange one item for another or subdivide a barter item. Indivisibilities refer to barter items that cannot be broken down into smaller pieces.

When I was a child, my friend Tommy traded his Schwinn bicycle with another boy named Teddy for a 100-card Topps baseball set. The Topps set had 90 players playing in the big leagues and 10 top rookies making their debut that season. I had about half of the 90 players and none of the rookies in my own baseball card collection. Tommy's parents scolded him for trading away the bike they had bought him for his birthday. I had an extra Schwinn. Tommy asked if he could trade the card set to me for my extra bicycle. Tommy thought it was a fair trade since he made the same exchange recently with Teddy. It made sense to me as well. The problem was I did not need the whole 100-card set; I only wanted about half the set. I couldn't take my bike, divide it in two, and give part of it to Tommy. He wanted the whole bike.

While Tommy and I had a double coincidence of wants (we both wanted what the other had), we had the problem of indivisibility. My bike could not be broken into smaller pieces and still be functional (Figure 1-1). We solved our problem when Tommy's parents paid me $20 for my Schwinn and I used the money to buy only the baseball cards I really wanted.

"My bike could not be broken into smaller pieces and still be functional."

Figure 1-1
Indivisible Bike

Operating in a barter economy presents many limitations that would easily paralyze commerce. Money and credit are those instruments that grease the wheels of commerce and make our economic transactions possible. Money is no different from the bike or the set of baseball cards – it is an economic good. Tommy's parents bartered money for another economic good, the Schwinn.

Money is the mechanism that addresses the limitation of double coincidence of wants and indivisibilities. It addresses the double coincidence of wants since an individual need not worry about what the other party desires. Likewise, the divisibility of money removes the barrier of having to consider subdividing a barter item where it is not feasible to do so - trying to divide the Schwinn bike. Our money is divisible since we have several denominations of paper money ($1, $5, $10, $20, $50, $100) and several denominations of coin money, which are fractions of a dollar.

In the early stages of an economy, any number of economic goods might be used as money. Eventually one type of widely available money will displace others. The shift is progressive until that money becomes the sole medium of exchange. Everyone must agree to the value of money. This value can be an actual representation of wealth or government can decree it. Legal tender is money by government decree – government tells you what it is worth regardless of how much it may actually be worth. Consider legal tender a misstep in our RCA.

Money & Wealth

What is money? Isn't it what you have in your wallet? What about what you have in a checking or savings account? Do you consider a 401(k) account money? Is any of this wealth? Is the equity in your home money or wealth?

The online Webster's dictionary defines money as,

> "*Something generally accepted as a medium of exchange, a measure of value, or a means of payment.*"

Webster's dictionary from 1968 says money is,

> "*Standard pieces of gold, silver, copper, nickel etc. stamped by government authority and used as a medium of exchange and a measure of value.*"

The Webster definition from 1968 is vastly different from the one today. Today's definition says nothing of gold or silver stamped by government authority. Why did the definition of money change so much? Does it really matter?

What is wealth? Is it something you possess? The forty-plus year-old Webster's text says wealth is "*much money or property.*" Adam Smith in his work, *The Wealth of Nations*, said that wealth was "*the annual produce of the land and labour of the society.*" I define wealth as a material item produced by human effort having exchange value. Exchange value means we can trade it or substitute it for something else. Consider wealth an accumulation of economic goods. Tommy's bike and my baseball cards were wealth but that did not make Tommy and me wealthy.

I define money as a medium of exchange, that is a unit of account (something measurable), and a direct store or representation of wealth. Money by itself is not wealth but a medium used for the exchange of wealth. If we use money for the exchange of wealth, it *should* represent wealth. My definition is more compatible with Webster's from 1968 since I stipulate that money has to represent wealth.

When Tommy's parents gave me twenty dollars of money for the Schwinn, I traded wealth (my bike) for something I trusted that represented wealth (the twenty dollars). I made the Schwinn for money exchange since ultimately I wanted the baseball cards and needed money to exchange for the cards. Trading half of a bike for the cards was not feasible.

Using the *modern* definition of money, bank accounts, 401(k) accounts, and the green bills in your wallet are money. The equity in your house is not directly money, but a lender can help you turn it into money. Using my definition, the bank accounts and the rest are not money since our money does not represent wealth. We exchange money for wealth in our economy but money does not truly represent wealth according to Webster's 1968 definition. Our paper money tells us what our money really is., "legal tender for all debts public and private."

Most of the economy's money does not look like the paper in your wallet but electronic entries called credit. The new definition of money is another misstep on our journey to identifying the root cause of our economic problems.

Money Evolution Early History

History shows us that confidence and wealth backing are the keys for a successful money system. For the majority of human history, tangible economic goods such as gold, silver, copper, brass and seashells formed the basis of money. The initial usage of paper money was likely in China around the time of the Tang dynasty in the ninth century. The Chinese government thought it prudent to issue this paper to relieve the weight burden of precious metal coin transport. Though the paper was not sanctioned by government for the payment of debt (i.e. legal tender), people accepted it. Acceptance continued until the government began to issue more paper money in relation to the existing coin stock. The government altered the wealth component of the money since there was more paper circulating without an equal amount of coins to back it.

Paper money survived for over 500 years in China. In 1455, paper money disappeared from China and did not reemerge for several hundred years. The increased issuance of paper money relative to the coin stock was an early example of what we call inflation. The Chinese government misstep reflects what can happen to the public's trust in paper with a loss of confidence in the system.

How many bikes could Tommy's parents have bought if they could make their own paper money? How many cards could I have bought if I had the same capability? If Tommy's parents could make their own paper money, what would happen if they got in a bidding war with another set of parents for my Schwinn?

Money in the Americas

In the history of the Americas, economic goods like cacao beans, seashells, and even feathers served as money (Figure 1-2). Modern forms of money emerged when Spain introduced its gold and silver coins into the New World. You could discern the value of a coin often times by its size. An eight-unit silver coin was bigger than the four-unit coin and so on (Figure 1-3). When regions of the Americas achieved their independence from Spain, they sought to have their own sovereign currency but did not have the means to fabricate coinage.

The solution for a young country like Costa Rica was to take an existing Spanish coin and use a die to stamp a mark over the top of it. This approach may seem to be an awkward attempt to create money though it was quite brilliant in two respects. First, placing a stamp on an existing coin was inexpensive. Perhaps most importantly, Costa Rica took an already accepted form of money as its own and eliminated any doubt of its legitimacy. The public had confidence the new currency had real gold or silver and that government could not simply create a bunch of it at will.

8 reales, 1759
Guatemala

Figure 1-2
Cacao Beans = Money

4 reales, 1768
Guatemala

2 reales, 1759
México

Figure 1-3
Coin value
based on size

Money During the Colonial Era

At one point in the history of the United States, gold and silver coins were also money. For reasons of practicality and safety, people stored coins in depositories issuing certificates redeemable for the coins. The depositories also charged a fee for storage. The public accepted these certificates as money and they served as payment for goods and services and for repayment of debt. Whoever presented certificates at the depository was entitled to the stated amount of gold or silver on the certificate.

The owners of these depositories recognized that at any point in time, the amount of metal on deposit was more than adequate to pay people redeeming certificates. This is perfectly logical since as long as the depositors and certificate users had confidence in the existence of gold or silver in the depository, there was no need to withdraw the physical metal. The owners of the depositories used this to their advantage. They began to issue certificates well in excess of gold and silver deposits. This additional issuance of certificates is another example of what we call inflation. More certificates were pursuing the same amount of goods and services in the economy. Each certificate had less purchasing power than before.

By issuing more certificates, the depository created no additional wealth - there was just more paper in circulation. Issuing more money in an economy does not make the economy wealthier. The market responds to the additional certificates through price increases on economic goods.

The depositories mentioned represent another culprit in the missteps surrounding our money. Like the previous Chinese example, the depositories found an easy way to create inflation. Their actions paved the way for government to do the same thing later.

Money During the War for Independence

During the American Revolutionary War, the new country needed vast sums of money to fight the British. One way of acquiring this money was to raise taxes though the colonists were in no mood for taxation given their beef with the British. Another method was to create money called the Continental Dollar (Figure 1-4). This money was credit extended to the government for buying goods and services. The colonists provided goods and services to the government to fight the war and the government paid people with Continentals instead of gold or silver. The Continentals were redeemable for Spanish milled dollars or the equivalent amount of gold since the Spanish dollar represented gold. Since no additional wealth, in the form of gold, appeared in the colonies to back the new Continentals, instant inflation occurred. This was inflation since the supply of Continentals increased relative to the supply gold.

The issuance of Continentals gave the government power to fight a war without having to pay for it directly. Government transferred the cost of war to the colonists indirectly through inflation. Throughout history, it has always been politically expedient for government to create money rather than tax its constituents. The continuation of this misstep carries grave implications today. How many wars would we fight if each household had to bear a direct tax?

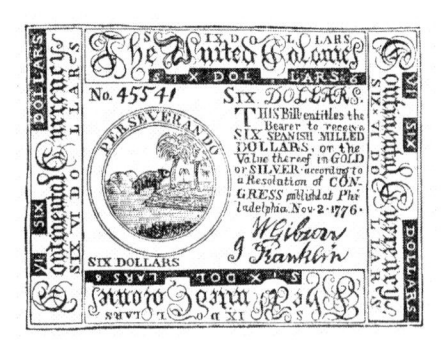

Figure 1-4
Continental Currency

Six years after the Continentals came into existence, the exchange rate was 146 Continentals to one Spanish dollar based on gold and 500 Continentals to a Spanish dollar based on silver (Figure 1-5). During those six years, what were you better off holding, Continentals or gold/silver? Anyone realizing what was occurring with the purchasing power of a Continental would have rid himself or herself of it before it lost value. This gives rise to something known as Gresham's Law.

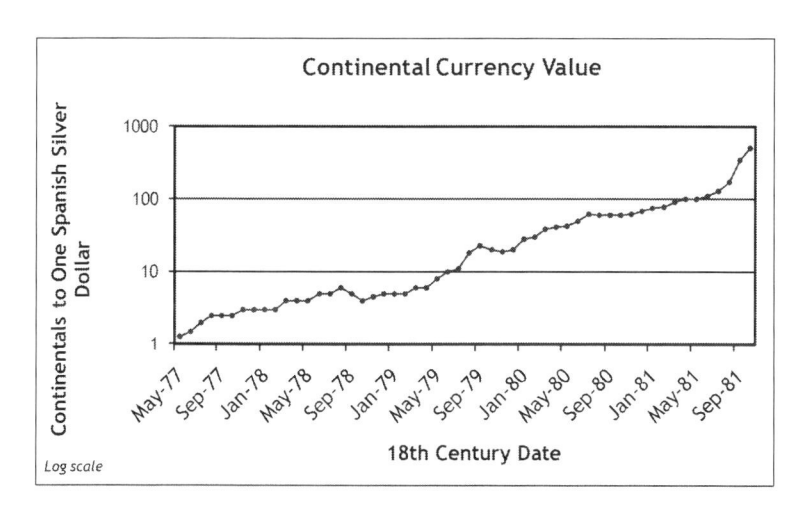

Figure 1-5

Want to own some Continentals???

Gresham's Law

Gresham's Law says that bad money drives out the good money. In the case of Continentals, the "bad" money was the Continental and the "good" money was the Spanish dollar or gold. The colonists were better off holding gold instead of Continentals. Even though the Continentals indicated they were worth an equivalent amount of gold, the colonists knew better.

A modern-day example of Gresham's Law is the U.S. Silver Eagle. The Silver Eagle is a coin issued by the U.S. Mint whose face value indicates it is worth one dollar. It is legal tender meaning the government says everyone must accept it as payment for goods or services. It also contains approximately 1 oz. fine silver. Would you drop the Silver Eagle in a vending machine or would you use the paper in your wallet with George

Washington's picture? Hopefully, you would use the paper dollar with George's picture because you know the Silver Eagle is worth more than a dollar even though the government says otherwise. The "bad" money, the one-dollar bill, drives the "good" money, the U.S. Silver Eagle (Figure 1-6), out of circulation.

Would you drop this coin in a vending machine?

Figure 1-6
One Dollar Silver Eagle

The Founding Fathers recognized Gresham's Law and understood inflation. Article I Section 10 of the Constitution says,

> *"No State shall enter into any Treaty, Alliance, or Confederation; grant Letters of Marque and Reprisal; coin Money; emit Bills of Credit; make any Thing but gold and silver Coin a Tender in Payment of Debts; pass any Bill of Attainder, ex post facto Law, or Law impairing the Obligation of Contracts, or grant any Title of Nobility."*

Note the specification of gold and silver coin for the purposes of tender to pay debt!

Money During the Civil War

The eruption of the Civil War created the same problem as in the Revolutionary War – how to pay for the war effort. Rather than create a tax to raise the funds, the government opted for the creation of United States Notes. The government issued the Notes, not redeemable in gold, and the people provided goods and services in return. The Notes were lawfully declared money, legal tender, for payment of public and private debts. Since the notes circulated as legal tender, their effect was inflation. The circulation of Notes was inflation since the supply of money increased without an increase in wealth.

Like the Revolutionary war, the misstep here was to create paper rather than raise taxes.

Central Banking

The money structure changed in 1913 with the creation of a central bank. Lawmakers felt a strong central bank could avert some of the financial panics caused by bank runs that occurred in the U.S. in the late 19th and early 20th century.

In the U.S. as elsewhere, banks could get in trouble by issuing banknotes in excess of gold held in vaults. This is similar to what occurred with certificate depositories. If that problem became acute, a bank run usually followed. Another way banks got in trouble was by creating excessive loans on their books. People unable to pay back loans caused bank failure. When banks failed, there was nobody to save them.

The rationale for central bank creation was to provide a bank of banks – an institution to save banks if necessary. Another reason was to provide additional capital for business expansion. There was a fear that without back end support, banks would be unwilling to provide inexpensive capital/low interest rates to business. The Federal Reserve Bank (Fed) was born (Figure 1-7).

Figure 1-7
Federal Reserve System Seal

I could write more about the rationale for creating the Fed but instead will focus on four areas:

- One of the Fed's responsibilities is to control the interest it charges its member banks for loans. Banks must maintain reserves on account with the Fed. When the reserves drop below prescribed levels, banks can borrow from the Fed. The interest rate at which they borrow is the discount rate.

- The Fed has their name on our paper currency also known as Federal Reserve Notes (FRN). FRN are legal tender, meaning the government tells you what they're worth. When people think of money, this is what they think of.

- The backing for the FRN is the assets of the Fed that are supposed to be U.S. Treasuries. The Fed buys these Treasuries by creating money out of thin air.

- The Fed also has the power to buy other assets it deems necessary to promote financial stability.

The Wizard of Oz has nothing on the Fed. By moving levers and pushing buttons, figuratively, they are able to "buy" U.S. Treasuries. The Treasuries they buy are the backing for the FRN they issue. Nothing but debt, which the Fed can buy at will, stands behind a FRN, and the FRN is but a promise to pay.

Roosevelt's Grab

Unfortunately, 16 years after the Fed's creation, a financial panic ensued that evolved into the Great Depression. The panic led President Roosevelt (Figure 1-8) to enact Executive Order 6102 on April 5, 1933 outlawing <u>domestic</u> ownership of gold coins, gold bullion and gold certificates. Roosevelt and his leadership reasoned that outlawing gold would help the economy out of the depression. People took their gold, except for small amounts associated with coin collecting and industrial usage, to Federal Reserve banks or branches and received $20.67 per ounce. After the public turned in their gold, Roosevelt raised its price to $35 per ounce.

He severed the linkage between money and wealth. A dollar no longer represented anything of value.

Figure 1-8
Franklin Delano Roosevelt

What effect did the gold confiscation and gold price increase have? The U.S. during part of the Great Depression era was on a gold standard mandating a certain percentage of the country's money be backed by gold. At any time, you could exchange paper certificates, by law, for physical gold. Taking away the public's gold eliminated that ability. No longer did the government have to worry about the public draining the gold stock. By taking away the public's gold, government could spend money more freely, and they could create inflation in the economy. When governments remove gold as backing for money we get inflation. The economic reasoning at the time felt that inflation was the only way to get the country going again. The public, drained by economic suffering, acquiesced.

The gold confiscation order did leave silver certificates (Figure 1-9) in circulation. Silver redemption ended, however, on March 25, 1964 when Treasury Secretary C. Douglas Dillon eliminated the public's ability to exchange the certificates for real silver. Congress ostensibly took this action since there were insufficient silver coins held in government stock to satisfy all of the silver certificates in circulation. For holders of those certificates, it meant the loss of wealth.

With the stroke of a pen, Franklin Roosevelt severed the link between money and wealth. The government convinced the public that having gold in their possession was the problem. With the public's surrender, government had more control over money than ever before and got us closer to the Land of Oz.

Until 1964, holding this was the same as holding real silver.

Figure 1-9
Silver certificate

Dollar Becomes the World's Money

The approaching end of World War II hastened the creation of a worldwide monetary structure that many concluded would lessen the chances of future, armed conflict and financial panics. A meeting convened in Bretton Woods, New Hampshire in 1944 and the eponymously named Bretton Woods Agreement emerged. The parties to this agreement vowed a fixed exchange rate between their country's money and the U.S. Dollar (USD). This was a tremendous advantage to the United States since all other currencies would be "pegged" to the dollar. To add further credence to the agreement, its architects made a decision to make a USD redeemable to foreign governments in gold at a rate of $35/ounce. Consider that an international agreement like Bretton Woods was only possible by having gold backing for the USD. That should tell you how important gold is with respect to money. The USD immediately became the world's currency and was as good as gold. Despite being unlawful for U.S. residents to own gold, a foreign government could demand the metal from the U.S. Treasury at a rate of $35/ounce.

Being the world's currency placed the U.S. in a unique position in the world economy. The U.S. could trade with overseas partners and have no worries about the exchange rate. A USD was worth 0.25 British Pounds, 15 Yen, or 3.33 Deutsche Marks. Since no gold was necessary to back domestic money, the U.S. could create larger amounts of money without worry. The larger amounts of money allowed the U.S. to spend freely with foreign countries. Foreign countries sopped up USD in the transactions and had the confidence of gold backing.

With an increasing amount of USD in circulation and with the USD pegged to other world currencies, a problem emerged. There were too many USD relative to the other world currencies.

Too many dollars circulated in the world due to U.S. government deficits as well as a growing trade deficit. Wars in Korea and Vietnam plus the addition of new social programs added to the deficit. The trade deficit meant the U.S. purchased more things from overseas than foreign countries purchased from the U.S. The twin deficits meant a greater number of dollars circulated in the world economy.

Foreigners got wise and decided they wanted to hold fewer USD and wanted gold instead. Under the terms of the Bretton Woods agreement, they could exchange USD for gold at a rate of $35/ounce. This began a gold drain on the US Treasury.

Nixon's Most Important Decision

Richard Nixon's presidential legacy for most people was the Watergate scandal. I suggest that the most significant event of his presidency was what he did on August 15, 1971. On this day, President Nixon effectively killed the Bretton Woods Agreement by eliminating the ability of foreign entities to redeem USD for gold. The money and spending policies of the U.S. had caught up with the nation. Foreign countries wanted to hold gold rather than USD. After his action, the currencies of the world "floated" relative to each other. The USD was no longer fixed to a foreign currency or to gold. Nixon wiped away the economic discipline of gold that held the world economy together for so many years.

Our brave new world would be one of managing currencies. The central banks and governments of the world would assume a more prominent role in the function of money. The ability to "manage" a currency introduced a speculative element to money that carries significant economic and political implications.

Watergate forced him to resign but killing Bretton Woods sent the country closer to the Financial Land of Oz.

Figure 1-10
President Nixon Resigning

The Wonderful World of Credit

Credit and debt are the two most important terms used in this book. Credit comes from the Latin "credere", meaning to believe. The definition of credit by Dictionary.com says,

> *"confidence in a purchaser's ability and intention to pay, displayed by entrusting the buyer with goods or services without immediate payment"*

You don't have <u>confidence</u> unless you <u>believe</u>. I have come up with my own set of economic laws to help you understand in concrete terms some of the key points in this book.

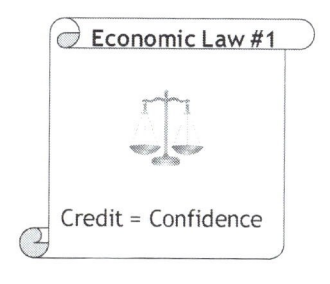

Economic Law #1

Credit = Confidence

Confidence implies credit and credit implies confidence – one does not exist without the other. In a loan, the lender extends <u>credit</u> and the borrower acquires <u>debt</u>. A loan only occurs when the creditor is confident in the debtor's ability to return the principal plus interest.

Making Credit (Part I)

Most of what we consider money today is not in the form of cash but in the form of credit. As of June 2010, there is approximately $13.8 trillion of credit extended to the United States Government (USG). Government needs this credit in order to fund its expenses when tax revenues are insufficient. Subtract tax revenues from government spending and we have the deficit equation:

Government spending – Tax revenues = Deficit

The USG has the unique ability to obtain large amounts of credit since the perceived risk of default is small due to its taxing power. In *theory*, the USG can retire its debt through taxation of the public. The fact the USG has to continue to borrow is reason to suspect they cannot retire their debt solely through taxation. Maybe the Wizard is not so powerful after all.

Federal agencies like Social Security extended credit to the USG, albeit more surreptitiously. Residents of the U.S. pay a tax for social programs like Social Security and Medicare. Our government leaders unfortunately diverted tax funds specifically allocated for those programs to other expenditures. What does the government give the social program trust funds in return? It gives them an IOU. The IOU is simply a promise by the government to pay itself. These IOUs are unfunded liabilities. The liabilities are unfunded since government used money specifically for Social Security and Medicare for other spending. All that Social Security has is an IOU, which is another form of credit. Projection of future unfunded liabilities of the USG total $63 trillion (cited in *Comeback America*). I will use this figure throughout the book.

The credit extended to government finds its way into the economy. Since there is no wealth behind any of this credit, government has been able to grow itself with very few limitations. The *only* limitation to government growth is the confidence of those holders of government debt.

What about private sector credit? As of June 2010, there is approximately $2.4 trillion of consumer credit, both revolving and non-revolving, down from $2.6 trillion at its peak. Revolving credit includes credit card debt and non-revolving credit includes auto, boat, mobile homes, education, and vacations. So where does all this credit originate? It comes from commercial banks, finance companies, credit unions, and pools of securitized assets - credit that is bundled and sold to others. Figure 1-11 illustrates the explosive growth of consumer credit. Note how the credit really explodes after 1982.

More private sector credit comes from mortgages. At the end of 2008, there was $14.6 trillion of outstanding mortgage debt. Seventy-five percent of mortgage debt belongs to single-family homes with the remainder allocated between commercial properties, multifamily units, and farms. So where docs this substantial amount of credit originate? Commercial banks, savings institutions, agency and government sponsored mortgage pools, and asset backed securities issuers create the vast majority of real estate credit. Figure 1-12 depicts real estate loans, originated by commercial banks. Notice the explosive growth of real estate debt beginning in 1982. In a later chapter we'll examine why 1982 was such a pivotal year in launching the credit boom.

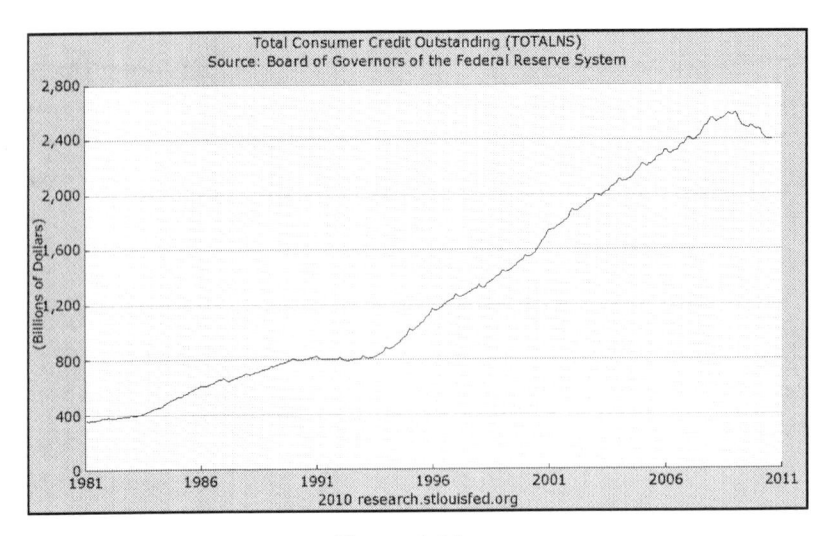

Figure 1-11
Total Consumer Credit

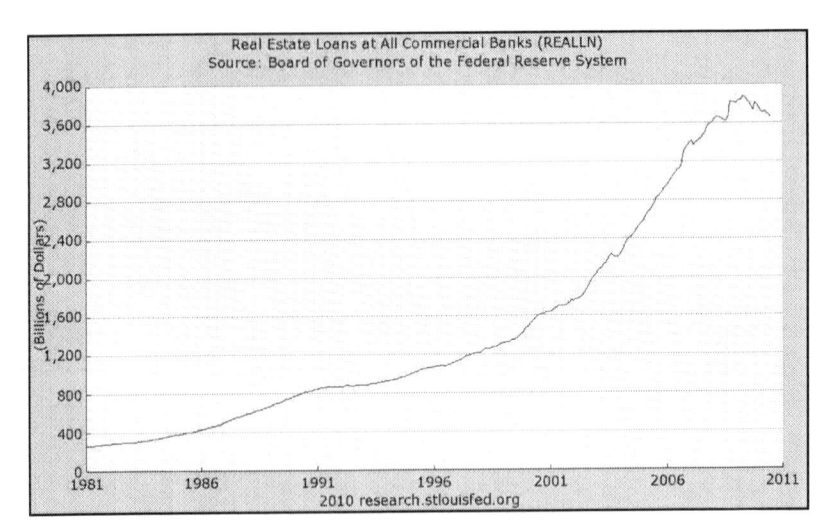

Figure 1-12
Real Estate Loans

We have credit extended to the government ($13.8 trillion), in the form of unfunded liabilities or government IOUs ($63 trillion), to consumers ($2.4 trillion), and for mortgages ($14.6 trillion). Recalling my first Economic Law, this means there is $30.8 trillion dollars worth of confidence in three areas and $63 trillion in another. How deep is the ocean? How high is the sky? How much confidence do we have?

Making Credit (Part II)

The Fed owns some of the government's $13.8 trillion of debt (Figure 1-13). How do they own government debt? When the US Treasury needs to borrow money, they sell debt instruments (bonds, notes, bills) to the public. The Fed buys these debt instruments from banks and financial institutions and increases the value of the U.S. Treasury's account. Where did the Fed's money come from to buy the debt instruments? *The Fed simply created the money* by increasing the value of the Treasury's bank account. Did the Treasury's wealth increase because of this transaction? No. By my definition, the Treasury did not receive anything that represented wealth. Does this constitute inflation? Yes, there was additional issuance of credit above the amount of wealth created. The Fed can create infinite credit in theory.

Another function of the Fed is to facilitate credit in the banking system. The member banks of the Fed lend under a practice known as fractional reserve. Historically, 90% of a bank's deposits became loans. These loans or credit flow into other parts of the banking system from which more loans occur. Additionally, banks have the ability to issue stock, bonds and other debt instruments and thus create a larger pool of funds for use as credit. Excessive credit creation plagued banks before we had the Fed so the only difference now is the implicit guarantee of Fed salvation.

One more key point.....Since all credit comes with interest considerations, where does the money originate for the interest. It *could* come from new wealth created. In the case of the government with $13.8 trillion in debt, where do the hundreds of billions of dollars in annual interest originate? Answer: the source of the interest payments is the same as the initial credit, which is to say, more credit! Thus, our present credit system relies on continuous amounts of credit creation in order to feed itself.

By allowing the Fed to make money where none existed previously, government has a lender of last resort. Rather than tax people to pay for its expenses, the government can rely on the Fed and the debt market for more credit. Politicians and bureaucrats use this to their advantage. This wizardry simply postpones the debt pain.

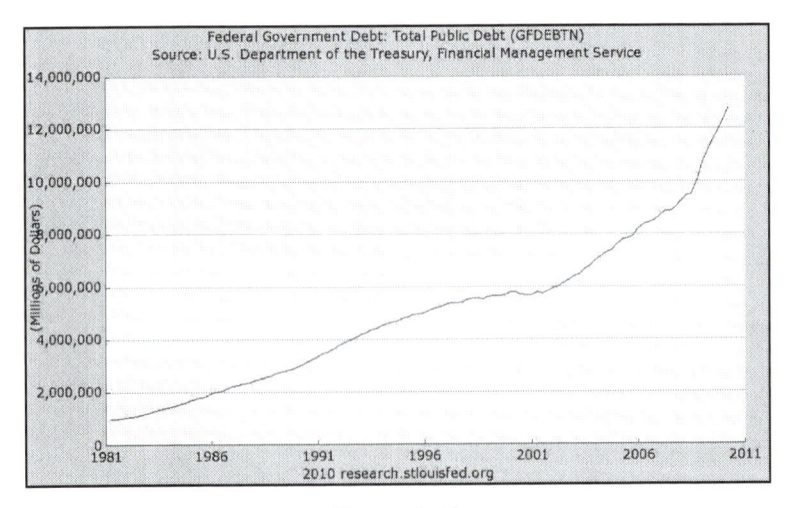

Figure 1-13
Public Debt

Making Credit (Part III)

We should also consider other forms of credit. Table 1-1 illustrates other forms of credit in the world economy.

Source	Amounts (trillions of $)
Foreign government debt	$16
Value of all listed stocks in world	$66
Corporate & municipal bonds	$25
Unfunded government liabilities [1]	$250
Reported derivatives	$683
Shadow derivatives	$800

Table 1-1

(1) – *includes U.S. unfunded liabilities noted earlier*

An in-depth discussion on derivatives is beyond the scope of this book but I will shed some light on the topic. Derivatives are contracts and can be an underlying asset. The best-known form of derivatives exist in the regulated commodity futures exchanges. In the commodity market, the futures contract serves a form of hedging for a producer or a consumer of some economic good.

Suppose a corn farmer just planted his crop that he will harvest six months later. The price of corn on the commodity exchange for delivery in six months is $4.00 per bushel. That price is good for the farmer as long as it remains in place until harvest. The corn market has its fluctuations so there is no guarantee it would remain at $4.00 per bushel. The farmer can enter into a futures contract that does guarantee his $4.00/bushel price. A cereal company also thinks $4.00/bushel is a good price. The cereal company and the farmer enter into a contract via the commodity exchange to complete the transaction. Six months from now the farmer and the cereal company have their guaranteed price in the transaction.

The preceding example is one of using derivatives for hedging purposes. Parties in commodity futures transactions also use derivatives for speculation. Some parties could enter the transaction above without any intent of selling or taking possession of corn. Despite the bad rap they often get, speculators add liquidity to a market. Liquidity is good for a market since it means there is more reliable and consistent pricing.

There is also derivatives activity that takes place outside of regulated exchanges and is harder to identify. Hedge funds, pension funds, investment banks and insurers expanded the practice of derivatives by engaging in "over the counter" transactions, which are essentially private trades. The good news for the participants is it gives them flexibility to propose deals that would be otherwise unsanctioned by regulated futures exchanges. The bad news is that investment risk is often unknown in these private arrangements making it difficult to assess what liabilities are involved. In regulated futures exchanges, everyone knows what the price of a bushel of corn is. With these over the counter products, it is anyone's guess. Billions of dollars are off the balance sheet of corporations and financial institutions in the form of these derivatives.

Derivatives are another form of credit in the economy. The amount of credit based on these derivatives and other forms of debt dwarf all other credit in the economy. These derivatives take confidence to a universally inexplicable level.

Our Money

The other money in the economy is cash - paper bills and coins. The Treasury Department is responsible for all currency notes and coins. The U.S. Mint produces the coins and the Bureau of Engraving and Printing produces the notes. Our notes are composed of 75% cotton and 25% linen. A nickel is actually only 25% nickel and the rest is copper. After production of coins and paper notes, the Treasury Department ships them to the Federal Reserve banks and branches.

According to a Federal Reserve Bank publication, as of 9/30/2008 there was $1.027 trillion of paper bills/coins in circulation. Of this amount, the Treasury had $275 million, the Fed had $189 billion, and the public had $838 billion. This cash does not represent wealth since it is not exchangeable for wealth. If you went to a bank and demanded gold or silver in return for your cash, there would be no cooperation on the teller's part. So what does this cash represent? We answer this question by looking at a Federal Reserve Note (that paper in your wallet with Washington's picture). It clearly states, *"This note is legal tender for all debts public and private."*

Legal tender means the government tells you how much the note is worth and that is acceptable as payment of debt. For example, after eating a steak in a restaurant, the establishment must accept your Federal Reserve Note by law. If you paid in cash and went home, the restaurant could not sue for non-payment since you provided legal tender. In the case of checks, credit card, debit card or other non-cash form of payment the restaurant is not obligated to accept these instruments.

You have probably been somewhere that had a sign saying, "Personal checks not accepted". Have you ever seen a sign saying, "Cash not accepted" ? A personal check is not legal tender since the government says nothing about its worth. Credit cards and debit cards by themselves say nothing and require some verification. The Federal Reserve Note brings no such question.

We did not always need government to tell us what money was worth. Silver certificates told us that a specific amount of the metal was on hand at the Treasury. Moreover, we could exchange the certificate for silver. We also knew that gold backed a percentage of our money. In the 20th century, government changed the definition of money. No longer did it represent wealth – you could not exchange it for gold or silver. Figure 1-14 illustrates how the definition of money has changed. In the 1920s, money was a certificate issued by the U.S. Treasury stipulating there was a deposit in the Treasury of a stated amount of silver. Our current money, Federal Reserve Note, makes no stipulation of any deposit of any kind in the U.S. Treasury.

The "backing" for the Federal Reserve Notes is the assets of the Federal Reserve and the full faith and credit of the U.S. Government and their ability to levy taxes. According to the U.S. Treasury's web site,

> "Federal Reserve notes are not redeemable in gold, silver or any other commodity, and receive no backing by anything. This has been the case since 1933. The notes have no value for themselves, but for what they will buy. In another sense, because they are legal tender, Federal Reserve notes are "backed" by all the goods and services in the economy."

This is a very circular explanation of our money. The Treasury says the goods and services in the economy back our money. Since the Treasury does not have possession of the goods and services in the economy, what backing does money have (Figure 1-14)?

Figure 1-14
Money Evolution
Top figure was exchanged for silver
Bottom figure is strictly for debt payment

Conclusion

Money takes the place of bartering in economic transactions. Since it replaces bartering, money is an economic good just like any other. In our earlier example, Tommy and I had an economic problem since we were trying to barter with something that was not divisible, a bike. We solved our problem by replacing our barter goods with money In order for money to replace barter goods, it must have value. The value can be something intrinsic like gold or the value can be by government decree. When government tells us what money is worth, they gain more control of the economy and can spend with less immediate pain. You, the next generation and I will deal with this problem.

Politically, it is much easier for government to fund expenditures by controlling money rather than taxing their constituents. Economically, we lost since government slowly removed the wealth component from money. Money has nothing backing it as it once did in our history. Money without backing allows the creation of massive amounts of credit by the banking system and government. Credit is addictive for both the public and government.

Governments historically tried to solve economic issues by attempting to control money. Government was averse to taxing its constituents for undertaking actions such as war. In other cases government wanted to repudiate business cycles and human action. Government action eventually set the stage for our economy having a system of easy credit.

Easy credit allowed governments to run unimaginable budget deficits. Running deficits was not enough. The U.S. Government made one of its most egregious missteps by siphoning money belonging to a trust fund and spending it. This will haunt the government for years to come. Most of our economic problems today result from excessive credit creation, tracing back to our system of money. Not all our problems stem from money but our altered money system is the root cause.

Summary

The following are key points from this chapter:

- We need money to facilitate economic transactions. Without it we could only barter goods and services.

- The public often thinks of money as wealth. The definition is valid as long as the money represents wealth. Today's money does not represent wealth.

- Gold and silver have a long history of usage as money. Replacements or substitutes for gold and silver led to inflation. The public perceives inflation as rising prices instead of a devaluation of their money.

- Public gold ownership was outlawed in the United States in 1933. The paper money previously representing gold was no longer exchangeable for the metal.

- For more than a quarter of a century after the end of World War II, the world economy operated under a system of fixed exchange rates. Currencies were "pegged" or fixed to some value of the U.S. Dollar (USD). The USD, in turn, had a value of $35 for an ounce of gold. The dollar-gold exchange privilege was only available to foreign governments.

- President Nixon decoupled the USD from gold in 1971. No longer could foreign governments exchange 35 USD for an ounce of gold.

- My first economic law says that credit equals confidence. There is no credit without confidence. Credit expansion tends to fuel more credit.

- The Federal Reserve Bank has the unique ability to purchase government debt (Treasury Bonds, Notes, and Bills) merely through bookkeeping entries. They purchase government debt and increase the value of the Treasury department's account.

- Legal tender means Federal Reserve Notes must be accepted for payment of debt. Even though this money does not represent wealth, government says you must accept this money as payment.

Chapter 2
Inflation

Our tendency is to think of prices always rising. You have heard the expression, "They aren't making any more land, so its price will always go up." Another popular expression is, "A dollar doesn't go as far as it once did." What about this one, "Buy stocks for the long-run." These expressions have probably been quite accurate for those readers not alive during the Great Depression. Inflation is part of who we are and ingrained in our investment philosophies.

Most people do not have a good understanding of what inflation is or what causes it. Chapter 1 provided a historical perspective on money and the inflation that came from it. This chapter provides more definition around the term *inflation*. Given the abstraction of thinking of inflation within the context of a multi-trillion dollar economy, I provide an inflation simulation in Appendix A. The mini-economy example in Appendix A will demonstrate that it is quite possible to have a working economy with zero <u>monetary</u> inflation. Prices can still rise in an economy but for reasons other than tinkering with the money.

Inflation & Wealth

People experience inflation as an increase in prices. More accurately, inflation is a reduction in the purchasing power or value of money. If there is more money chasing the same amount of goods and services, the value of the money decreases.

Emily runs a lemonade stand in your neighborhood. She sells each glass for $1.00. In any given day, Emily sells 10 glasses of lemonade netting her $10. Bobby moves into the neighborhood and begins to buy Emily's lemonade, all 10 glasses. The rest of the kids can't figure out how Bobby is doing it since they all get the same allowance. What they don't know is Bobby has been borrowing money from his parents who are paying him his allowance many weeks in advance.

Emily may be able to sell her lemonade for more than $1 per glass since she knows Bobby has a bunch of money and other kids want lemonade too. With all the new money in this little economy, Emily decides to raise the price to $1.50 per glass. She sells it all and nets $15. As long as Bobby can continue to borrow ahead in his allowance, the extra money chases the lemonade. Inflation hit the lemonade business since prices are now 50% higher. The little lemonade economy seems wealthier since now the sales total $15 instead of $10. The little economy feels wealthier but is only so because of the borrowing by Bobby. An economist would say the Gross Domestic Product (GDP) of the lemonade economy grew by 50% since the value of all sales went up by 50%.

What happens when Bobby can no longer get advances on his allowance? What do you think will happen to the price of lemonade when Bobby removes his money from the lemonade economy? Here's a hint: There won't be as much money chasing lemonade. If the price of lemonade reverts to $1.00, is that economy in a recession since the GDP is now \$10? Is that economy suddenly less wealthy? By modern economic measures, there is a recession even though Emily sold the same amount of lemonade. The lemonade economy probably feels less wealthy since Bobby withdrew his money but that does not consider that it felt wealthier due to Bobby's *borrowed* money.

People feel wealthier during inflation. The price of their home increases. Banks are willing to lend on the increased value of a home. Your stock portfolio may have increased in value. That piece of art hanging in your living room now fetches twice the original purchase price. Your salary continues to increase every year. Your debt load might be higher but you feel you can service the payments since you anticipate higher income in the future. That wealth you feel is on paper or in the form of greater credit. Until you cash out your stock portfolio, all your gains are on paper. Though you live in a bigger home, you have a larger mortgage to go along with it.

I defined wealth as *"a material item produced by human effort having exchange value."* Paper increases in value or increased debt does not represent increases in wealth.

The Bedouins understood wealth. In the 1962 big screen hit *Lawrence of Arabia,* the Bedouin Auda Abu Tayi (Figure 2-1), played by Anthony Quinn, finds a stash of Turkish paper money and scatters it wildly in an open area with complete disdain. Quinn's character only desired true wealth – gold or silver coins. He did not trust paper produced by a government. He instinctively knew that the issuer of the paper had the ability to devalue it by producing more of it.

Bedouins like in the movie Lawrence of Arabia knew money was more than a piece of paper with numbers on it.

Figure 2-1
Bedouin

Causes of Inflation

Our experience with inflation is only partially the result of increased issuance of paper money. The inflation we witnessed is mostly a product of credit creation. Credit is an IOU or an obligation to pay. These IOUs reside in the banking system or on government books. When the supply of these IOUs expands, the price of those things purchased by the IOUs goes up.

Credit creation is the cause of our <u>monetary</u> inflation. Credit creation not matched by an equal amount of wealth creation, allows more money to chase goods and services. This causes their "price" to go up. The reality is, the "price" is not going up but rather the value of the money is going down.

The Colonists recognized inflation since they had real, wealth-based money circulating alongside Continentals. It became quickly apparent when the Continentals lost their purchasing power. Few wanted the Continentals and hoarded gold coins. This was inflation front and center. In our bout of inflation, we have not had wealth-based money for many years so a comparison is harder. All we knew was Federal Reserve Notes and IOUs. There was no money for us to hoard since none of it was wealth-based [1]. Inflation was just something we accepted.

Here's another way to know the value of money is going down. Suppose that in the lemonade example Emily accepted a Topps 1973 Lou Brock baseball card (Figure 2-2) for a glass of lemonade when the price was $1 a glass. If she continued to accept the same Topps card for a glass when the price went to $1.50, then we can say the value of the Topps card stayed constant while the value of the money went down.

Regardless of the dollar price of lemonade, you could always trade one of these for a glass.

Figure 2-2
Lou Brock Card

Monetary inflation results from excess credit creation or paper money issuance. It is possible to have another type of inflation. If Emily lost part of her lemon supply and the kids in the neighborhood wanted the same amount of lemonade, she could demand more money for a glass. If the kids accepted the higher price, then there was inflation for reasons of supply – this is not monetary inflation.

[1] *I omit gold and silver coins since their usage is not widespread.*

If there is a constant supply and demand for an economic good, the price of that good will increase as the supply of money increases. We call this monetary inflation (Figure 2-3). If there is a constant demand for an economic good and a constant supply of money, the price of that good will increase as the supply of that good decreases. We call this inflation due to economic scarcity.

The Wizard always had a hand in the inflationary process. The public accepts the Wizard's explanations on inflation and reconciles that it will always be part of the economic narrative. Some inflation is seen as being economically healthy. Tinkering with money will come back to haunt the Wizard through a condition he cannot control called deflation.

This is serious inflation. Look at all the zeroes!

Figure 2-3
Turkish Note

Summary

The following are key points from this chapter:

- The ability to create money or credit is the cause of monetary inflation.

- Credit creation not matched by an equal amount of wealth creation, allows more money chasing goods and services. This causes their "price" to go up.

- The <u>effect</u> of inflation is increasing prices. Prices increase since money loses its value. The concept sounds counterintuitive and is different than most people understand.

- Increasing prices create the appearance of more wealth in the economy. GDP, a measure of economic activity, goes up with inflation regardless of how much debt was created.

Chapter 3
Deflation

Deflation is a difficult concept to understand. Everyone knows <u>inflation</u> since we hear, "a dollar does not go as far as it used to" or "cost of living allowance". We never hear "the dollar goes farther than before". The administration of former U.S. President Gerald Ford popularized the fight against inflation with the slogan "WIN" or "Whip Inflation Now" (Figure 3-1). Ever see a slogan saying, "Whip Deflation Now"?

Will we ever see a button that says "WDN" (Whip Deflation Now) ?

Figure 3-1
Whip Inflation Now

Deflations are associated with economic depressions. The Great Depression ushered in the most recent period of sustained deflation in the United States. Prices of many assets fell. Politically, the "D" word is highly undesirable. One of the last words you will hear out of government is "depression". That word just has too many bad connotations. In order to avoid any appearance of depression, government leaders try to create the appearance of wealth through inflation.

Inflation helps an important economic statistic, GDP, or the total value of all goods and services in the economy. While GDP is increasing, depression can be held at bay even if it is on the back of debt. Debt is less of a problem during inflation since the debtor will have more dollars in the future with which to pay off loans. The same applies to governments. Inflation helps their debts too.

Deflation does the opposite to debt. Debt is harder to pay back since there is less credit in the economy. Deflation occurs in areas that previously experienced the most inflation. Today, this is the real estate market.

Deflation is a monetary and psychological phenomenon. Inflation means confidence and belief. Deflation means the opposite. The psychological component is the expectation of lower prices. During a deflation, people will hold out for lower prices. Why buy now when prices will be lower in the future?

Four conditions indicate the arrival of deflation:

☐ Shrinking credit
☐ Greater cash holdings
☐ Fall in asset prices
☐ Business slows

What is Deflation?

If inflation is the expansion of credit above the amount of wealth, what is deflation? Deflation is the reduction of money and credit outstanding. The public incorrectly defines inflation and deflation as rising and falling prices respectively. This relationship is a misnomer. Rising prices result from the increase in money sloshing through the economy chasing things like homes, cars, private schools etc. Money increases when lenders and others issue more loans or lines of credit. Falling prices are the result of a reduction in money or credit. When there is less money chasing homes, cars, and private schools, prices have to fall to meet demand.

Prices can fall for other reasons. If you were ever the first person to buy the latest electronic gadget, you know what I mean. When your friends bought the same gadget a few months later, they paid less. Your friends paid less since there was more supply due to greater production or an improved production process that reduced the price of the gadget. What we are discussing in this chapter is <u>monetary</u> deflation.

Think of deflation in the following manner. During inflation, the public recognizes that the purchasing power of their money is constantly falling. The public needs more credit to combat their money's decreased purchasing power. The house you were looking at that was $150,000 is now $200,000. Unless you suddenly inherited $50,000, you will need to borrow an extra $50,000 for that house. During inflation, your lender is able and quite willing to extend the additional $50,000 to you. If by chance you weren't a great credit risk, your lender still had a product for you, a sub-prime loan. During an inflationary boom, lenders expand the number of people qualifying for loans.

During a deflation the opposite occurs. Banks tighten credit. You would not have qualified for that extra $50,000 and perhaps not any type of loan. If you are far enough in the deflationary process, the $150,000 house might sell for $125,000, which would be good for you if you could get a loan. If the price fell to say $75,000, you might think it a bargain, if you could get a loan. If you had $75,000 in cash, you have instant purchasing power that someone waiting on credit does not. In a deflation, the purchasing power of money increases. Cash is king.

Remember Emily's lemonade stand? If Bobby's parents quit giving him multi-week advances on his allowance, there would be less money in the lemonade economy. Removing Bobby's allowance advances would mean less money chasing the same amount of lemonade, which in turn should lead to a price drop.

The inflationary credit system relies on continuous amounts of credit creation in order to feed itself. With deflation, since lenders reduce credit, the effect on the system is severe. When an economy experiences a reduction of credit, old or existing credit experiences stress due to refinancing needs. Banks are not as eager to roll over loans or grant new financing. During times of credit expansion, old or existing credit is rolled into new credit. Deflation also stresses those in debt who may be unable to cope with interest payments. This leads to my second Economic Law.

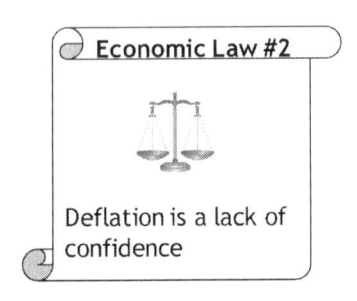

Economic Law #2

Deflation is a lack of confidence

DEFLATION

Deflation is a lack of confidence since lenders are less willing to lend and borrowers are less willing to borrow. I postulated with Economic Law #1 that credit = confidence. Borrowing and lending are all about confidence.

Another condition for deflation is the inflation that preceded it. Without the increase in the amount of credit, there is nothing to deflate. This leads to my third Economic Law.

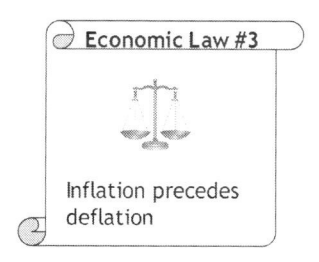

During a deflation, since the amount of outstanding credit contracts and debts are still payable, debtors must find another funding source. The source is typically assets. Asset liquidation must occur in order to raise the funding necessary to service previous debt. Liquidation forces the price of assets down. The current devaluation of home prices is an excellent example. Furthermore, deflation encourages cash retention on the part of the public for two reasons:

a) The psychological expectation of lower prices.

b) The psychological expectation of less credit in the future.

Let's go back to our lemonade stand. Bobby's parents stop giving him advances on his allowance. Bobby still wants to buy Emily's lemonade but now he has to come up with cash to do so. Bobby has a stash of Topps baseball cards much coveted by the other kids and sells some of his collection. He is able to raise money but only by selling his "assets". He sells so many of his cards at one time that kids are no longer willing to pay the same prices. Some of the kids expect the price of Bobby's cards to drop. Soon this becomes a self-fulfilling prophecy.

There could be other reasons for falling prices though that has nothing to do with deflation as I have defined it. Improvements in productivity can result in lower prices. If Emily finds a type of lemon that yields twice the juice for the same cost, she should be able to produce more lemonade for a smaller unit price. Consumers in the economy benefit from innovation that lowers prices.

Another scenario that could lead to price reductions results from changes in the supply of Federal Reserve Notes or cash money. If the amount of cash or Federal Reserve Notes decreases, the money chasing goods and services falls. This fall would cause a reduction in prices. Other than a physical destruction of Federal Reserve Notes or their hoarding, it is difficult to imagine a reduction in cash. I cannot see Federal Reserve Notes being destroyed other than for reasons of wear and tear. Even in this case, there would likely be a replacement of the Notes. If for some reason, people were to hoard cash that means there is a lesser form of money in circulation as we discussed in the Chapter 1 reference to Gresham's Law. At this time, there is not a lesser form of money in circulation in the U.S. economy.

The majority of the U.S. public does not comprehend deflation. Deflation is not something with which the public has much, if any, experience. The two major deflationary bouts in the U.S. occurred in the 1830s and the 1930s. Because the public doesn't understand deflation, not understanding it can prove financially fatal.

What Sets Off Deflation?

As long as lenders are willing to lend and borrowers willing to borrow, credit can continue to expand. Of course another prerequisite of credit expansion is the ability of borrowers to pay back or at least roll over their loans.

The catalyst for deflation may be any number of events. It could be a bank failure caused by a run on a bank or investments that soured. It could be the failure of a municipal or corporate bond. It could be the failure caused by home foreclosures. It might be large numbers of poor credit risks unable to pay their bills. It could be sheer saturation of credit strangling borrowers.

After large numbers of borrowers are unable to pay their debts, a psychological component takes hold. The confidence expressed during the credit expansion turns to pessimism. A downward spiral ensues.

- Pessimism makes lenders more cautious so they lend less.
- Pessimism makes borrowers more cautious so they borrow less or not at all.
- Borrowers stressed to pay loans begin to liquidate assets in order to raise cash. If they are unsuccessful, they default.
- The demand for cash increases. People hoard cash and are less likely to spend it.
- Businesses restrain their expansion and production plans.
- Consumers are reluctant to spend since they anticipate lower prices.
- These behaviors reduce the velocity of money or the speed with which money circulates to make purchases.
- Prices go down.

Deflationary Signs

☑ Shrinking credit

If deflation is a reduction of outstanding credit in the economy, how will we know when it arrives? If deflation were here, we should see a reduction in credit by the banking industry. Figure 3-2 illustrates the deflationary effects in our economy by revealing a reduction in credit at commercial banks. Not only was the rate of credit growth declining from late 2008 to 2010, credit was actually shrinking. Credit growth began its decline near the stock market top in the fall of 2007. While the rate of credit decline moderated somewhat, it still shows no growth. Figure 3-2 says it all. If credit equals confidence, then confidence is in severe decline.

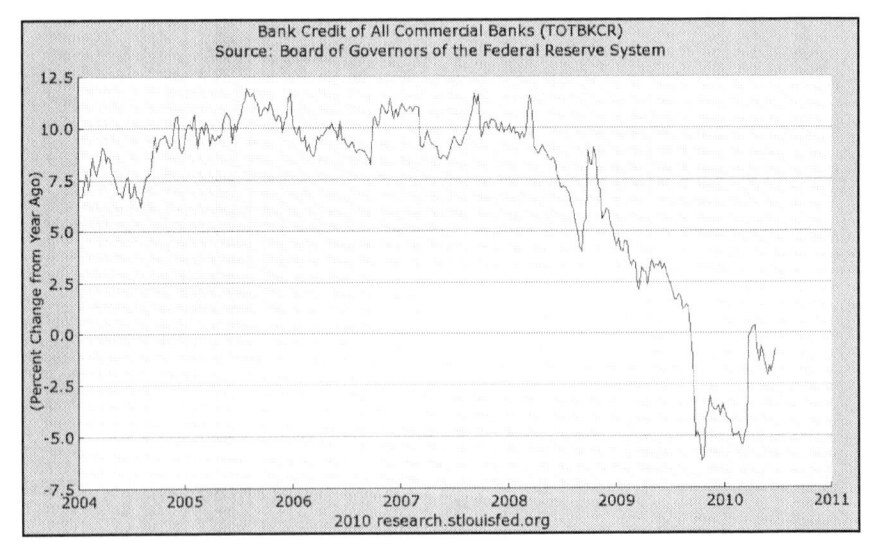

Figure 3-2
Shrinking Credit

☑ Greater cash holdings

Another event indicating the arrival of deflation is the state of cash. Cash becomes more desirable during a deflation. Figure 3-3 illustrates the sharp rise in public cash holdings in the period after the stock market top of 2007 and the financial panic of 2008. The chart illustrates a monetary statistic called M1. M1 is a measure of the money supply that includes coins, currency held by the public, traveler's checks, checking accounts, and NOW accounts (interest-bearing checking). The statistic is a measure of the cash or near-cash in an economy. These forms of money become dearer to people when the other source of money, credit, goes away.

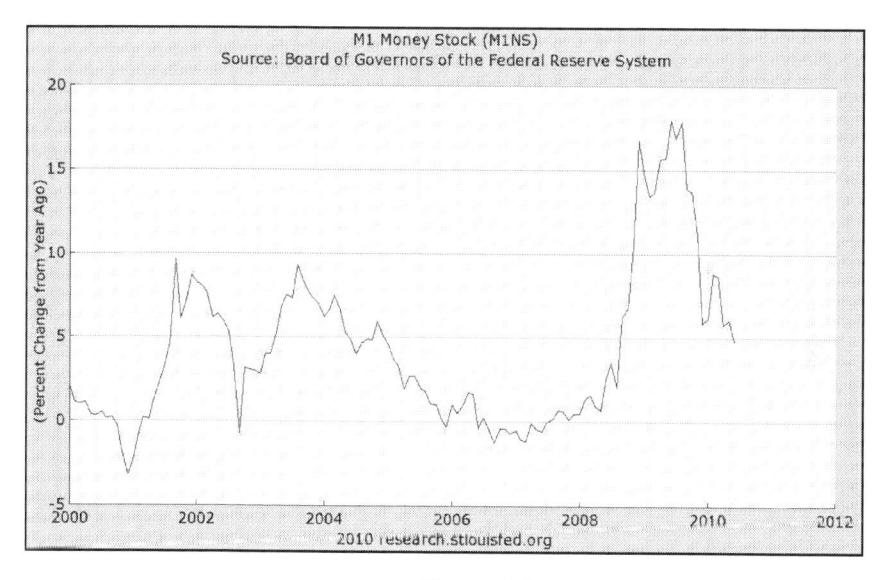

Figure 3-3
Cash/Near Cash Holdings

Notice how Figure 3-3 is the inverse of the previous chart (Figure 3-2) illustrating bank credit. When bank credit started to shrink, cash holdings started to rise. The large spike in cash holdings followed by its relative decline reflects a temporary rise in confidence on the part of the public, who believe government pronouncements about the end of the recession. Something else that will affect cash holdings is the economy itself. As more struggle with paying bills, there will be more dipping into cash reserves. This will be a devastating condition – people wanting to save but unable to for survival.

☑ Fall in asset prices

We should also see a fall in asset prices. The fall in asset prices would be most noticeable in the area that experienced the most inflation. Arguably, we experienced the most inflation in real estate. As a result, we should expect to see this asset class fall in value. Figure 3-4 illustrates what happened in the real estate market.

Another well-known asset that fell in price is the stock market. Stocks made their highs in the fall of 2007, and despite a furious rally have yet to approach their former heights.

☑ Business slows

Industry should also slow down during a deflation. How is industry responding? Figures 3-5 & 3-6 illustrate what happens as deflation takes hold. Softening demand and more restrictions on business loans by banks show up as a contraction in the United States' industrial output. Industrial production declined sharply in 2008 and 2009. Business inventories increased sharply in 2008 and 2009. Not only were we producing fewer goods, they were piling up in warehouses or stores unsold.

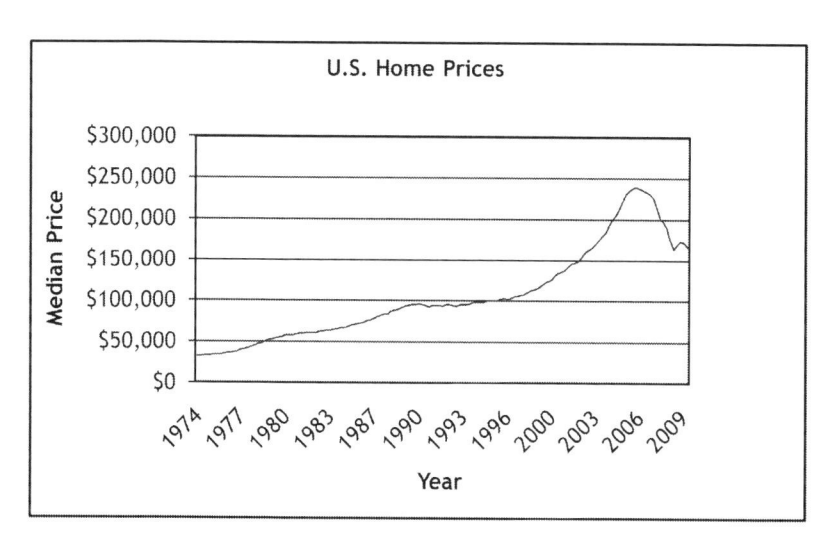

Figure 3-4
U.S. Median House Prices

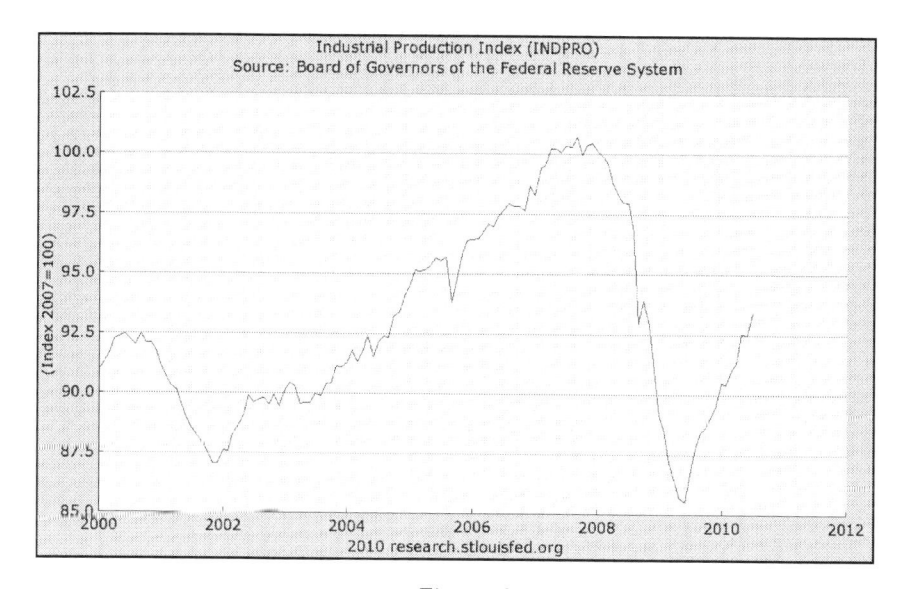

Figure 3-5
U.S. Industrial Production

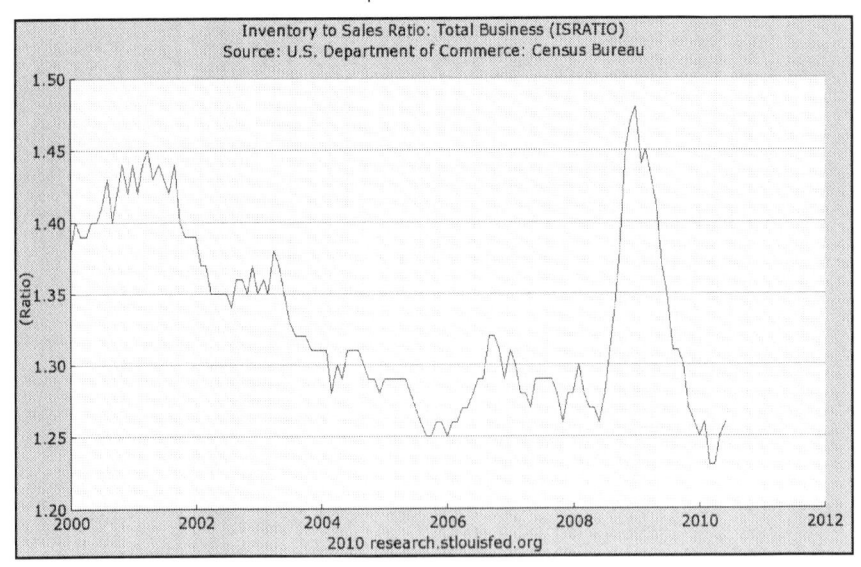

Figure 3-6
U.S. Inventories Relative to Sales

Consider the timing of the events:

- Bank credit – fell sharply starting in the fall of 2007

- Cash holdings (M1) – increased sharply starting in the fall of 2007

- Home prices – peaked in 2006 and fell sharply

- Stock market – made its high in the fall of 2007 and then fell sharply

- Industrial production – fell sharply starting in the fall of 2007

- Business inventories – increased sharply starting in the fall of 2007

All these significant deflationary events started around the same time. This is no coincidence. If just one of these events occurred, it might not be enough to conclude deflation. All of them initiating at approximately the same time fits well within my model and definition of deflation.

Some may suggest that both industrial production and business inventories improved from 2009 to 2010. This is true. The reasons for these improvements center on government efforts and renewed economic confidence. Government programs and lower interest rates did stimulate demand, but this stimulation came through borrowing. Government action sends false signals to the market creating the impression of greater prosperity but this illusion was only possible through borrowed money. This type of money borrowing does not add wealth to the economy; it only adds debt.

Other Deflationary Signals

Let me mention other clear signs of deflation that are not on the checklist in this section. If people don't have money or credit to conduct economic transactions what else could they do? In Chapter 1, I discussed how economies evolve from pure bartering towards money usage. Deflation can make this process go backwards.

Bartering

Bartering allows participants to exchange goods and services in the absence of credit or money. In 2009, the classified ad website Craigslist reported a 125% increase in barter transactions. A Google search on "barter networks" reveals hundreds of networks in existence in the U.S., Canada, and Latin America. A disillusioned real estate seller in Florida launched his own house-swapping website that has morphed into an exchange for houses, businesses, yachts, boats, and even aircraft.

Barter networks are deflationary since they characterize people unable or unwilling to acquire more credit for economic transactions (Figure 3-7). It may be someone unwilling to part with cash needed for other expenses where bartering is not practical. It may be a case where bartering is perceived to be a less expensive alternative. Regardless of the situation, the effect is one of reduced demand for credit, which is deflationary.

Figure 3-7
Paying for a subscription with birds

A casualty of barter network proliferation is government. Bartering exchanges are taxable events in the U.S. reportable on Federal income taxes. It is certainly not beyond the realm of imagination that many will not report these transactions on their tax returns. An increase in these types of barter networks is particularly harmful to government coffers already strained by declining tax revenues. The disintermediation of government shows up in other areas of the economy as well.

Scrip

The conditions precipitating the expansion of barter networks are giving rise to the issuance of scrip. Scrip is a currency substitute issued by private enterprises and is a form of credit. Unlike our Federal Reserve Note, scrip is not legal tender since no government authority decrees its value. Scrip has emerged in the early stages of our economic woes in cities like Ithaca, NY and Detroit, MI. During the Great Depression, scrip usage was a popular way to conduct economic transactions when there was insufficient money or credit. A business might pay its workers with scrip that could be used at other establishments accepting scrip. As defaults increase and government institutions are unable to provide support, individual creativity will mark the day. Scrip will simply be a survival mechanism available (Figure 3-8) .

Concentration Camp Scrip

Scrip used by military personnel in Okinawa

Figure 3-8
Examples of Scrip

Currency & Credit Substitutes

Another example of currency substitution has emerged with the creation of Bitcoin electronic currency. A Bitcoin is a peer-to-peer digital currency that does not rely on a central authority to issue it. All Bitcoin transactions occur in an encrypted secure fashion through the internet without involvement from a middleman. If there is adoption of alternate forms of credit/ currency, there is less need for existing forms. This lessening demand for currently popular forms of credit is deflationary.

The number of businesses accepting Bitcoins is limited but steadily growing. I have only provided a very brief overview of this currency. You can read more at (www.bitcoin.org).

Decline in M3

The broadest measure of our money supply is a statistic known as M3. M3 has several components outlined in Table 3-1.

Money statistic	Type of money included
M1	Notes & coins (cash), traveler's checks, demand deposits, NOW accounts,
M2	M1 + savings deposits, time deposits less than $100k
M3	M2 + large time deposits, institutional money market funds, short-term repurchase agreements and other liquid assets

Table 3-1

The M3 measure of our money supply has been contracting for a couple of years and is contracting at its fastest rate since the Great Depression. This contraction has deflationary consequences since it means there are fewer dollars available to chase economic goods. The revelation of a contracting M3 is even more shocking considering how much the Fed and government have done to provide stimulus.

Other Deflationary Signs Recap

Bartering, scrip, and digital currencies are processes that diminish the need for credit. If I can barter, use scrip or digital currencies, I don't need credit. I can conduct my economic transactions outside of the banking system and avoid the influences of central banking. All of these things reduce demand for credit, which is deflationary.

What Will Make This Deflation Different?

In order to understand what makes this deflation potentially the most severe in history, we need to understand the inflation that preceded it (Economic Law #3). The primary difference between previous bouts of inflation (China in the 9th century, Continental currency, Civil War U.S. Notes) and the current inflation is the issuance of credit in electronic form.

Inflation in the previous bouts was a function of physical paper issuance. The government or a certificate depository issued more paper certificates than the wealth, usually precious metal coins, they represented. The price of goods and services went up relative to the paper. The tangibility of the paper made the effects of inflation more obvious since it often circulated next to precious metal coins so people could see the devaluation of the paper more clearly. Gresham's Law (bad money drives out the good money) came into play since the public had a tendency to hoard the precious metal coins and spend the paper. The paper certificates eventually lost value as people migrated back to gold or something that represented gold.

Today we don't have real wealth circulating as money, so it is difficult for people to compare bad money to good money. We didn't experience the hoarding of good money since we don't have any to fall back to. The lack of alternate money allowed inflation via credit to grow even faster – we had little choice.

During the Great Depression thousands of banks failed, which is highly deflationary since there was much less lending occurring in the economy. The balloon representing the Great Depression deflation was the size of a beach ball. The amount of air representing our potential deflation would fill one of those airships you see floating above sporting events (Figure 3-9).

Figure 3-9
Deflation 21st Century Style

Inflation in this bout arose from the creation of massive amounts of debt or IOUs. These IOUs appeared on the books of banks and governments. Creating these IOUs was easy with a money system that does not represent wealth. Alarmingly, the amount of IOUs created is beyond the ability of our economy to pay them.

Imagine borrowing money for things like cars, vacations, big screen TVs, and houses and reaching such a point that you could not make your monthly payments. Absent a significant inflow of money, you have three options:

- You borrow more money just to be able to make your payments. This is a temporary solution since you are borrowing money to service payments for previously borrowed money. At some point, nobody will lend you any more money.

- You default on your loans. This solves your debt problem but your lender owns your car and your house. Your lender will sell your house and car to cover the loan loss meaning fire sale prices.

- You sell off some of your assets (home, car, TVs) to raise cash in order to pay off your loans. This forced sale of assets drives their price down.

The example I just mentioned relates to tangible assets like homes and cars. What about something less tangible like financial assets (stocks & bonds)? They can also fall in value during a deflation. The prices of stocks and bonds increase when a buyer and seller agree to a higher price. Once a single buyer and a seller agree to the higher price, the market sets for everyone else. Others owning stocks or bonds feel the same price effect without having conducted any transaction. The same thing can happen in reverse. When just one buyer and one seller agree to a lower price, the market falls for <u>everyone else</u> owning that asset.

A declining market in stocks or bonds is highly deflationary. The value many thought they had in their stock or bond portfolio falls and with that fall comes the feeling of lesser wealth. The value of the portfolio literally disappears. One day the brokerage statement shows $50,000 in the account and the next it shows $35,000. Where did the $15,000 go? These financial assets were

IOUs or stock certificates that the market said were worth $50,000. Now the market feels differently and the portfolio is valued at $35,000. Ultimately, financial values are agreements in the minds of those participating.

The scope of our crisis is more severe than the deflationary episodes of the 1830s and 1930s. In those deflationary episodes, we did not have this many IOUs or the overall reliance on financial assets.

What Ends Deflation?

Deflation is a product of the previous credit boom. In his opus, *Human Action*, the Austrian economist Ludwig von Mises postulated that prices of material and labor reach excessive levels during a credit boom. Prices of both must come down before consumers will spend and businesses can be profitable again. Consumers get tapped out and can no longer purchase things at current prices. Businesses abstain from purchasing materials or hiring workers until prices and wages adjust to the actual state of the market. Consumer and business action are necessary to have supply/demand return to balance in the economy and end the deflation. Wages and prices fall.

Saturated debtors, no longer able to deal with crushing payments, begin to sell off assets in order to pay off loans. The prices of those assets fall since those with cash understand what is happening and hold out for lower prices. Forced asset sales are devastating but necessary in order to restore proper valuations in the economy.

Another component that helps vanquish deflation is default. Borrowers default on their loans and creditors go out of business. While extremely painful, this necessary process will also help rebalance supply and demand. At the balance point, willing lenders and borrowers return to more normal economic activity. Finally, when the deflationary process is complete, confidence will slowly return to the system.

All the steps described above bring pain and suffering. This is simply the price for massive credit inflation. For those with cash, it will be a time to pick up assets or investments at great bargains. For those in debt, austerity lies in their future.

As mentioned in the foreword, our credit bubble grew like a balloon whose skin got stretched very tight – almost to the point of tearing and popping. The balloon wants badly to deflate but the Wizard keeps trying to put the air back in. Deflation can end naturally, albeit with significant pain. Attempts to ward off the deflationary effects in an economy merely prolong the balloon's pain. As von Mises said, "*...any attempt of the government or the labor unions to prevent or to delay this adjustment merely prolongs the stagnation.*"

What Lies Ahead?

We stand at the precipice of the greatest credit deflation in history. When you, I, and the rest of the people in the economy grow debt beyond the point where we can sustain it, confidence crashes and the economy soon follows. The flow of credit also crashes.

The destruction of credit places tremendous strains on the collateral against which this credit was given. For example, in the real estate market, a loss of home value causes the size of the loan to be greater than the value of the home. The loss of home value makes lenders very uncomfortable. Lenders are not keen about loans where the collateral, the home, is worth less than the loan. If it was a matter of a borrower defaulting, and the home value was greater than the loan, the bank could take possession and sell. While not a desirable outcome for the bank, at least they could recover their loan value. If the value of the home falls below the loan amount, not only does the bank need to sell the home but now it must take a loss.

Tighter credit standards will evolve and the deleveraging process lies ahead. Deleveraging means the reduction of debt. The intent to reduce debt leads to the selling of assets at lesser and lesser prices. If the sale of assets is insufficient to retire the earlier debt, default occurs. As defaults become more rampant, the lending institutions find themselves unwilling to grant new credit. Banks will also fail in greater numbers since many borrowers will be unable to pay them back. Insolvency is already present for many banks and the total would be higher were it not for the wizardry of the Federal Reserve Bank action. Fewer banks mean less credit. Those fortunate enough to retire their loans create more deflation since the loan payoff reduces the amount of credit in circulation. The events in this paragraph are deflationary.

The United States and other governments sensed the deflation and attempted to counteract the effects of the deflationary spiral through their own spending; they replaced consumer spending and investment with their own (Figure 3-10). Unfortunately, in the case of the U.S., there was no rainy day fund to save the economy. The U.S. borrowed and added to its formidable debt pile – they borrowed money to deal with borrowed money. It is impossible for the U.S. Government to replace private spending and investment by raiding the U.S. Treasury since they have no rainy day fund. At this point, a Treasury default or restructuring becomes likely or a drastic reduction in government spending ensues.

Figure 3-10
Government Efforts to Fight Deflation

Summary

The following are the key points of the chapter:

- Deflation is a reduction in money and credit outstanding. With reduced credit, there is less purchasing power chasing goods and services.
- Deflation is a lack of confidence.
- The following events reduce credit:
  - ☐ Loan default
  - ☐ Restricted lending by banks
  - ☐ Diminished borrowing by borrowers
  - ☐ Loan payoff

- Falling prices do not cause deflation but are a consequence of deflation.

- Inflation precedes deflation.

- Deflation is ignited by the inability of borrowers to pay their debts.

- The ignition of deflation sets off a series of events that are psychologically driven.

- Deflation ends when prices and wages adjust to the actual state of the market.

- The current economy showed signs of deflation based on the following:

  - ☑ Bank credit fell.

  - ☑ The public increased its cash holdings.

  - ☑ Industrial production fell and inventories increased.

  - ☑ The stock market remains off its highs.

  - ☑ Housing prices are down.

- The current deflation will be unlike previous bouts since the recent inflation was mostly a product of IOU creation and not physical paper money. IOUs were much easier to create than paper money. There is a whole lot more to deflate this time.

Chapter 4
Human Behavior

Ever wonder why social, political, or economic events give the impression of chaos or a lack of order. Can you sort out why something occurred and what might occur next? Nature gives us predictable cycles. For example, we know that a day is approximately 24 hours and a year is 365 days. We can also predict high and low tides. We know that a human gestational period is approximately 9 months and that a woman's fertility cycle is approximately 28 days. If we did not know these things, a day would have no meaning and ocean tides would confound anyone building sandcastles. Pregnancies would seem random. We understand these things because science discovered models that are predictable and based on cyclic events.

There is research applying cycles to human behavior. Human behavior is part of nature's fabric. We can model human behavior or mood if we can find cycles that exert influence. Fortunately, researchers have found cyclical relationships affecting human behavior. I offer a word of caution. These cyclic relationships will not be as precise as tidal activity or celestial events. This lack of precision is not a shortcoming. People have free will and individuals do not have to conform to some unseen cycle. If enough individuals feel this way, the cycle could shift. As a whole though, people tend to act in groups (Figure 4-1).

People in groups exhibit a herding response I call "crowd following". In the absence of information, people tend to align themselves to a larger group. The desire to belong to a group is a powerful, emotional motivator that creates a psychological dependence eventually producing a trend. The trends change when a crisis or other mitigating circumstance causes some in the group to alter their course. Then the rest of the crowd follows. Presto, we have a cycle.

Think of teenagers wearing high top tennis shoes. Initially just a few teens have them. Then more teens *need* them in order to look like their friends. Soon other teens implore their parents to buy high tops. Now everyone has high tops. One evening on TV, a music star appears wearing old school low top shoes. A small group of teens discards their high tops in favor of the new low top shoes. Their friends do the same. Then other teens *need* to have the low top shoes because everyone is wearing them. Presto, we have a cycle.

Figure 4-1
We like to follow crowds

My intent is to show you how human behavior will affect areas like politics, social mood, economics and investment trends. Anticipating human behavioral changes will allow us to understand why events unfold and how they may affect investments and wealth preservation.

Cycles

Cycles require an understanding of how people perceived time. Over the course of human history, time was chaotic, linear, or cyclical (Figure 4-2). Chaotic time meant that events occurred randomly. For primitive man, this was how time progressed – events had no correlation. If the sun rose yesterday in the eastern sky, tomorrow's rise in the same sky was unpredictable.

Linear time features a distinct alpha and omega – a beginning and an ending. The linear view holds that the future is a straight-line move of the recent past. How would you answer the following questions?

1. The major league home run record set by Babe Ruth in 1927 stood until broken by Roger Maris in 1961. Mark McGwire broke the record in 1998 and Barry Bonds broke McGwire's record in 2001. How many years until someone eclipses Bonds' record?

2. The average price of a house in the U.S. was $25,000 in 1972 and $100,000 in 1995. What if I asked you in 1995 what the price of a house would be in 2005 or 2010?

3. In 1985, the Dow Jones Industrial Average was 1,200. What would your prediction have been at that time for the Dow in 2002 or 2008?

The linear view extrapolates the future from recent trends. Since the home run record was broken in quick succession in 1998 and 2001, maybe the new record should have occurred by now. People buying homes in 1995 certainly expected them to be worth a whole lot more by 2005, just as those buying in 2005 expected their homes would be worth more by 2010. Most people in 1985 would predict a much higher Dow in 2002 just as those in 2002 would have predicted a higher Dow in 2008.

Well, the 2001 home run record stands, no doubt influenced by Major League Baseball's clampdown on performance enhancing drugs. Home prices *fell* after 2005 due to some of the deflationary triggers mentioned in the last chapter. The Dow fell in 2008 to levels below that in 2002. Linear time blew up in these areas.

Cyclical time emerged when ancient civilizations identified natural cycles based on planetary events. Those cycles also became associated with human actions like sleeping and wakefulness, seasons of the year, and planting and harvesting. Despite cyclical time's natural rhythm, linear time achieved greater prominence through history. Early Christians invalidated studies in alchemy and astrology due to their associations with cycles.

Technology aided linear time's victory by providing artificial light, refrigeration and heating, year-round crops, and advanced life-support measures. Artificial light disrupted the natural cycle of a day. Refrigeration and heating mitigated the effects of the seasons. Advanced life support measures altered the natural course of a human lifetime.

Our society also evolved to a point where events appeared more random – an embrace of chaotic time. Many believe history provides no guide whatsoever and somehow this time is different. Unfortunately, that societal segment does not understand that history is the glue that connects people through time.

My discussion in this chapter focuses on cyclical time. A number of prominent cycles appear in areas such as precipitation, stock prices, population, temperature, panics, and grain prices. The existence of these cycles illustrates that it is possible to forecast things other than tides and celestial events. One aspect of working with cycles is to appreciate their variability. Cycles can vary over time and even disappear altogether. It is important to recognize the existence of cycles and to use them as <u>guidelines</u> rather than rules.

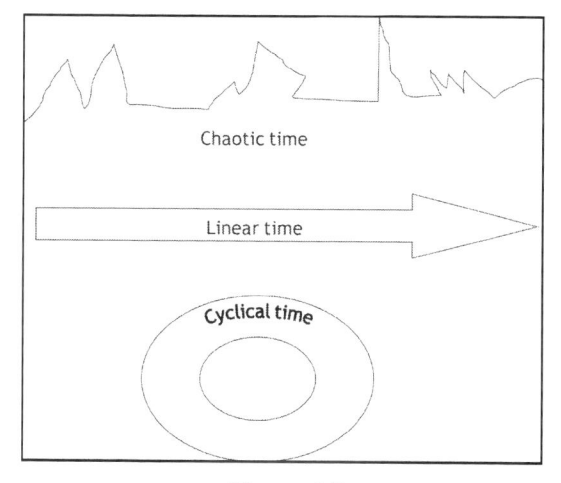

Figure 4-2
Representation of Time

Kondratieff Waves

A prominent cycle in the world of economics is the Kondratieff cycle or "K-Wave". The K-Wave is a business and economic cycle that symbolizes spring, summer, autumn, and winter. The K-Wave is named for the Russian economist, Nikolai Kondratieff who analyzed economic statistics and concluded that developed economies fluctuated in cycles of 50 to 60 years in what he termed "long waves". This work was so controversial that Stalin jailed Kondratieff in 1930. Kondratieff's crime was to suggest that an economy's long-term performance was cyclical – not what a socialist like Stalin wanted publicized.

Kondratieff acknowledged public mood as influential in the rise and fall of prosperity. The public's responses to economic activity formed the basis of his wave theory. He believed the public acted differently over time in a repetitive pattern - the trends I talked about earlier in this chapter. The discussion of human affairs is not something you hear in a discussion about economic theory so it is fair to say that economists seldom accept Kondratieff's work.

Kondratieff felt that economies had periods of accumulation followed by periods of overconsumption. While prices are relatively cheap, people accumulate assets. As prices increase, consumption of assets is necessary to maintain the same standard of living. At some point, prices get too high and the economy begins a decline in order to moderate prices so that a new growth cycle can begin.

The K-Wave has four distinct waves or dramatic mood changes determining the tone of individuals involved in the economy. If you have knowledge of these phases, you can anticipate economic changes and the prevailing psychological mood.

Wave I (Spring)

The growth phase begins from a depressed economic base. In the depression preceding Wave I, the public is mentally exhausted and has little interest in investment. Production expands and the increased volume of goods requires a higher money velocity. Unemployment falls, wages rise and prices remain stable.

Wave II (Summer)

This is a primary recession phase where excess capital produces a shortage of resources. Wars seen during this period produce economic strains increasing the inflationary impacts. A dramatic fall in output, a rise in unemployment and a severe recession characterize the phase. A conservative shift in popular mood arrives.

Wave III (Autumn)

This is a plateau period. The economy moves to a period of relatively flat growth and mild prosperity. The economy becomes consumption oriented. Strong feelings of affluence terminate in a feeling of euphoria. The combination of an inflated price structure and the desire for consumption produces rapid increases in debt. Consumption expands beyond practical limits and the economy slips into a severe and protracted depression.

Wave IV (Winter)

The excesses of the plateau period culminate in a collapse of the price structure. The exhaustion of accumulated wealth forces the economy into a sharp retrenchment. This is just another way of describing deflation. Kondratieff viewed depressions as an enema allowing the economy to readjust from the previous excesses and to build a base for future growth.

Kondratieff Wave analysis suggests we've moved beyond the plateau period (Wave III) into the throes of the economic winter (Wave IV) (Figure 4-3). It is fair to suggest our economy became quite consumption oriented with pronounced feelings of euphoria. Our Wave III did not feel like a plateau and probably felt more like a Wave I due to the accumulation of debt.

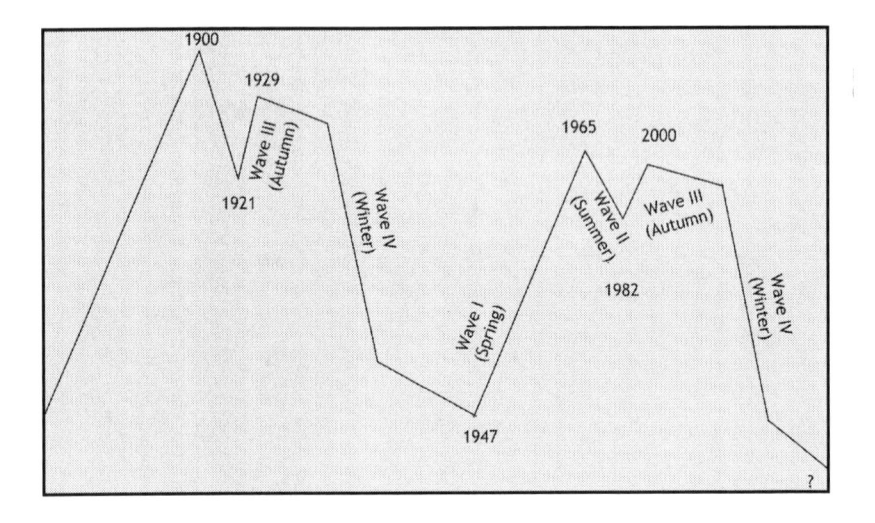

Figure 4-3
Kondratieff Waves

Elliott Waves

Ralph Nelson Elliott developed another useful tool for analyzing economic rhythm in the 1930s. He studied market prices, identified repetitive forms or patterns, and developed another set of waves. Much like the K-Wave, Elliott Waves show distinct patterns of growth and decay. Within larger Elliott Waves exist smaller ones and within these smaller ones exist smaller ones still and so on (Figure 4-4). This embedding of waves is important in Elliott Wave analysis since it gives a sense of how strong the wave pattern will be. The largest wave pattern is the Grand Supercycle, the next largest is the Supercycle and the one following it is the Cycle. There are more wave names defining smaller increments. When various waves culminate at the same point in time, the movement up or down tends to be quite powerful.

Elliott postulated that in markets, progress occurs in the form of five waves with an alternation between "up" and "down" waves. The progress pattern is Up-Down-Up-Down-Up (waves 1,2,3,4, and 5) and the waves have no predefined length (Figure 4-4). The other side of Elliott Waves is what occurs when the progress pattern completes. Elliott identified three corrective waves that alternate in a Down-Up-Down pattern (waves A, B, and C in Figure 4-4).

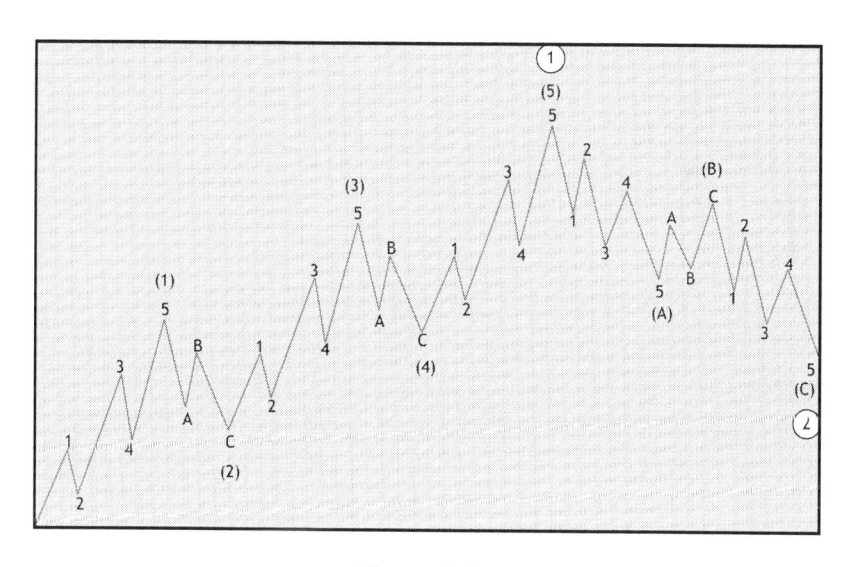

Figure 4-4

Elliott Waves

Each wave in the Elliott Wave sequence is a reflection of the mass psychology of either optimism or pessimism. Wave counts can tell us where we are in that spectrum of mass psychology and where we are headed next. The basic Elliott Wave pattern is described further in Table 4-1.

Robert Prechter is a current practitioner of Elliott Waves who makes forecasts on the economy and the stock market. He makes the following comments regarding the current Elliott Wave structure of the stock market (Figure 4-5):

- ☐ Grand Supercycle Wave (III) began in 1784 and ended in 2000. The Grand Supercycle is the largest waveform.

- ☐ Supercycle Wave (V) began in 1932 and ended in 2000. There are 5 Supercycle waves within the Grand Supercycle.

- ☐ Cycle Wave V began in 1974 and ended in 2000. There are 5 Cycle waves within a Supercycle.

These waveforms end in the year 2000. The confluence of all these waves ending at the same time sets up the potential for a powerful move to the downside. The influence of the Grand Supercycle wave should make the down move more pronounced than that of the Great Depression. Prechter goes on to conclude that we are actually in the corrective process of the waveforms and in the early stages of Wave C of the Cycle wave, the tsunami.

Wave	Description
I	First impulse wave. A portion of this wave creates a base from which a much larger advance can take place. A slow but steady increase in optimism is evident after the previous bottom. The degree of optimism depends on how severe the previous bottom was. The more severe the previous bottom, the slower the buildup of optimism.
II	First corrective wave. The movement of Wave II will not go beyond the start of Wave I though it can experience a retracement severe enough to convince the public that a persistent downtrend has begun.
III	Typically the most powerful wave. If it is not the most powerful wave, it is never the shortest. The wave is strong and broad, and public optimism expands. *Confidence,* that word so often used in this book, returns energetically.
IV	Second corrective wave. The movement of Wave IV will not go into the territory of Wave II. Deterioration in this wave sets the stage for weakness in the fifth wave. Confidence and optimism take a slight breather and there is even justification of the corrective wave in people's minds.
V	Last impulse wave. This wave appears strong but in many respects is weaker than Wave III. At this point, the public is "all in" and optimism and confidence run high.

Table 4-1
Elliott Wave Description

Wave	Description
A	Initial wave of decline. An arrogant complacency is in place and reflected in economics, politics and government. In the investment world, it is the start of the bear market. The public, however, only views the reaction as a point from where the next advance may begin.
B	The pyrite wave. Pyrite is more commonly known by its nickname, "fools gold". Wave B tricks people into believing the advance is the start of something big. Fundamentals of the investment world and the economy weaken subtly. There is a continuation of the euphoria and a denial of what lies ahead.
C	Tsunami of all waves. Social mood starts to break down and the economy follows. Investment markets start to crumble and safe havens are few. Prices begin a downward slide. Cash is a good place to be.

Table 4-1 (continued)
Elliott Wave Description

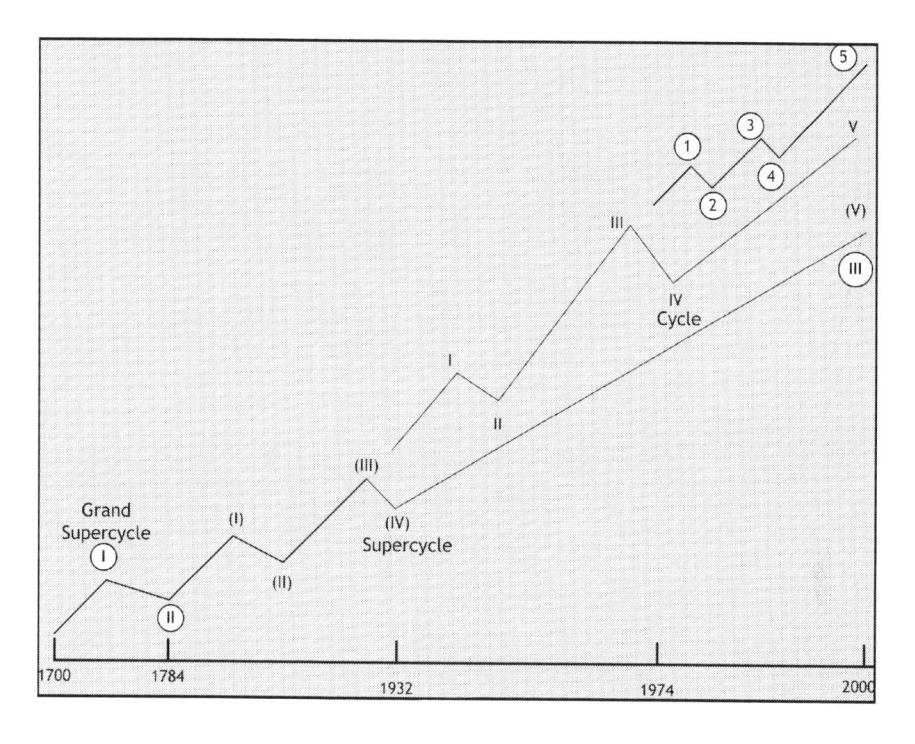

Figure 4-5
Elliott Wave Cycles

Millennium Waves

There is another, longer cycle available to evaluate economic and social progress. The Millennium Cycle, as the name implies, identifies turns that occur in 1,000-year cycles. The cycle has five circled "up" waves (labeled 1 ,2 ,3 ,4 , and 5) which have an Up-Down-Up-Down–Up pattern and 3 circled "down" waves (labeled A, B, C) which have a Down-Up-Down pattern. These waves comprise the Grand Supercycle. Each Grand Supercycle wave has a five-wave subdivision within it called a Supercycle labeled (1), (2), (3), (4), and (5). Likewise, each Supercycle wave has another wave pattern within it called a Cycle with five waves labeled I, II, III, IV, V. The Millennium Cycle breaks down with the following Grand Supercycles:

Wave	Description
① (1000 – 1320)	Revival of European cultural activity and the dominance of France. Though the period featured the Crusades, knowledge in areas such as science medicine and architecture transferred from the Islamic world to the western world. Logic and dialectics facilitated intellectual inquiry.
② (1320 – 1485)	The epidemic known as Black Death decimated Europe and caused a fall in population of 40%. The Hundred Years war destroyed much of the peasant population in France.
③ (1485 – 1650)	Transition from medieval times to a more modern way of life. Finance, commerce and industry began competing with agriculture. Period famous for the Renaissance, the Reformation and a reaction against the teachings of the Church. Time of Shakespeare and Martin Luther. The discovery of the New World. Business expanded and prices rose.
④ (1650 – 1789)	Time of persecution for witchcraft, fanaticism, the Inquisition and economic depression.
⑤ (1789 – 2000?)	American Revolution and the formation of the Constitution. Rise of the U.S. as a world power, the Industrial Revolution, the emergence of communism and socialism, the conquest of outer space, an explosion in world commerce, and the creation of the largest credit bubble in history.

Table 4-2
Millennium Cycle
(Grand Supercycle Waves)

Now let's take a look at some of the Supercycles within Grand Supercycle Wave ⑤ (1789 – 2000).

Wave	Description
(1) (1789 - 1837)	The end of this wave marked a prosperous period culminating in the Panic of 1837. The Panic of 1837 was a financial crisis built on speculative fever.
(2) (1837 - 1857)	The end of this period was marked by the Panic of 1857 that included a downturn in the economy. From 1852-1857 the stock market declined 66% compared with inflation.
(3) (1857 - 1929)	This was the second phase of the Industrial Revolution. This was also the Gilded Age, which marked a period where the U.S. grew at an extremely rapid rate.
(4) (1929 - 1932)	Marked the initial stages of the Great Depression. The year 1932 is very important since it marked a historic stock market bottom.
(5) (1932 – 2000?)	The ending sub-wave in the sequence marks the greatest stock market run in history.

Table 4-3
Grand Supercycle Wave ⑤
(Supercycle Waves)

Let's examine Supercycle Wave (5) (1932 – 2000) and each of the Cycle waves within it. I will mention a few key points in terms of the stock market.

Wave	Description
I (1932-1937)	Nineteen thirty-two (1932) was the major stock market bottom and 1937 was the high for the Great Depression period.
II (1937- 1942)	Nineteen forty-two (1942) was a significant low. The only lower point was the 1932 low.
III (1942-1973)	The Dow went from a level of approximately 95 to 1000, a ten-fold gain.
IV (1973-1982)	The Dow oscillated in a 400-point range for much of this time making a strong low in 1982.
V (1982-2000?)	This period marks the greatest bull market run in history.

Table 4-4
Supercycle Wave (5)
(Cycle Waves)

According to Millennium Cycle analysis (Figure 4-6) we have completed the entire Millennium Wave cycle that includes Grand Supercycle Wave (5) (circled), Supercycle Wave (5), and Cycle Wave V. The next wave should evolve into a depression. The effects will not merely be economic. Culture, politics, social structure, and money itself will be transformed during this wave change.

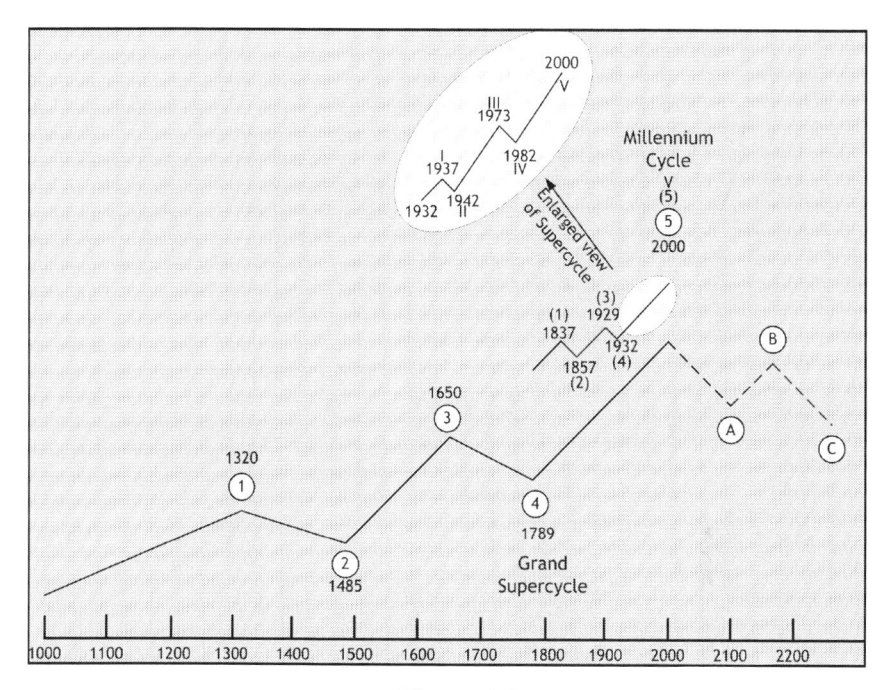

Figure 4-6
Millennium Cycle

The Economy and Waves

How do you test the validity of the waves with respect to economic performance? I use three figures of economic performance, GDP, Industrial Production, and Capacity Utilization to illustrate how the U.S. economy fared during the various wave periods (Figure 4-7). If wave patterns have merit, we should see weakening economic fundamentals as we move towards the end of the various cycles. We should also see weaker performance in the growth waves. For example, K-Wave III should be weaker than K-Wave I, Elliott Cycle Wave V should be weaker than Cycle Wave III, and Millennium Cycle Wave V should be weaker than Cycle Wave III.

K-Wave

Wave I shows better performance than Wave III in GDP and industrial production. Capacity utilization figures were only available for the period encompassing Waves II and III. Despite Wave III supposedly being a growth wave, there was less capacity utilization than in Wave II. This is not a healthy economic sign.

Elliott Supercycle (V)

This Supercycle shows a contraction in GDP and industrial production from Cycle Wave III to Cycle Wave V. In fact Cycle Wave IV, a down wave, had better figures in all three categories versus Cycle Wave V. So even though the period from 1974 to 2000 felt like a boom for people, it was actually quite a bit weaker than the growth period of 1942-1966.

Millennium Wave Supercycle V

In a similar manner to Elliott Waves, this wave shows a weaker Cycle Wave V than Cycle Wave III in the areas of GDP and industrial production. Capacity utilization was higher in Cycle Wave IV (a down wave) than Cycle Wave V, which is supposed to be a stronger wave.

	GDP (average % annual growth)	Industrial Prod (yearly average of monthly changes)	Capacity Utilization (average monthly value)
K - Wave			
IV (1929-1947) [1]	3.8	4.1	
I (1947-1965)	4.1	4.8	
II (1965-1982)	2.9	2.5	83.3
III (1982-2000)	3.7	3.4	81.1
Elliott Supercycle (V)			
I (1932-1937)	3.7	12.3	
II (1937-1942)	7.1	8.2	
III (1942-1966)	4.3	4.6	
IV (1966-1974)	4.0	4.2	85.1
V (1974-2000)	3.1	2.7	81.3
Millennium Supercycle (5)			
I (1932-1937)	3.7	12.3	
II (1937-1942)	7.1	8.2	
III (1942-1973)	4.2	4.4	
IV (1973-1982)	2.9	1.5	82.5
V (1982-2000)	3.3	3.4	81.1

Note [1]: Excluding World War II years, GDP growth drops to 0.6%

Figure 4-7
Waves & the Economy
[Shaded boxes not to scale]

All three waves were consistent in demonstrating weakening economic measures. If I add unemployment data to the mix, we see persistently worse unemployment. Elliott Cycle Waves III and V show a worsening average unemployment rate from 4.9% to 6.5% respectively. The same worsening figures show up in the K-Wave and the Millennium Wave.

Compounding this worsening of economic fundamentals, we have the following conditions as we progress through the various waves:

- ☑ Households had fewer liquid assets and more debt.

- ☑ Federal debt as a percentage of our GDP is much higher.

- ☑ The trade deficit went from a surplus to a large deficit.

For all of our debt, we aren't getting the same bang for our buck in economic performance.

Wave Interpretation

As I noted at the beginning of the chapter, human behavior cycles are not precise. Because we are talking about people, the cycles identify tendencies and are not rules but guidelines. The lack of cycle precision is not a shortcoming since people have free will. On the other hand, people tend to act in a collective behavioral pattern so the use of cycles is appropriate. I presented K-Waves, Elliott Waves, and Millennium Waves as expressions of human progress and decline. Some readers will have doubts these waves can have any predictive value. I will agree that we cannot use them in the same manner as predicting tides or celestial events. If you are married to the concept of linear time, nothing I can present will dissuade you. If you can accept the influence of cycles on human behavior, then these waves can provide a guide to our future.

Where do I think we are with respect to these waves? During the most recent economic upswing, people had a strong desire to feel prosperous. In the United States, much of that prosperity was on the back of debt. Demand for debt increased and the need for saving decreased. This was evident in both the public and private sector. The public and government forgot how to save. These behaviors are symptomatic of K-Wave III, the ending wave. Our growth in this wave was more tepid and it was built on the back of debt. Elliott Cycle Wave V and Millennium Cycle Wave V show a similar slow-growth pattern.

I'd like to make a point about the use of the year 2000 as the end of the cycles. The year 2000 is but a reference point. I could use 2007 for the end of the K-Wave and the Millennium Supercycle. As I showed in Chapter 3 on deflation, 2007 was an important year for a number of deflationary events. Elliott Wave technicians use 2000 as the terminal year for Grand Supercycle Wave (III), Supercycle Wave (V) and Cycle Wave V. According to Robert Precther, the doyen of Elliott Wave analysts, we are in the early stages of Cycle Wave C, the tsunami.

All three wave interpretations arrive at a similar conclusion. We are entering a period of contraction. I cannot predict the degree of contraction but I do know we have a large balloon to deflate. The effects of the contraction have been largely muted thus far because of debt added to the economy. All we did with debt was postpone the inevitable. I will present other cycles in this chapter that are of shorter length to provide further support for these longer time cycles.

The Saeculum

Perhaps the most important cycle affecting you personally is the cycle of birth and death. This cycle has a name – the Saeculum. A Saeculum is a unit of time roughly encompassed by a human lifespan. The human lifespan, as defined by the ancients, ranged from 80 to 100 years. Each Saeculum is comprised of four generations. A generation is the period between a mother giving birth and her offspring doing the same - roughly 25 years. The Saeculum progresses through youth, growth, maturity, and decline much like a person advancing into older age. The most well known generations are the Millennials (1982-2007), Generation X (1961-1981), and the Boomers (1940-1960). These years are approximate.

Each generation tends to have different characteristics in their behavior and their values. The Boomers grew up in the aftermath of a crisis – World War II and the Great Depression. They were indulged as children, became absorbed in the cultural crusades of the 60s and 70s, and emerged as moralistic midlifers – remember he did not inhale. Gen Xers grew up as under-protected children, were alienated as young adults and will have an important role in shaping society as they enter middle adulthood.

In the late 1960s, Boomer college freshmen asserted in a 2 to 1 majority that "developing a meaningful philosophy of life" was more important than "getting ahead financially". Responses from college freshmen from Generation X gave the complete opposite answer.

Behavior and generational values tend to repeat at similar points in the Saeculums. Boomers and Gen Xers tend to mimic the same grouping, four generations prior. History also shows that during a crisis, the generations are in the same relative position in their lifespan. During the last crisis, occurring with K-Wave IV (1929 – 1947), the generation corresponding to Boomers moved into elder adulthood (65 and over) while the generation corresponding to Gen X moved into midlife (42 and over). Boomers brought an idealism to society while Gen X will have to bring a pragmatic philosophy for dealing with our challenges.

Boomers unquestionably exerted the most influence in our society. They were born during a high birth rate period and became socially active during the 1960s and 1970s. That period ushered in civil rights, the women's movement, and urban reform. The same generation became more conservative during the 1980s and 1990s. Stock ownership achieved great breadth through the proliferation of mutual funds. The Boomers presided over a credit and stock market boom unlike any in history.

The generation that paralleled the Baby Boomers, those born four generations prior, exhibited similar behavior. The parallel Boomers of the period from the 1900s to the 1920s ushered in the Progressive Era with its similar idealism of the 1960s and 1970s. The 1900s to 1920s idealism brought us alcohol prohibition, women's suffrage, and a focus on alleviating the conditions of the poor. After 1920, the Progressive Era faded and brought in conservative presidential administrations. The 1920s brought a soaring stock market and interest in investment trusts that were the mutual fund equivalents of that day.

Generational research has also shown that baby booms tend to precede periods of high activity and high inflation while declining birth rates tend to precede periods of low activity and low inflation/deflation. The Boomers were born during K-Wave I and Elliott Supercycle (V), Cycle Wave III, which are powerful growth waves. Lower Gen X birth rates set the stage for a subdued, conservative economic environment ahead as this generation moves into the next stage of the Saeculum. This generation was born during K-Wave II and Elliott Supercycle (V), Cycle Wave IV, which are contraction waves. Generation X will be thrust into positions of leadership to deal with the aftermath of the influential Baby Boomers.

Social Rhythm

The sociologist Peter Harris published a monograph that concluded that a number of American social indicators demonstrated a twenty-two year cycle. Using 300 years of data, indicators such as birth rates, marriage age, wage growth, social mobility and political activism seemed to vary every twenty-two years. He also suggested that the mood of the country proceeded through cycles closely following his twenty-two year metric. Harris' twenty-two year cycle approximates the generational pattern discussed earlier. These cycles will affect various societal components as outlined in this chapter section.

Incarceration and Drug Use

A social rhythm change I anticipate is a relaxation of views towards incarceration of non-violent criminals. Consider that a large portion (perhaps 50%) of the prison population in the U.S. consists of non-violent criminals. A 2008 story in the Washington Post cites 1% of the adult population in the United States is in prison. The 2.3 million prisoners place the U.S. at the top of world statistics for incarceration – far ahead of the more populous China. State governments spend $50 billion and the Federal Government spends $5 billion to house prisoners.

Predictably, with state budgets straining from diminished tax collections, some states are starting to consider reducing their prison population. Illinois announced the early release of up to 1,000 inmates incarcerated for drug offenses or non-violent property crimes with less than a year remaining on their sentences. Voters will begin to question why non-violent inmates are in jail in the first place. Many of the non-violent inmates in the system are convicted drug offenders. Those are easy targets for thinning the prison ranks.

In order to thin the ranks of convicted drug offenders, drug possession will be viewed in a new light. I predict a gradual decriminalization of drug possession. Presently, 13 states have decriminalized non-medical marijuana. Some states, most notably California, have many legal medical marijuana dispensaries that operate under state though not Federal protection. Federal law states that cannabis (marijuana) usage is illegal even for medical purposes despite what any local or state law indicates. This has created quite a conundrum.

As state and Federal budgets become more strained and as government provides fewer services to its citizens, legislators will see this type of decriminalization as an opportunity to divert scarce funds to areas of greater need. The decriminalization of marijuana and perhaps other drugs allows governments to create something otherwise dwindling for them, tax funds. A sales or value added tax could be the logical extension of the decriminalization or legalization of certain drugs. Another result of this effort will be the reduction of law enforcement activity dedicated to policing drug usage. Additionally, the use of medical marijuana should increase as the public shoulders more responsibility for their health and welfare.

While there are economic forces influencing the potential decriminalization of some drugs, there are social effects in play. A positive social mood tends create strict thought around moral issues and a waning mood tends to relax these attitudes. Using our cycle indicators like K-Waves, Elliott Waves, and Millennium Waves, we can identify high and low human behavior periods. We would expect a greater relaxation of the feeling surrounding drug use during low periods and more restrictions in high periods (*no pun intended*).

In 1937 (a high point in the stock market), the Marihuana Tax Act levied a tax of roughly one dollar on people dealing commercially in cannabis, hemp or marijuana. The Act, however, did not criminalize its usage. Ironically, the Act passed despite opposition by none other than the American Medical Association.

In 1942 (a low point in the stock market), a sociological study was commissioned in New York City entitled, *La Guardia Committee Reports*, which concluded the following regarding marijuana usage:

1. It does not lead to addiction.

2. It does not lead to the commission of other crimes.

3. It does not lead to the usage of heroin, morphine, or cocaine.

In the bull market period from 1942 to 1973 a number of pieces of legislation including the Boggs Act (increased penalties for drug abuse), the Narcotics Control Act (more increase in penalties), and the Controlled Substances Act clamped down hard on marijuana and other drugs.

During the bear market period from 1973 to 1982, several measures emerged softening the stance on drugs. The Shafer Commission recommended the decriminalization of marijuana and President Carter made a similar recommendation.

Once the bull market resumed after 1982 the clamp down began again with the Anti-Drug Abuse Act, President Bush's (41) speech on the "War on Drugs", and a Supreme Court ruling on medical marijuana.

Our social mood now has led to the American College of Physicians releasing a position paper urging the government to remove marijuana from its Schedule 1 classification. Schedule 1 substances imply no medical usage and a high potential for abuse. The U.S. Attorney General, Eric Holder announced that Federal agents would not target medicinal marijuana use where state law sanctioned it.

Whatever you conclude about the studies or the laws, what is important is to consider the cyclical nature of these events. My anticipation of decriminalization or outright legalization of some drugs is not a political or moral argument. What I see are economic realities faced by governments and a change in societal attitudes towards some types of drugs. If a police department sees its budget axed, will they want to dedicate scarce resources towards narcotics or basic citizen protection? As the public becomes more concerned with their economic welfare, the focus on the increasingly violent war on drugs will no longer be important. At a minimum, decriminalization of some drugs will enter the discussion. A discussion on the decriminalization of drugs would have been unthinkable during the Reagan Administration, remember, "Just say no." We are entering a different social rhythm now.

Welfare

Another economic reality is how we might deal with social welfare. Charles Murray concluded that in the 30-year period from 1950 to 1980, social welfare costs increased 13 times but the number of poor people was the same in 1968 and 1980. Americans have gotten used to cost-of-living increases in Social Security and recently the nation expanded health care coverage. As you will see in an upcoming chapter, the U.S. Government simply cannot fulfill all of its social welfare covenants. The public may call for a rollback of the welfare state and this will affect those in various economic strata, not just the poor.

Fallen Heroes

The changing social rhythm will affect well-known personalities too. During our cycle uptrend, many personalities achieved prominence in their respective fields but now the cycle downtrend turns these personalities into what I call "Fallen Heroes". The Fallen Heroes are people formerly occupying the pantheon of their respective fields that for some reason or another, fell into disfavor. It was not so much that the individuals changed, it was how public mood turned against them. Examples of these former heroes are listed in Table 4-5.

Wave	Description
George W. Bush	Enjoyed stratospheric popularity after 9/11 and left office with exceptionally low approval ratings
Mark McGwire	Credited with "saving" baseball now reviled for potential steroid abuse and for an awkward appearance before Congress
Barry Bonds	Baseball's all-time home run king now reviled for potential steroid abuse and Federal indictments
Bernard Madoff	Respected New York investment advisor accused of perpetrating the largest Ponzi scheme in history
Alan Greenspan	Credited with having a magic touch propelling Wall Street to higher levels. Now criticized for not having the wisdom to forecast the stock market meltdown and housing bust.
Eliot Spitzer	New York Attorney General lauded for fighting corruption later associated with prostitution while serving as governor.

Table 4-5
Fallen Heroes

Another Fallen Hero includes Jim Cramer, the CNBC stock market maven. Comedy Central's Jon Stewart chastised Mr. Cramer for failing to call out the speculative excesses of Wall Street. The dressing-down of Mr. Cramer was inconceivable just a few years ago when his flashy, loud persona made him "must see" television. Beyond Mr. Cramer, Stewart took CNBC to task for cheerleading Wall St. and failing in their duty to educate viewers on what was driving momentum in the stock market.

While the recent bear market rally eased some of the pressure on Mr. Cramer, he will slide more deeply into the Fallen Hero category once the market resumes its slide.

There are also Fallen Heroes in the institutional ranks including General Motors (GM). At one point, GM was the largest auto producer in the world. What was good for GM was good for the country it was said. In 2001, GM pension funds began a period of chronic underfunding. Later in 2004, as the financial mania pushed forward in consumer goods and housing, GM was obtaining 87% of its profits from its financing arm, GMAC! GM fell to the point where it was at the mercy of government for loans and had its CEO dismissed by government. Taxpayers at one point owned 61% of GM leading to the derisive term, "Government Motors". Government is now in the car business.

Another fallen institutional Hero was Indy Mac bank. The lending institution that failed in July 2008 was intimately involved in the creation of low quality loans eventually sold to the secondary market. Despite evidence that such low quality loans originated with this bank, regulatory agencies disregarded these events. Rating agencies that should have been vigilant over the types of loans made by financial institutions fell asleep at the wheel. Such negligence was typical of other ratings agencies recommending companies before their stocks tanked.

The Fallen Heroes in Table 4-5 probably are not very different people now than when they were at their pinnacle of success. Alan Greenspan did not suddenly become a bad central banker. Bernard Madoff (Figure 4-8) did not suddenly emerge as a bad investor for his clients; his Ponzi scheme was many years old. What changed was society's attitude. The general optimism of the social uptrend shifted towards diminished confidence and increased hostility.

As economic conditions worsen, so will societal attitude. There will be calls for more Congressional investigations looking for scapegoats responsible for the financial mess. There will be less overall trust of institutions and government. Society will not have as many heroes as before.

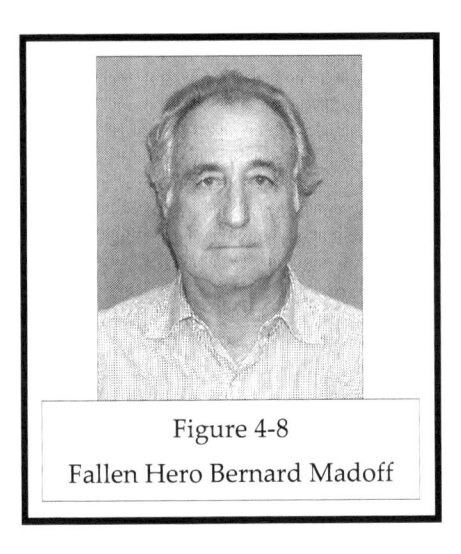

Figure 4-8
Fallen Hero Bernard Madoff

Political Rhythm

Arthur Schlesinger Jr. coined the term "patterns of alternation" in 1985 to describe an ebb and flow in the cycles of American politics. Schlesinger predicted the 1990s would be a period of greater government involvement reminiscent of the activism of the Roosevelt and Kennedy era administrations. The Ross Perot campaign of 1992, while quite successful in popular support, did not echo the political rhythm into which the nation was entering. The country was not ready for broad scale discussion of fiscal responsibility. Schlesinger went on to say that, some time at the end of the first decade of the twenty-first century, the public would grow tired of government activism. The general elections of 2010 and beyond will feature more discussion on how government spends money.

If you doubt we had an activist government in the two decades after 1990, look at how government spent money. Federal debt exploded from 1990 to 2010. It did not matter if a Democrat or Republican was in the White House. It did not matter if the GOP or the Democrats were in charge of Congress. Debt increased regardless. Easy credit conditions seduced our political leaders eager to satisfy every single constituency.

A call for less active government emerged during the acrimonious town hall meetings of 2009. The electorate appeared more politically active than it had been in several years. As congressional leaders found out during these meetings, their titles no longer insulated them from verbal harassment. People openly questioned the need for more government spending.

The more involved electorate should also give rise to new political activism. The Tea Party has emerged at the center of political activism. While they may never coalesce into a third party, the politics is ripe for a viable third party to compete with the GOP and Democrats.

Foreign Affairs Rhythm

The scholar Frank L. Klingberg discovered an alternating pattern to America's foreign policy. The pattern alternates between an inward-looking approach to one of greater foreign involvement. His pattern lasts forty-seven years or roughly two generational periods. Klingberg predicted the period from 1967 to 1987 was to be one of introspection while the period from 1987 to 2014 was to be one of greater foreign involvement. The Vietnam War ended in the early part of Klingberg's introspection period and military action was limited compared to the ensuing period. Military activity since 1987 featured the invasion of Panama, Gulf War I, Gulf War II, the occupation of Iraq, involvement in Bosnia/Serbia, and significant military action in Afghanistan. Even in the interim period between Gulf War I and II, the U.S.

had an active military presence in the Gulf region.

Due to some of the fiscal challenges and the anticipated political rhythm, I forecast a retrenchment of American involvement in foreign affairs. The presence of American troops in peaceful geographies will draw scrutiny from those countries and from within the United States. It will be very difficult for American politicians to justify troops overseas while government drowns in a sea of debt. Government generosity overseas in the form of grants and aid should also see curtailment. There will be more discussion on how the U.S. prosecutes the War on Terror.

The nation's debt will place the U.S. in an awkward position with its creditors. It's going to be much harder to carry a big foreign policy stick when the country is beholden to others financially. The change in our foreign affairs rhythm could very well signal the end of American hegemony on the world stage. America will have to retreat to being a republic and not an empire.

Lack of Investment Vigilance

A feature of the economic upswing was the investor who stopped asking questions. In their haste to make money, investors became a rather trusting lot. Bernard Madoff was *the* seminal figure in this area. Madoff ran what appeared to be a very successful investment fund (Bernard L. Madoff Investment Securities) and was a prominent figure in the New York scene. What is truly stunning about the Madoff incident was the breadth and scope of the fraud. Just a couple of months before the Madoff fund collapse, investors thought they had $64.8 billion in their accounts. It has become apparent that the Madoff fund was never legitimate.

While investors demonstrated little vigilance, the Securities and Exchange Commission (SEC) was one organization whose job it was to be vigilant. In a well-documented effort, financial analyst Harry Markopolos reported his deep suspicions of the Madoff fund to the SEC a full nine years before the fund collapsed. The only reason he undertook his research was that his own company wanted to understand how the Madoff fund performed so well. Markopolos concluded that Madoff's results were not possible absent an active Ponzi scheme or another illegality. His efforts continued for several years without any attention from the SEC.

Beyond Bernard Madoff and other high profile Ponzi schemes, here are some other lower profile examples as documented by the FBI:

- Jan 2009 – four defendants from Florida were charged with running a $1 billion Ponzi scheme
- Jan 2009 – Heber Springs, AR man charged with defrauding investors of tens of millions between 1996 and 2008
- Feb 2009 – grand jury indicted three men with operating a $65 million Ponzi scheme in Seattle
- Feb 2009 – a Minnesota man charged with defrauding 519 people nationwide of $30 million out of a company known as Joshua Tree Group
- Mar 2009 – a Folsom, CA man was charged in a Ponzi scheme that bilked 150 investors of $40 million, many of whom he met at his church.

There are _many_ more beyond these. The cases provide an interesting geographical cross-section. Investment fraud was not strictly a Wall St. phenomenon. The frauds spanned coast-to-coast, and in the last case, a fellow parishioner was in on the swindle.

Moreover, it's not just a fellow parishioner who led people astray. An Anglican bishop in St. Louis, MO is accused of bilking some of his worshippers and country club associates to the tune of $45 million. This is another great example of affinity fraud where close associations promote an overwhelming amount of trust.

The breadth of fraud is indicative of the end of a cycle where the public suspended disbelief in the hopes of achieving fabulous wealth. The next cycle will bring greater public scrutiny and perhaps an utter lack of trust in the area of investment.

Public Anger

As a society, we were so confident that critical thinking went the way of the dinosaur. Having a healthy dose of skepticism was often a recipe for ridicule. The new cycle will foster public anger in ways that were formerly unimaginable.

On April 15, 2009, protesters gathered in 300 locations in all 50 states to stage "tea parties" akin to the Boston Tea Party of 1773. What was interesting about the gatherings was that no political party or other well-organized group sponsored them. The viral nature of the Internet allowed disparate groups of people to organize via blogs, Facebook or chat boards without a larger body for leadership. Many of these self-organizers never participated in these types of rallies. Politicians attempting to score points with the protesters were rebuffed and not allowed to speak at these rallies. Who were these people forming the tea parties? They were ordinary citizens, fed up for one reason or another (Figure 4-9).

Public anger reached center stage during the town hall debates and the passage of the health care legislation. Some analysts and Democrats blamed the Republican Party for the backlash. The backlash featured racial epithets, nasty voicemail messages, and property destruction. The issue is not simply GOP vs. Democratic Party.

Overall, there is a groundswell of discontent without party affiliation with the Tea Party receiving the most attention. To consider them an organized political party at this point is premature. Politicians from the Republican Party, however, see an opportunity to capitalize on the discontent by addressing Tea Party rallies. The Tea Party has been consistent in its assertion that it wants no part of political affiliation. They simply want their voices heard.

Figure 4-9
Tea Party Rally

Less than one year from their humble beginnings, none other than former Presidential candidate John McCain and Vice-Presidential candidate Sarah Palin where stumping for votes at a Tea Party rally to help Senator McCain in his Arizona senatorial campaign. This would have been inconceivable in 2009.

While the Tea Party itself may not become an organized political party, it may serve as the basis for a viable third party in the United States. Perhaps that third party is nothing more than an independent party in name. The new cycle will bring ideas forward on how to combat the pressing financial issues of the day and quell public anger. The danger with public anger is its potentially volatile nature. Extreme candidacies for political office tend to emerge from a torrent of public anger.

Financial Conservatism

The years ahead will be a time of greater financial conservation. The primary impetus for this conservation will be the overhang of massive debts in the government sector and personal finance. The consumer is unwilling to acquire more debt unlike government, once again behind the curve, who is attempting to replace consumer spending. An April 2010 survey conducted by Bankrate asked what individuals would do with their 2009 IRS tax refund. Fifty-eight percent (58%) indicated they would either pay down debt or save the refund, 26% indicated they were going to spend the refund on necessities and a mere 7% indicated they would spend it on discretionary items like a vacation. The Personal Saving Rate illustration (Figure 4-10) is a reflection of this financial conservation trend. Notice how far the savings rate is from the level of 1982. The public will attempt to reach those previous savings levels in the years to come.

Another aspect of financial conservatism is the diminished use of leverage. Leverage is the ability to control an asset with borrowed funds. In the commodities market, a trader puts up a "margin" to control a large contract. This margin may be as little as 10% of the actual contract value so their leverage is 90%. For example, $5,000 of margin may control a contract worth $50,000. If the value of the contract increases by $1,000, the trader has made 20% on their money (1,000/5,000). Conversely, if the value of the contract falls by $1,000 the trader loses 20%. In either case, the $1,000 move on the $50,000 contract is 2% of its actual value but the trader feels the move as 20%. When the trader experiences a loss of $2,000, 40% of the margin put up is lost. The trader may still control the contract but their brokerage asks for more money, known as a "margin call". That margin call serves as an early warning that something is wrong with their position.

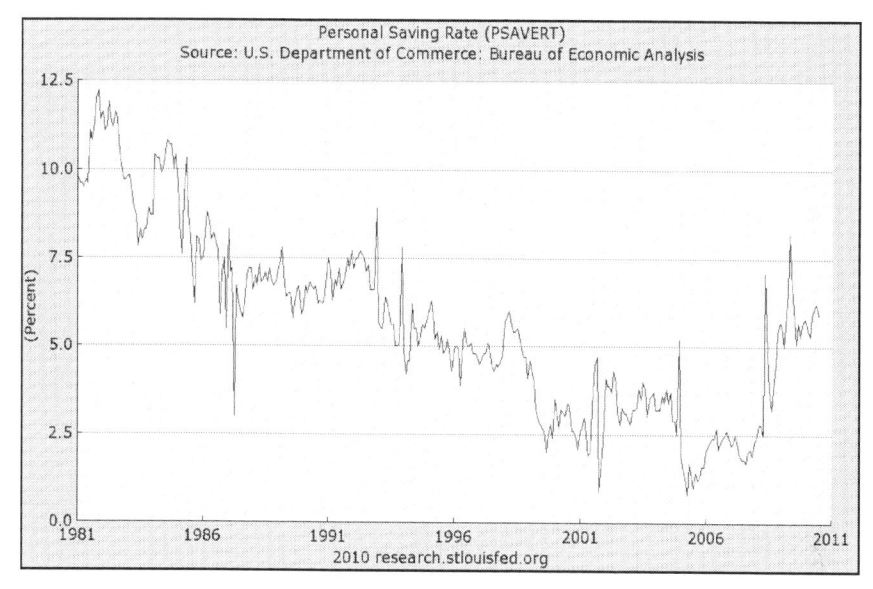

Figure 4-10
U.S. Savings Rate

The recent credit cycle fostered a period of increased leverage. The margin call in the commodity-trading example is nothing new in that industry. Margin calls are protection for investors from becoming too leveraged. What emerged in the recent credit cycle was the use of leverage in an asset class that turned into investment – home ownership. The roof over people's heads turned into an unprecedented speculative orgy made possible with leverage. The increased leverage resulted from lower down payments, adjustable rate mortgages with low introductory teaser rates and the anticipation of higher home values. The move to over-leverage one of the public's most precious assets, the roof over their head, was symptomatic of the euphoria of the period. Over-leveraged homeowners had no margin call to warn them of the collapsing value of their asset.

The public's use of debt and leverage will change sharply. The future homeowner will see the roof over their head as simply that, a roof over their head. Many will simply opt to rent. For some it will be a matter of preference. For others it will not be a matter of choice. The stain of the leverage experience will haunt many for years to come much as the Great Depression haunted those coming of age during this period and instilled a sense of conservation.

Putting It All Together

The purpose of this chapter was to acquaint you with the idea of cycles in the realm of human behavior. I will emphasize again that these cycles are guidelines and not rules. Just because one cycle alternates in a pattern of 54 years does not mean the next cycle will be 54 years. The cycle could be 49 years or 60 years. What is important is to understand the cyclical nature of human behavior. Cycles are not unlike biological processes in that they exhibit periods of growth and decay. The period of growth and the period of decay can have variability, but the cycle will still occur.

We are transitioning through various cycles both large and small. All of these cycles are related since they involve the action of human beings. The evidence of these cycle changes are all around us, they are subtle in some cases but they are there. Not so subtle changes are evident in our economic performance.

There is evidence of long-term deterioration in our economy. Even through ostensibly strong portions of our cycle, our economic performance lagged. More disheartening is the fact we have such lagging performance on the back of great increases in debt.

Cycles will also affect how we view actions presently considered criminal like drug usage and incarceration. A waning human behavior cycle will remove attention from the war on drugs and place it in areas like economic survival. This distraction will allow governments to focus their attention on the potential tax revenues to be gained from decriminalization of some drugs—revenues they will desperately need.

Socially, some of the people we thought were heroes are no longer occupying a fond place in our hearts and minds. Many people got burned by investment scams and we are becoming more financially conservative. Public displays of anger and growing discontent are being vented towards a government seen as increasingly decoupled from economic reality.

The economic downturn caught many experts and government leaders by surprise. The prevailing wisdom implied that our financial and economic markets suffered from a temporary setback that we could work our way out of through the application of government money – this is linear thinking. The reality was a government fighting a powerful cycle. The Wizard is still behind the curtain pushing buttons and pulling levers. Policymakers not attuned to the new economic rhythm will be overwhelmed when their intervention methods fall short. The accumulation of debt during the long-term upswing makes the upcoming cycle more treacherous. Recognition of the cyclical change will not make the problems go away but should make you more aware of alternatives to protect your family's wealth.

Summary

The following are key points of this chapter:

- There are cycles available that can provide a guide to social behavior. They are guides and not rules.

- The K-Wave is a cyclic indicator of business and economic activity. The K-Wave embodies spring, summer, autumn, and winter.

- Elliott Waves provide another approach to evaluating business and economic activity. These waves show cyclic patterns of growth and decay.

- The Millennium Cycle is one of the longest available. This cycle focuses on activity occurring at thousand year intervals.

- The Saeculum is a cycle the length of a human lifetime. Four sub-cycles, called generations, comprise the Saeculum.

- Cycles are important since they provide a glue connecting people through time.

- Distinct rhythms are associated with cycles in politics, social indicators, foreign affairs, and economics. These rhythms produce behavioral changes in society creating identifiable patterns or trends.

- A consequence of these rhythms is how society views those formerly in the pantheon of their field. As the rhythm becomes more negative, more of these popular figures and institutions will fall into disfavor.

- The euphoric mood of a cycle causes people to be less diligent in their approach to their investments. The changing mood revealed many swindles that took place during the euphoria.

- As the mood worsens and people feel betrayed by individuals and institutions, public anger will grow. The anger eventually finds its way into politics. This creates a potentially dangerous situation as demagogues may rise to power.

- Individual financial conservatism is a natural consequence of coming down from the euphoria. Government is usually behind the curve on this but eventually they will have to rein in their finances as well.

PART II

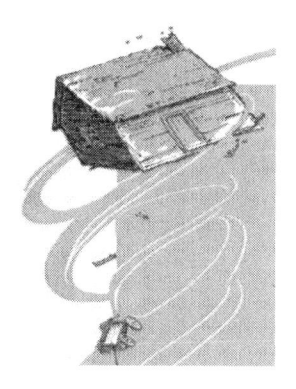

THE CRISIS

Part II focuses on how we arrived in this financial crisis. The earliest mention of the word "crisis" occurred in 2008 with the bankruptcy of Lehman Brothers. From there government came forward with a series of bailouts and stimulus packages. Throughout the crisis we have come to rely on government, our own Wizard, to save the day. Government is not the Wizard many think it is. At some point, we will draw back the curtain and see what government is capable of doing.

To shine the spotlight strictly on government and financial institutions is to ignore a fundamental component of most financial crises. Speculative bubbles and investment manias usually precede a financial crisis, and the public has a great role in them.

Chapter 5
How Did We Get Into The Crisis?

The Global Financial Crisis caught many investors and governments by surprise. The Treasury Secretary of the United States (Figure 5-1) was reported to have gotten on his knees before the Speaker of the House to beg for quick passage of a bailout plan. He used terms like "seized" and "frozen" to describe the financial system and placed the fate of the world's economic well-being at the foot of Congress – a presumptuous conclusion. Eventually Congress passed the bailout plan, Troubled Asset Relief Program (TARP), much to the dismay of some who questioned the wisdom of expanding governmental involvement in the financial markets.

After TARP, reports surfaced of lavish bonuses paid in firms benefiting from government assistance. The aftermath of these reports led to public scorn and Congressional skewering of banking officials and leaders of investment companies. The public was furious. How could these companies need government help and be so generous to their employees? Someone had to be responsible for this whole mess. So who is to blame?

Reasons for the economic crisis lie in four key areas. Our money system provides the basis for extensive credit expansion that lies at the heart of excessive speculation. There will always be speculation but the magnitude of our crisis would be smaller with a better money system. The economic policies of the U.S. and many countries favored spending versus saving. When you have credit expansion and an inclination to spend, you create the foundation of debt accumulation. Government had a hand in the whole mess since they pass laws or create regulations that favor speculation. No you say? Government is accountable to its people so they must accept responsibility; that is the reason we elected them. Ultimately, we have to look within. We were complicit in the speculation and credit expansion so we can't just blame others.

Did he have to beg for passage of TARP by placing the world's financial fate at the feet of Congress?

Figure 5-1
Treasury Secretary Paulson

Credit

The *fundamental* reason for the financial crisis is our money. Cyclical influences in human behavior will create financial crises but our flawed money system lays the foundation for excessive borrowing and bad investment. Chapter One described money and more importantly, what truly represents the majority of our money today, credit. It simply was too easy to create large amounts of credit and spread this credit around. When we create too much credit, it tends to cluster in "cones" of investment or areas of the economy (Figure 5-2). The cones can be a deliberate effort on the part of government, like the housing market, or it can be a byproduct of their efforts, like mortgage-backed securities. Other cones simply materialize and cannot be forecasted since it is just money chasing the latest hot investment. These cones of investment, once full of credit, become overly speculative and create bubbles. The bubble environment leads to greater demands for credit and higher prices. Unfortunately, these prices are not sustainable and a crash ensues.

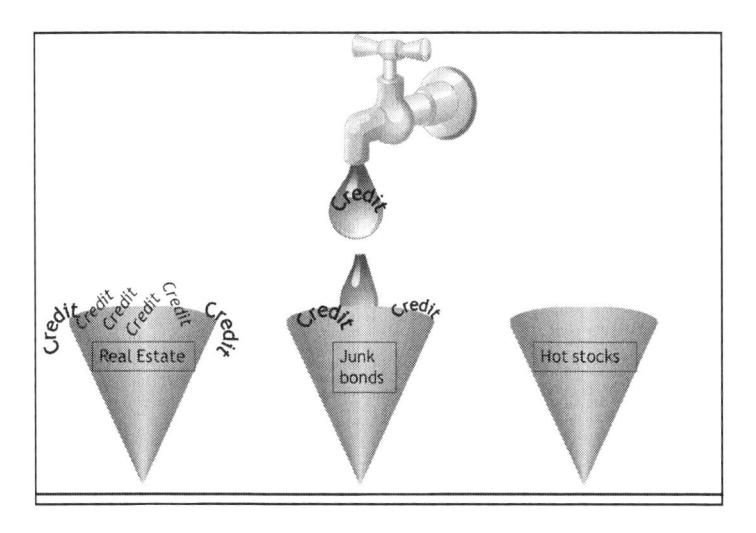

Figure 5-2
Credit Cones

Our government and central bank guide our credit policies. Our central bank, the Fed, controls our credit supply by regulating bank lending. The process of fractional reserve banking means that banks can pyramid loans well in excess of the deposits they actually have on hand. When the gold depositories of our history pyramided their gold stores by issuing excess certificates, inflation ensued and the depository failed.

The central bank, through the banking system, determines how much credit needs to be available in order to provide an adequate supply of money for the economy. We used to make light of communist bureaucrats deciding how much their factories needed to produce. Central banks are doing the same thing. They are telling our economy how much money it needs. Consider that for much of the United States' history, and the history of other countries, economies operated without a central bank. The absence of a central bank did not hamper economic growth, and our money actually represented wealth. The issue of central bank existence is outside the scope of this book but rest assured that there are copious amounts of information on this topic if you would like to research it further.

Our money no longer represents wealth. Government tells us that our paper money is legal tender for the payment of public and private debt. Remember, legal tender means you must accept it by law. If you went to a restaurant and paid with paper money, the merchant would have to accept your payment. No establishment that I know of displays a sign saying, "Cash not accepted".

The banking system makes credit rather seductive. It is so easy to add credit to the economy that many think we are suddenly wealthier. Adding credit to the economy reduces the purchasing power of outstanding credit. More credit in the economy does not mean we have more labor, goods, or natural resources. The early spenders of the credit might gain an advantage by spending before some prices rise. The late spenders experience the higher prices or decreased purchasing power.

When the banking system creates excess credit, speculation tends to follow, hence the term "bubble". The credit flows easily to those cones of opportunity mentioned earlier. Excess credit flows to areas that ordinarily would not receive it. In our recently popped bubble, those areas receiving excessive credit were real estate (commercial and residential), some commodities, and financial instruments.

Credit creates debt, which is an obligation to pay. We can pay this debt out of savings or through production. Savings is deferred consumption. As an economy, we accumulated debt too fast. In order to pay off debt, we created more debt. Since this is not a long-term solution, default usually follows. Debt default contracts credit, which is deflation. Since we had so much easy credit, saving was less important. The scale tipped far in the direction of spending versus saving. What we have now is credit saturation and a banking system reluctant to lend.

Our Economic Policy

The economic policy of the U.S., regardless of whether a Republican or Democrat is in office, centers on a theory called Keynesianism. Keynesianism receives its name from John Maynard Keynes, an influential British economist of the early 20th century (Figure 5-3). Keynesianism presumes that government knows how to stimulate the economy via spending. Government has to know a heck of a lot to understand all the intricacies of an economy.

He's the architect of modern economic policy.

Figure 5-3
John Maynard Keynes

I came up with another law as a way to visualize an economy.

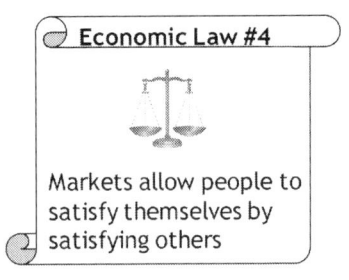

Economic Law #4

Markets allow people to satisfy themselves by satisfying others

Economic Law #4 says that markets are a collection of people satisfying themselves by satisfying others (Figure 5-4). Read this Economic Law carefully. There is a genuine selfish interest on the part of market participants (<u>satisfying themselves</u>) that must be balanced with an unselfish interest (<u>satisfying others</u>). It is a remarkable balance occurring naturally and without planning or coercion. I have wants and needs. You have wants and needs. Through an unfettered market, we can <u>both</u> satisfy our wants and needs. We satisfy these needs by providing a good or service to each other.

Can Keynesian economic policy figure out what all these people want?

Figure 5-4
Marketplace

The market dynamics described are what the Austrian economists believe. To them, a market is not a machine but an ecosystem composed of many participants each acting independently. It is beyond difficult to presume that anyone has a mathematical model or can engage in central planning determining what people want. What people want can change endlessly. Why would we think a government could accurately anticipate the changing wants and needs of so many people? With modern Keynesianism, government borrows money and has to figure out how to spend it. Once they figure out where to spend it, they have to grow to manage all the new spending.

Fans of *Star Trek The Next Generation* remember an alien race known as the Borg (Figure 5-5). The Borg's mission was to assimilate all conquered life forms into a mass collective of thought. The Borg had no independence. They traveled in a massive cube where all life forms integrated into the cube behaved as one. While this represented a powerful force with which to reckon, any sense of individuality was lost. The Borg's constant mantra was, "you will be assimilated."

In response to the crisis, government tried to assimilate more of the economy through fiscal (government spending) and monetary (Federal Reserve) policy. More and more money is going to fund the operation of the massive government cube. When government decides to spend money, it can't be spent where the market wants. As large as government has become, it is still no match for the markets. The Borg were eventually destroyed when they tried to assimilate the free will of all their conquered life forms. As government continues to increase in size, it will encumber the market's free will. This is not a battle it can win.

These guys tried to assimilate all life forms they encountered. Government is trying to assimilate more of the economy.

Figure 5-5
The Borg

Government

Since credit was abundant, there was more to spend. People spend according to price signals derived from supply and demand. Government legislation and regulation favoring specific industries altered price signals. A seminal example of this distortion occurred in the housing market. For years, politicians in the U.S. and abroad wanted to encourage broader home ownership. As far back as 1987, Margaret Thatcher vowed to increase home ownership in the U.K. from 62% to 75%. What could be better politics than increasing home ownership?

In 1999, Fannie Mae (Federal National Mortgage Association), the country's largest underwriter of home loans, came under pressure from the Clinton Administration to expand loan programs for low and moderate-income people. Fannie Mae is a publicly owned, government-sponsored enterprise (GSE) that purchases mortgages from lenders and resells them to investors.

This corporation, chartered during the Great Depression, packages mortgages backed by the Federal Housing Administration (FHA). Who is the FHA? The FHA is another Depression Era Federal agency that insures lenders against loss on residential mortgages.

To be fair, the pressure on Fannie Mae also came from shareholders, anxious to maintain profit growth, and the banking industry. The banking industry wanted Fannie Mae to facilitate more loans to subprime borrowers. The term subprime implied those borrowers whose credit ratings did not qualify for conventional loans. Those borrowers were relegated to paying much higher interest rates with finance companies.

Government created a distortion in the housing market by expanding the pool of money otherwise available to borrowers. Banks could lend more since their risk was passed to the Federal Government. Less qualified borrowers could obtain home mortgages at far lower rates than the market would have dictated. Ultimately, these programs were the foundation for the housing crisis we see today. Regrettably, government thought they were doing right by their constituents. In reality, they were laying a foundation for an economic nightmare (Figure 5-6).

In 1999, the United States Government laid another foundation for our crisis by repealing the Glass-Steagall Act - the Banking Act of 1933. Congress passed the Glass-Steagall Act after the stock market bottom of 1932. Government frequently passes legislation trying to prevent something after it has already occurred.

Congress passed the Glass-Steagall Act to deal with excessive speculation that was rampant before the 1929 stock market crash. That speculation eventually led to overvaluation in areas like stock prices and real estate; does this sound familiar? A rash of bank failures also rocked the country and precipitated a significant deflation. Remember credit equals confidence. When banks fail, confidence goes out the door. With fewer banks, there was a whole lot less credit.

Specifically, Glass-Steagall expanded the abilities of the Federal Reserve and permitted paper currency to be part of the Fed's war chest. Secondly, the act separated the functions of investment and commercial banking. Why? The second portion of the act allowed banks to either lend or be involved with investing, but not both. The mixing of commercial and investment banking created increased risk for depositors leading to more bank failures. By limiting a commercial bank to accept deposits and make loans only, the legislation mitigated the risk of speculation. The banking industry lobbied for many years for the repeal of the act. Banks argued the act's repeal would make them more competitive. They finally achieved their goal in 1999. In one swift stroke of the pen, Congress discarded what seemed prudent for 66 years.

Deposit banks were now free to engage in investment banking. After Glass-Steagall's repeal, sub-prime loans increased from 5% of all loans to 30%. Citibank, a recipient of bailout funds, expanded rapidly through underwriting and investing in mortgage-backed securities, collateralized debt obligations, credit default swaps and similarly risky investments. These developments hastened our journey to Oz and made our landing much rougher.

Government is the ultimate Wizard. The public has this perception of government operating a giant console of buttons and levers and making things happen. While they can make things happen, their motivation is short-term satisfaction. Of course, for every action, there is a reaction. Government does not always consider the future effects of their actions. After you pull back the curtain, you will see government as it truly is. There is no magic. The Wizard behind the curtain is just like you, me and everyone else.

Fannie Mae made it easier for banks to lend to subprime borrowers so they could buy homes.

Figure 5-6
Fannie Mae Head Franklin Raines

Look in the Mirror

You are probably wondering how YOU can be blamed for the economic crisis. The economic upswing experienced from the early 1980s until recently created a euphoric condition for people not unlike the best hallucinogenic. Like the addict who needs more to maintain the high, our economy required greater and greater doses of credit to maintain the euphoria. The addict, like the participants in the euphoric economy, cannot tell their core is rotting.

The U.S. simply became too reliant on easy credit and forgot what it meant to save. Saving is deferred consumption or delayed gratification. Our economy, however, did everything it could to make gratification instantaneous. Need a home loan? No job? No income? No problem. A whole cottage industry emerged with loans requiring low documentation or no documentation. These "liar loans" allowed lenders to look the other way on questionable loan applications. Borrowers also looked the other way on these loans by not assessing the riskiness of this financial proposition.

One story struck me as emblematic of the problems in the home mortgage industry. The case involved a young couple with a small child living in a nice neighborhood in the Phoenix, AZ area. The husband had sporadic work in the construction industry and the wife was a full-time student. They had very little in savings. Despite their financial condition, the bank ponied up a loan to accommodate them in $300k+ home. This couple's financial margin for error was virtually non-existent. Predictably, they found themselves in quite a pickle when the market value of their home dropped. They were unable to meet the mortgage payment and soon landed in foreclosure. Even if the bank wanted to make this loan, why did this couple enter into such a contract when the margin for error was nil?

Need a 125% loan on your existing home? No problem. Why would any lending institution provide a loan on a home for more than it is worth? Why would a borrower enter into such a contract?

Can't pay now? No problem, we'll defer payments for one year. See the pattern here. We can hurl venom at the leaders of commercial and investment banking but the reality is, we went along for the euphoric ride and ignored basic principles of personal financial management. In typical herd-like fashion, we saw others doing this and thought this must have been okay for us to do it too. This is the innate human desire to belong to a group and the powerful cyclical forces noted in the last chapter.

Conclusion

There is a whole lot more that could be written on the causes of the financial crisis though such a discussion would be well beyond the scope of this book. My intent was to focus on four areas: money, economic policy, government, and you. You probably never considered money as a problem, though I hope you have a greater understanding of the implications of our unsound money system.

Our economic policy of Keynesianism presumes that government can figure out how to spend money instead of the public (Figure 5-7). If you give this some thought, think about how difficult it would be for politicians and bureaucrats to decide how much and where to spend money. In the present crisis, this becomes a dicey proposition when there is no money to spend. Politicians have a vested interest in satisfying their constituencies. What could be more satisfying to constituencies than their elected officials making home ownership a reality?

The public ultimately was the recipient of easy money and the economic policies that went along with it. It was too intoxicating to have discipline to control spending and save like we used to.

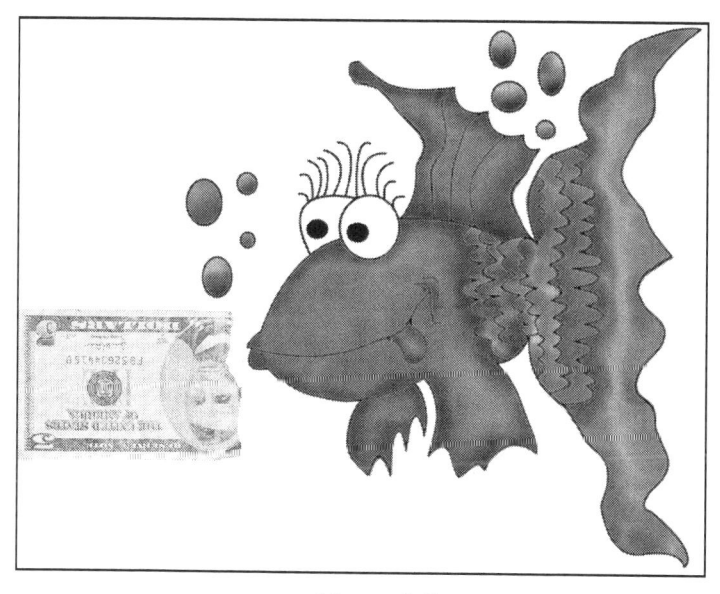

Figure 5-7
Government Spending (Keynesian Style)

Summary

The following are the key points in this chapter:

- Our credit system makes it very easy to create excessive borrowing.

- Excessive borrowing and credit creation leads to speculative bubbles.

- Bubbles collapse when borrowers can no longer service their debt.

- Economic policy contributed to the crisis through a theory called Keynesianism.

- Under Keynesianism, government presumes to know market needs and how to spend money. Central banks presume to know how to set interest rates and intervene in the market.

- Economic Law #4 shows that an economy is a collection of people selfishly acting in their own interest for the interest of others.

- The larger government becomes the less economic freedom you have.

- Government legislation contributed to the crisis by repealing laws previously designed to lessen economic risk. Government also created agencies contributing to the excessive borrowing problem.

- Individuals also shoulder responsibility for the crisis. The euphoria of the speculation took individuals' attention away from their rotting core.

Chapter 6
Government Action

Government has an interesting habit of contributing to a problem and then trying to solve the problem they created. The financial crisis was no exception. Government action in this crisis was without precedent. The action ranged from chastising the banking industry and Wall Street to massive spending and rescue programs. Politicians satisfied their constituents with Congressional dog and pony shows. In keeping with the Keynesian economic philosophy, government had no qualms proposing and implementing massive spending programs.

The government and the Fed see themselves as wizards behind the curtain pushing buttons and pulling levers applying borrowed money to problems. The notion of government wizardry saving the day is something this chapter hopes to debunk. Government is a large player in the economy just like any other. However, a different set of rules do not apply to government.

Role of Government in Economy

If we have an unfettered market with participants knowing

their wants and the wants of others (Economic Law #4) and if we have a unit of money that represents wealth, what else does the economy need for proper functioning? The only remaining market need is the safety or protection of the market. If market participants had to worry about bodily harm or other forms of crime, how much economic activity would occur? If those same participants had to worry about someone not fulfilling their end of an economic transaction, how much economic activity would occur? The protection of the market occurs through laws. Laws emanate from two principles:

a) Do unto others as they would do unto you – the basis of criminal law

b) Do what you said you were going to do – the basis of contract law

If you lived in a society where these principles did not exist, it would be hard to have a market. There would be constant fear that someone would be trying to inflict physical harm or that you could not trust your market transactions with others. Government is responsible for creating an environment in which a market can operate safely. Government provides the legislative process for the law, the judicial process for the interpretation of the law, and a body for the enforcement of the law. We need government to provide these functions because without them we would have chaos. These two principles are the basis for the market's protection. In societies where government does not support these principles, there is no viable economy.

Size of Government

The size of government today is greater than needed to support these principles. Table 6-1 is a comparison of the size of the U.S. Federal Government 100 years ago and now.

	1910	2010	Change
Population	92.2 million	308.9 million	Up 235%
GDP [1]	$33.4 billion	$14,624 billion	Up 43,684%
Federal Budget [2]	$0.840 billion	$3,721 billion	Up 442,876%
Federal Deficit [3]	$0.035 billion	$1,556 billion	Up 4,445,610%
Funded Debt [4]	$2.6 billion	$13,786 billion	Up 530,130%
Unfunded Debt [5]	N/A	$63,000 billion	Infinite

Table 6-1
Government 1910 vs. 2010

(1) GDP (Gross Domestic Product) - The market value of all final goods and services made within the borders of a country in a given year.

(2) Federal Budget – What it costs to run government. The amount includes Social Security, Medicare/Medicaid, Defense and other programs.

(3) Federal Deficit – Spending minus revenue

(4) Funded Debt – Monies officially borrowed historically to cover Federal Deficit

(5) Unfunded Debt – Promises made to recipients of Social Security, Medicare and other programs for which no money currently exists.

In 1910, it cost $9.11 per person to run the Federal Government. Unfunded liabilities from the likes of Social Security & Medicare did not exist. The funded debt was a mere $2.6 billion.

In 2010, it cost $12,045.97 per person to run the Federal Government, the funded debt is $13+ trillion and the unfunded debt is an unfathomable $63 trillion. What changed in the last 100 years? Here are some noteworthy events:

1. Central bank creation in 1913 - permitted the growth of credit.

2. Institution of income tax in 1913 - transferred money from citizens to government coffers.

3. Abolition of gold ownership in 1933 - removed government spending discipline.

4. Creation of Social Security in 1935 – sacred covenant politicians established with voters.

5. Creation of Medicare in 1965 – another sacred covenant politicians established with voters.

6. Decoupling the U.S. Dollar from gold in 1971 – allowed government to expand faster.

If you think government growth occurred only at the Federal level, Table 6-2 provides a sobering view of state and local government growth.

Year	Full-time equivalent employment (FTE)
2000	15.077 million
2008	16.668 million

Table 6-2
Government Employment

If you take the 16.668 million FTE in state and local government and add the 6 million employed by the Federal Government (not including military personnel), you arrive at 22.668

million people out of 154 million in the civilian labor force who work for the government. Roughly 15% of the U.S. population works for the government. These figures are from 2008.

Government has grown at a much faster rate than our economy (Figure 6-1). The Federal Government budget is 4,429 times larger now than 100 years ago. It costs 1,338 times more per person to run the Federal Government today than it did 100 years ago. In 2008, the median household income in the United States was roughly $50,000. In 1910, the average salary was $750 per year. While your household definitely makes more money than your great grandparents did (67 times more), it certainly didn't expand the 4,429 times that government did!

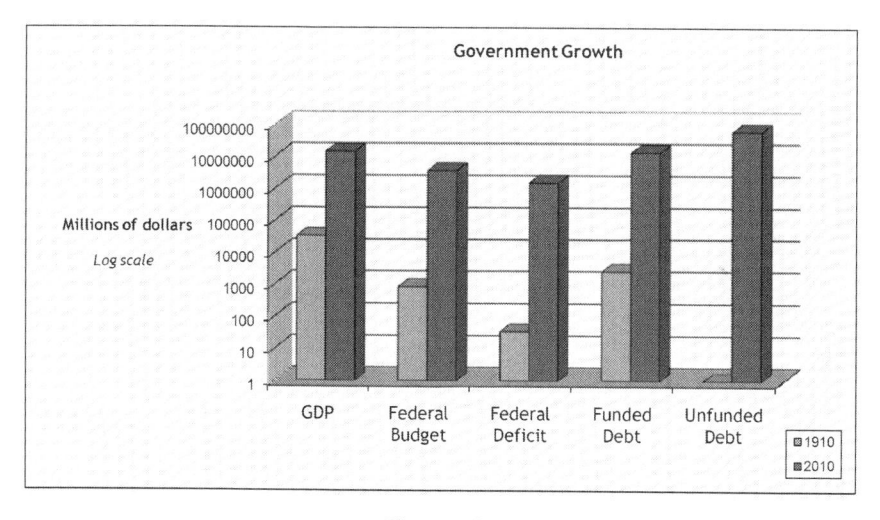

Figure 6-1
Federal Government Growth

If you believe the Federal Government has a unique ability to save the economy, why are they so far in debt? Why does it cost so much to run government? Why has GDP not been impacted more given how much government spends? No lever pulling and button pushing can spur economic growth effectively without incurring more debt.

Government Attempting to Help

Government efforts to "fix" our economic problems dominate the headlines. Beginning early in 2008, we had the Bush stimulus package of approximately $170 billion. There were $200 billion funding efforts for Government Sponsored Enterprises (GSE) like Fannie Mae and Freddie Mac. In the fall of 2008, a massive government bailout program called "TARP" (Troubled Assets Relief Program) worth several hundred billion was rushed through Congress under the guise that without it, our credit markets would remain frozen and economic collapse was nigh. Predictably, the automobile industry, witnessing the largesse extended to other parts of the economy, wanted their share of bailout money. Congress obliged.

The American Recovery and Reinvestment Act (ARRA) added $787 billion in government "rescue" funds and separately, a controversial $75 billion housing rescue plan. Over $2 trillion was committed to various rescue plans to "get the economy going again". Is all this a bunch of wizardry or will these programs help the economy?

To understand the answer to that question we need to understand what government is capable of doing. Government taxes and spends. Let's start at the state and local level. State and local funding comes from taxes, Federal Government funds, and extensions of credit like bond issues. Unlike the Federal Government, states and municipalities do not have the luxury of spending more than they have. When they do spend more than they have, they have to cut back on the services they provide, raise taxes, ask Washington for more funding, or all of the above.

The Federal Government's funding is supposed to come via taxes and tariffs. When they spend more than they have, funding comes from other sources. The Federal Government historically has the reputation as the best credit risk so investors both foreign and domestic are willing to lend money through Treasury sales of bonds, notes, and bills. The Treasury also has a unique link to the Federal Reserve allowing Fed purchases of U.S. Treasury debt. The Fed "lends" money to the U.S. Treasury by creating bookkeeping entries and "buys" Treasury debt (Figure 6-2). The money from these bookkeeping entries emerges out of thin air – now that's what I call wizardry! The Federal Government has capabilities that others do not. However, will these capabilities really help the economy?

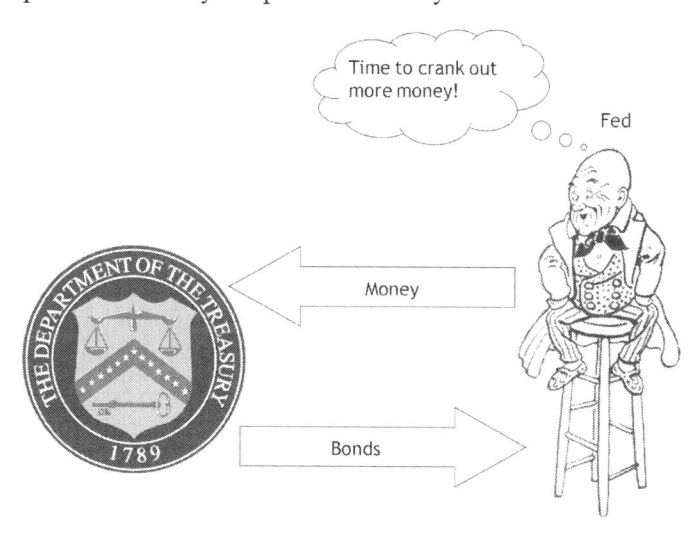

Figure 6-2
Federal Reserve Purchases of Treasury Debt

While government is playing a larger role in the economy with all the rescue attempts, it is still a market player ultimately judged by other market participants. The first bank rescue plan, Troubled Assets Relief Plan (TARP), had the Treasury purchasing toxic assets, or assets that had unknown value, so banks could resume the business of lending. Since there was no market for these assets, how much should taxpayers have paid for them? Why would the American taxpayer want to purchase toxic assets?

Predictably, banks, still reeling from years of bad loan underwriting, chose to retain the money given to them. Their posture led to public and congressional outcry. Look at it this way. Banks are in the business of lending money. Banks got burned with bad loans and questionable investments. Why would they be in a hurry now to lend in an environment they fear? Remember, credit equals confidence. Banks have little confidence and that means there is little credit.

Despite intensive efforts, government can't force banks to lend or people to borrow. Government can tax and spend but it cannot force the credit markets to do what it wants.

Infrastructure Stimulus

What if government hires a bunch of people for infrastructure projects? Won't that help? Government stimulus plans proposed are a mixture of public works, infrastructure repairs, mass transit, build/repair Federal buildings, and energy projects. The efforts are not wrongheaded since our infrastructure does need repair (Figure 6-3) and other projects in the plan *may* be worthwhile. The scope and timing of the plan raises issues.

> I. In order to run these projects, government must increase in size. Bigger is not better.
>
> II. The government made the decision NOT to embark on these projects before. What makes these projects desirable now?

III. Projects deemed worthy by bureaucrats take capital out of the market since government must borrow. This capital might be better served elsewhere.

If we turned the clock back to 2007 at the height of the stock market and before the financial crisis, how would the American people react to stimulus?

Figure 6-3
Old Bridge in Allegheny National Forest

Stimulus spending sounds good until you consider its costs. The cost of stimulus will be felt immediately and in the future since government had to borrow. The total cost is not just the initial price tag but all the years of paying interest as well. A proportionately small amount of spending cannot move an entire economy. This is spending few wanted or thought of just three years ago.

Cash for Clunkers

When I introduced this chapter, I said government often has a habit of creating a problem and then solving it with another. Cash for Clunkers is a beautiful example. In 2003 Congress passed legislation offering up to a $100,000 tax credit for business owners who purchased vehicles weighing *6,000 lbs or more* – the credit had been $75,000. Not coincidentally many SUVs fit that description. What happened to large SUV sales? According to the watchdog group Taxpayers for Common Sense, 100,000 people claimed the credit in 2002 out of 3.6 million large SUVs sold.

In 2009, government brought us a program derisively called "Cash for Clunkers". The actual name was Car Allowance Rebate System (CARS). Under this stimulus program, consumers received $3,500 - $4,500 towards the purchase of a more fuel-efficient vehicle. The intent was to boost sales of reeling automakers while at the same time allowing buyers to go "green".

Think of the irony here. In the 2003 program, government encouraged large SUV purchases. Taxpayers having no interest in large SUVs subsidized those qualifying for the program. The market for large SUVs was not in a state of decline given the 3.6 million units sold. If I recall, in 2003 we were still trying to curtail our reliance on foreign oil so why encourage sales of gas guzzling SUVs. What then was the purpose of the program?

With Cash for Clunkers, government now rewarded many of those same purchasers of the large SUVs. The Clunkers program unfortunately removed used cars from the market since dealers were required to scrap or disable vehicles traded in. People dependent on the used vehicle market saw the supply of available cars diminish (Figure 6-4).

Let's look at the Clunkers program on a monetary cost/benefit basis. Approximately $2.877 billion of rebate applications were received by the program deadline covering 700,000 vehicles. This translates into approximately $4,100 per vehicle. Under the rules of the program, the trade-in clunker had to be rated at 18 MPG or lower with lesser values for large pickup trucks and cargo vans. For the sake of this analysis, let us say the average MPG of all 700,000 vehicles traded in was 15 MPG. If the new vehicle rated 4-9 MPG higher than the trade-in, the buyer received $3,500. If the new vehicle rated 10 MPG or more than the trade-in, the buyer received $4,500. Given that the credit per vehicle was an average of $4,100, I will estimate 22 MPG as the average mileage of the new vehicles for a savings of 7 MPG.

The EPA estimates the average car is driven 12,000 miles per year. Figures from 2009 indicated Americans were driving even less. For the sake of these calculations, however, we will use 12,000 miles/year. With a 7 MPG fuel savings, Americans will save roughly 255 gallons of gas per car per year for a total of 178.5 million gallons. Using a gas price of $2.50/gallon the total savings equates to $446 million.

The program vouchers cost the government $2.877 billion. This does not include the extra costs the Transportation Department expended resulting from labor increases required to handle processing of applications. It also does not include the costs to finance $2.877 billion since the government had to borrow money for the program. If the voucher cost was financed with Treasury Notes of 10 years with a 3.5% interest rate, the yearly interest cost is approximately $100 million or $1 billion for 10 years. Using a shorter term for financing, say 5 years, with a 2.375% interest rate translates into $68 million per year in interest costs or a total of $340 million. We can estimate the total cost of the program to be $3.217 billion ($2.877 billion + $340 million) using the 5 year financing option. If we use a 10-year financing option, the cost is $3.877 billion.

For a cost of $3.217 billion, we saved approximately $446 million/year in fuel costs. At that yearly fuel saving figure, it takes more than 7 years to equal the program's total cost. If we use the 10-year finance option, the figure is closer to 9 years. A more thorough economic analysis can be undertaken. Benefits like environmental impacts are not included. The economic cost of clunker cars destroyed is also not included; this would make the analysis even less favorable. Just looking at these rough numbers though, could you as a taxpayer justify the program?

Cars traded in under this program were destroyed or disabled.

Figure 6-4
Cash for Clunker

A program I call "Cash for Golf Carts" illustrates another noble attempt by government to stimulate sales while going "green". This government program provided tax credits between $4,200 and $5,500 towards the purchase of an electric vehicle. Separate incentive plans provided by the states could make the purchase of the electric vehicle nearly cost-free. So what does this have to do with golf carts? The IRS ruled that a golf cart could qualify as an electric vehicle as long as it was roadworthy. Add some safety features such as side mirrors and 3-point safety belts and presto, you have an electric vehicle! As one golf cart dealer delighted, "The purchase of some models could be absolutely free. Is that about the coolest thing you've ever heard?" Cool indeed. With no limit to the amount of golf carts qualifying under the government plan, enterprising people scooped them up for later resale (Figure 6-5).

I could elaborate more on the economic virtues or lack thereof of these programs. My point is to show you how government decisions have unintended consequences which then cause them to come up with another misguided plan to address the first one.

Is this really what the government had in mind?

Figure 6-5
Cash for Golf Carts

How a Market Operates and Government's Role

Government became so large, costing $12k+ per person in the U.S., that it is now a bigger player in the economy. The economy is in a continual state of change. The economy adjusts due to changes in judgment on the part of its individual participants. A snapshot of the economy at any point in time reveals the price or exchange rate for something. The price is an agreement between two parties - nothing more, nothing less. As Ludwig von Mises (Figure 6-6) said in *Human Action*, "*The market process is entirely a resultant of human actions.*" The two key words in the quote are "human actions". Human actions create the economy.

"*The market process is entirely a resultant of human actions.*"

Figure 6-6
Ludwig von Mises

Markets tell producers what to produce and in what quantities to produce them. Markets also tell consumers what to consume and in what quantities to consume them. If the price of filet mignon were $0.10 per pound, how would consumers react? Imagine the price of filet going to $1,000 per pound. How would consumers react then? In both cases, the market dictates behavior. The market is telling government that it can continue to borrow large amounts of money for low interest rates. How long will this continue? In the next chapter we will see if the market is judging the U.S. appropriately as a borrower.

If government's role is to <u>protect</u> the market, it has to be a <u>participant</u> in the market. Government plays a role in the market through the purchase of raw materials, equipment, and labor. Please understand this point. The government, like anyone else, is a market participant. Unlike what government officials would have you believe, bureaucrats are no wizards with special powers over the market.

The government, as we know it, has expanded well beyond merely protecting the market. Government stimulus programs attempted to grow its participation further. While some contend that government's increased participation speaks of socialism, Mises argued in *Human Action*, that an economy is either socialist or capitalist. If the economy is socialist, then government plans everything – government is the economy. If the economy is capitalist, then the market dictates what happens. As large as government has become, it remains a minority player in comparison to the rest of the economy.

The U.S. Government, as the world's largest debtor, is getting to a point where its current and future creditors will judge its actions more harshly. Some of this judgment will be financial and some will be political. It's no coincidence that one of Secretary of State Clinton's first overseas trips was to China. U.S. financial supremacy is under scrutiny. Treasury Secretary Geithner found out the hard way when he was laughed at when he told a Chinese university audience that the U.S. debt they owned was safe (Figure 6-7). Who would have imagined that a U.S. Treasury Secretary would be the object of laughter for a university audience?

The government is the people. The people are the market. The government is in the market like anyone else albeit now by spending $3+ trillion (Figure 6-8). Therefore, the government cannot divorce itself from the effects of the market. It is not separate from the market since it is *in* the market. Whatever the government does in the market affects you, me and everyone else. For the same reason you, me, and everyone else judge government actions in the market. That is what a market is all about, human action.

Her first overseas trip was to China. He was laughed at by Chinese university students.

Figure 6-7
Secretary of State Clinton &
Treasury Secretary Geithner

Conclusion

Government has a very specific role in the economy, which is to protect it with laws. Unfortunately, government grew well beyond the role of economic protector and now finds itself deeply in debt. Despite this debt, government moved forward with unprecedented spending to revive the economy and rescue us from the financial crisis. Since government does not have this money to spend, the overall costs include not just the initial expense but all the years of paying interest as well. For government to do all these things, it has to jump in the market and compete for goods and services like other market participants. Government does not add anything to market resources; they can only take them away and redirect them where they want. The market sees government sucking up resources and begins to question its spending. This questioning places the U.S. in a difficult position since it is not used to being in a situation where their spending gets questioned by others.

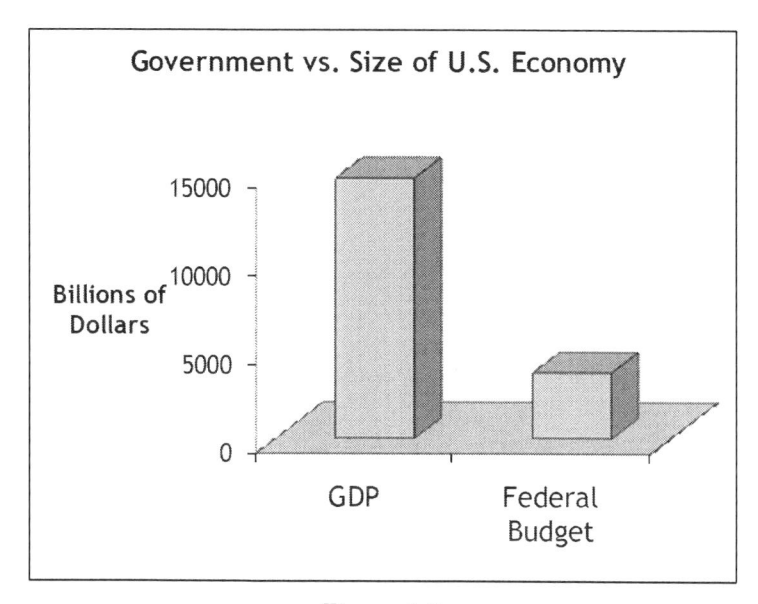

Figure 6-8
Size of Federal Budget Relative to
Economy

Summary

The following are key points in this chapter:

- Government solutions to economic problems often create other problems.

- Government does not have any magical effects on the economy. It is a player in the economy like any other, albeit a large one.

- Government's fundamental role is to protect the economy. They protect the economy through support of criminal and civil law.

- Government expanded well beyond its fundamental role. The Federal Government of the U.S. spends 1,338 times more per person than it did 100 years ago.

- Government tried to soften the economic crisis through stimulus plans and bailout efforts.

- Stimulus plans involved spending on projects not considered essential just before the crisis.

Chapter 7
Is Government A Good Borrower?

The last chapter discussed some of the ways government tried to help in the economic crisis. Any help they gave was accompanied by historic borrowing. Government expanded their scope to spend 1,300 times more per person to operate than 100 years ago. Even before the crisis, government grew to be a leviathan. The U.S. is the world's number one borrower. Borrowing and lending are all about confidence, so how good of a credit risk is the United States?

Government FICO Score

The following is a hypothetical exercise. The U.S. Government wants to play a larger role in the market but it has to borrow to do so. Not all borrowers are equal. Fortunately, we have a metric that judges the creditworthiness of individual borrowers. This metric is the FICO score. A FICO score is a standard lending industry measure for determining the creditworthiness of a borrower. As a participant in the borrowing market, what would the government's FICO score be? Table 7-1 provides the criteria and weighting for judging. The table provides government's information to compute the FICO score.

- ☐ Payment History – 35%
- ☐ Amounts Owed – 30%
- ☐ Length of Credit History – 15%
- ☐ New Credit – 10%
- ☐ Types of Credit Used – 10%

Criteria	Experience	Qualitative Score
Payment History	Never missed a payment	Excellent
Amounts Owed	$13+ trillion	Very bad (debt is 5x income)
Length of Credit History	200+ years	Very good
New Credit	Much	Bad
Types of Credit Used	Wide variety / many creditors	Fair

Table 7-1
Government FICO

Suggested FICO score: Below 620

While the above is an academic exercise, it illustrates how the market might view the creditworthiness of the Federal Government. The suggested FICO score places the government in a sub-prime category, meaning it would not qualify for the lowest rates of interest since it presents a higher risk profile (Figure 7-1). If a credit counselor were to advise the government on improving their FICO score, they would suggest a reduction in "Amounts Owed". What do you think the government should do to reduce its $13+ trillion in debt?

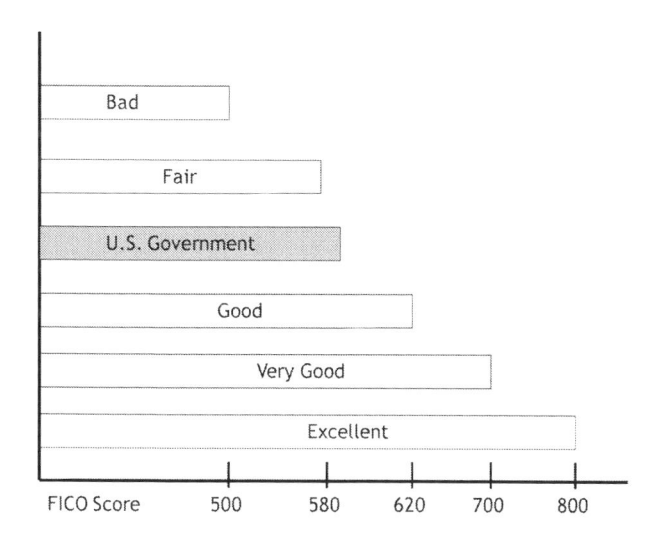

Level shown is bottom end of range

Figure 7-1
FICO Score Range

The above analysis does not consider all of the unfunded liabilities of the government. These liabilities are the promises of Social Security, Medicare, and the recent health care legislation. The staggering total for these promises is approximately $63 trillion. These are all monies for which the government will be liable for which it does not have a penny. If we considered these liabilities in the FICO score, you would have few if any lenders to the government of the United States. What would a credit counselor say then?

157

Fortunately, for the government of the United States, they do not have to worry about a FICO score. Officially, the creditworthiness of the U.S. government is determined by ratings agencies.

Rating Agencies

The assessment of the U.S. government's FICO score was hypothetical since these scores do not apply to governments. There are agencies, however, that rate the creditworthiness of governments. Three agencies, Moody's, Fitch, and Standard & Poors represent the most well known rating agencies. They rate the credit quality of companies and countries. Their credit ratings allow investors, investment banks, and governments to assess relative credit risk from an independent, non-biased source.

These agencies came under heavy criticism during episodes where their accuracy was less than stellar. For example, during the Enron debacle, ratings for the company remained at investment grade just four days before the company declared bankruptcy. Another problem is that the very companies rated by the likes of Moody's and others often pay to be rated. This creates a potential conflict of interest. Most recently, the agencies came under fire for not identifying the problems with mortgage securities.

In analyzing a country's debt rating, there is also a potential conflict of interest. A credit rating agency could be conflicted assigning a poor credit rating to a country if they felt that government could impose stricter regulation on their operation. How would it look if all of the U.S.-based ratings agencies took an unfavorable view of U.S. Government debt? Downgrading U.S. debt would mean instantly higher interest rates for the government at a time of greatly expanding debt. Congress would no doubt get involved and ask for an investigation into the matter.

The heads of all these agencies would be asked to testify before congressional committees. Politically motivated congressional representatives would grill the agencies on how they arrived at such a conclusion.

If you doubt such a thing could happen, witness the events of June 2, 2010. On this date, the Financial Crisis Inquiry Commission (FCIC) held a hearing to investigate the role of ratings agency Moody's in the financial crisis. What is the FCIC? The following statement is taken from their web site, *"The Financial Crisis Inquiry Commission is a bipartisan commission that has been given a critical non-partisan mission — to examine the causes of the financial crisis that has gripped the country and to report our findings to the Congress, the President, and the American people."*

On this date, the chair of the commission, made some very telling opening remarks. Here are some excerpts:

- *"To be blunt, the picture is not pretty. From 1998 to 2007 Moody's revenues from rating complex financial instruments like mortgage securities grew by a whopping 523 percent. From 2000 to its peak in 2007, the company's stock price climbed more than six fold. Moody's did very well. The investors who relied on Moody's ratings did not fare so well."*

- *"From 2000 through 2007, Moody's slapped its coveted Triple-A rating on 42,625 residential mortgage backed securities. Moody's was a Triple-A factory."*

- *"In 2006 alone, Moody's gave 9,029 mortgage backed securities a Triple-A rating. That means they put the Triple-A label on more than 30 mortgage securities each and every working day that year. To put that in perspective, Moody's currently bestows its Triple-A rating on just four American corporations. Even Berkshire Hathaway, with its more than $20 billion cash on hand, doesn't make that grade."*

None other than Warren Buffett, a large investor in Moody's through his company Berkshire Hathaway, appeared before the commission that day. His comments like those of many others centered on the fact that nobody could foresee the collapse of the housing bubble (Figure 7-2). I strongly disagree with his conclusion. I also find it ironic that Buffett didn't question a ratings agency, in which he was an investor, not giving his own company a AAA rating. The ratings agencies certainly threw bouquets at mortgage securities so why not Berkshire.

If ratings agencies had such a difficult time assessing mortgage securities, how good will they be assessing the debt of an entire country? If they were more critical in their assessment of sovereign U.S. debt, what do you think the FCIC would ask them? Rest assured Congress would rake any ratings agency over the coals that looked unfavorably at U.S. debt.

"Mr. President, I did not see the housing collapse coming."

Figure 7-2
Warren Buffett & President Obama

Financial Condition of the United States

Pretend you work as an analyst at a ratings agency and was assigned the task of assessing the financial condition of the United States. You find a Treasury Department publication providing details. The Treasury's 2009 fiscal year report noted how the present economic crisis weakened the country's financial position with tax revenues declining $400 billion. The report highlighted increased expenditures in mandatory programs like Unemployment Insurance, Medicare, Medicaid, and Social Security (Figure 7-3). Spending in the mandatory programs are "automatic stabilizers". In other words no matter what happens to the government's revenue, the mandatory programs do not change. If your own household budget had such a revenue decline, you would immediately cut your spending. The U.S. Government <u>did not</u> cut its spending.

It was obvious there was no cut in spending by what you discover next. In fiscal year 2009, the Federal Government took in about $2.1 trillion in receipts. That was roughly the same amount that government paid directly to individuals via some sort of transfer payment (Social Security, Medicare etc.). Roughly every dollar the U.S. government took in went directly to individuals in some manner. All other spending required borrowing.

Your anxiety reaches a new threshold when you discover what happens to the U.S. budget in 2020. <u>Spending on the major entitlement programs and interest on the national debt will absorb 100% of Federal revenue by 2020</u>. That means that for every dollar the government takes in, 100% is earmarked for mandatory obligations – nothing else remains. After reading the date on the report, you determine it was written *before* the recent health care legislation was signed into law. You then surmise this condition will likely happen well before 2020 especially if interest rates increase.

You become rather alarmed about what you read and delve further into the issue of the health care legislation and its effect on the government budget. Former Congressional Budget Office (CBO) director Douglas Holtz-Eakin said,

"Removing the unrealistic annual Medicare savings ($463 billion) and the stolen annual revenues from Social Security and long-term care insurance ($123 billion), and adding in the annual spending that so far is not accounted for ($114 billion) quickly generates additional deficits of $562 billion in the first 10 years."

He estimates that by 2020 the government's annual deficit will be $1.2 trillion with $900 billion necessary just to pay interest on the debt.

After reading information from Treasury Department documents and commentary from a former Congressional Budget Office director, you conclude that the FICO score determined earlier in this chapter is too generous. Economists, however, take exception to your analysis. Many economists like to cite the figure of public debt relative to the size of an economy or GDP. Many claim that the United States need not worry about public debt since the economy is large enough to handle it. After investigating that claim of economists, you find a great book on the subject of debt to GDP - *This Time Is Different*. In the book, the authors go to great length to provide a history of debt crises throughout the world. Government debt default or restructuring can occur at many levels of debt to GDP. The mistake often made by policymakers is to assume that this time *is* different, it cannot happen now. What if policymakers are wrong?

A colleague of yours hands you a review by the Federal Reserve Bank of St. Louis from 2006. In the review, Lawrence Kotlikoff suggested the U.S. Government was essentially bankrupt insofar as it would be unable to pay its creditors. This declaration came in 2006 well before the recent government-spending binge!

You read more reports from the government indicating their anticipation of trillion dollar deficits every year for the next decade. You conclude there simply is not enough taxing power, value creation, or willing lenders to support these projected deficits. At this point, you decide you no longer want to be an analyst for a ratings agency. The conclusions are simply too overwhelming to digest.

Little did they know what this would do to the budget.

Figure 7-3
President Johnson signs Medicare bill
with former President Truman watching

Rating Country Debt

After reading the previous section on the financial condition of the United States, how creditworthy would you say the U.S. is? The ratings agency Standard & Poors says the United States is a AAA rated country and its outlook is stable. Here are two other countries, and their debt ratings, in the news recently for their country's debt problems:

Greece: BB+

Spain: AA

Since many economists feel a country's debt to GDP ratio is important in assessing creditworthiness, we present the following external debt to GDP ratios:

US - approaching 100% (98%)

Greece -167%

Spain - 176%

Japan – 227%

Spain and Japan, countries with a higher external debt to GDP figure than Greece get a higher rating from Standard & Poors. This analysis is a simple one but it does create some question around debt rating.

You might conclude the U.S. debt rating should be higher than either Spain or Greece. After all, the U.S. economy can handle the strain given the size of its economy. What the above analysis does not include are all the other liabilities of the United States (Social Security, Medicare). If you add another $63 trillion to the country's existing debt load, now you get a figure approaching 600%. While it is true these liabilities are not debt *right now*, they certainly *will be*. The only reason these liabilities are not debt right now is there is not a formal loan arrangement like a Treasury bond, note, or bill. All Social Security and Medicare have are IOUs. Please do not conclude the money for these social programs will somehow materialize either. There simply is not enough taxing power or potential economic growth to come up with this money.

So what can we make of country debt ratings? I revealed apparent inconsistencies in country debt ratings using an often cited figure of economic strength, a country's Gross Domestic Product. The ratings agencies place countries like Greece and Spain in their crosshairs and investors get nervous. This nervousness causes those governments to propose spending cuts and other austerity measures. In the United States, there has been little thought of withdrawing government stimulus. How can the rules for the U.S. be different from Greece and Spain? What about Japan? Should severe austerity measures occur in Japan given how indebted that country is compared to the ones with the bull's eye on their back?

Earlier I said that a potential conflict of interest exists with U.S.-based agencies rating U.S. debt. What does a non-U.S. ratings company say about U.S. debt? The Dagong Global Credit Rating Co. based in Beijing does not look as favorably on U.S. debt. They assign the U.S. a "AA" rating, which is two rungs below their top grade. Their best grade, "AAA", goes to Norway, Denmark, Switzerland, Singapore, Australia, and New Zealand. They do not include their own country, China, in the highest rated category; China received an "AA+" rating. Dagong believes it is important to rate country debt on the ability to repay, a novel concept indeed! The only way for a country to repay its debt is to have the ability to create wealth. At some point, creating new debt to pay for old debt stops working. Unfortunately, this is the U.S. model.

There is so much U.S. Treasury debt in the world today that downgrading it to levels commensurate with other economies would cause problems not just in the U.S. but abroad too - think China here. A downgrade of U.S. debt would do two things:

1. The interest rate on newly issued debt would go up and that would cost the government more in yearly interest. That is the worst possible outcome for a budget under stress.

2. The holdings of those owning U.S. debt would fall in value. When interest rates increase, bond prices fall. There is more coverage of this topic in Appendix C.

Getting the U.S. debt problem under control (Figures 7-4 & 7-5) promotes something much discussed in this book and that is confidence. Good debt ratings inspire confidence. Ratings agencies cannot indefinitely award pristine debt ratings to the U.S. while the country continues its fiscal slide. While it is in the interest of investors worldwide that U.S. debt at least appear healthy, that game will not last long. The problem now is that once the ratings agencies call one country's debt into question, it opens up Pandora's Box for the rest, including the U.S.

Figure 7-4
Social Security Card

Figure 7-5
National Debt Clock

We have to get Social Security under control before the Debt Clock improves.

Summary

The following are key points in this chapter:

- A hypothetical FICO score for the U.S. Government indicated it was a Fair credit risk at best.

- Ratings agencies like Moody's, Fitch, and Standard & Poors rate debt quality.

- The ratings agencies came under fire for their poor record with mortgage-backed securities. These securities are the same ones associated with the housing crisis.

- A U.S. Treasury Department document concluded that by 2020 the entire Federal budget would be spent on entitlement programs and interest on the national debt – nothing will be left over for anything else. This was assuming no increase in interest rates and no consideration for the new health care legislation.

- A former CBO director estimated an additional $562 billion in deficits from the new health care legislation alone.

- Ratings agencies have taken an unusually harsh approach in assessing the debt of countries like Greece and Spain in comparison to Japan and the United States. Despite a proportionately higher level of debt, Japan receives a much higher debt rating from Standard & Poors.

- There are economic and political ramifications of downgrading U.S. debt since so many investors own this debt.

Chapter 8
Speculative Bubbles

We did not arrive in the Financial Land of Oz by mere happenstance. It took many years, a bunch of credit, and a favorable speculative psychology. Ultimately, many people had a hand in this journey.

What causes people to speculate wildly with investments? It's almost as if they are following the orders of legendary St. Louis Cardinals announcer Jack Buck when he implored his listeners, "Go crazy folks. Go crazy!" During the dot com bubble, there were companies that had no earnings, no immediate prospect for earnings and yet their stock price kept increasing. There were even anecdotal stories of angel investors leaving checks in mailboxes just for the opportunity to invest in something.

This chapter examines bubbles, which are dramatic expressions of investment euphoria. Bubbles occur due to the innate human instinct of herding. The investment public tends to act as followers. People without good information simply follow others. Imagine stepping outside on a sunny day to find all your neighbors with their umbrellas up. You could have looked online at a weather forecast or on TV for color weather radar, but you did not. Instead, you figured if all your neighbors have their umbrellas up that you best go get yours. You herded with your neighbors since you had no better information to tell you it was going to remain sunny.

Bubbles climb a "wall of worry". People worry about being left out and do not recognize the herding impulse of the bubble. The public may not realize a bubble exists since rationalizations of investment values are always abundant. Remember the term "New Economy"? For those realizing they're in a bubble, the investment quickly becomes a hot potato. When there are enough hot potatoes, the mania's peak arrives and the bubble bursts. Dorothy's bubble burst when Glenda, the good witch, told her she would have to get started on her journey home the long way. We have a long road ahead as well.

Bubbles

Bubbles, the final economic frontier. This is the voyage of the market. Its multi-year mission is to explore strange new manias; to seek out new investors and new sources of credit; to boldly go where no market has gone before. *(Star Trek music playing in the background)*.

While a bubble is not as vast as the space explored by the starship Enterprise, it can trap many unsuspecting investors. A bubble is a speculative investment mania. The investment can be anything from vehicles traditionally considered investments (stocks, bonds, real estate) to something organic like a flower (Figure 8-1). Yes, you read that correctly, a flower! During a bubble, the public takes investment values to levels previously unimaginable. The valuations reach these levels when the price of the investment is wildly higher than its intrinsic value. See Appendix B for a dramatization of a bubble.

These pretty flowers once caused a speculative bubble!

Figure 8-1
Tulips

In the world of stocks, the book value per share is the net asset value of a company divided by the number of shares outstanding. The book value is what the company's financial statement says each share is worth. The book value is what I call the intrinsic value. The difference between the actual price of a stock and the book value per share is what I consider implied value.

Book value per share = Net asset value / # of shares outstanding

Book value per share = Intrinsic value of share

Implied value of share = Price of stock – Intrinsic value

If the book value of a stock is $50 per share and it is selling for $100 per share, then we have $50 of intrinsic value and $50 of implied value.

Here is another example of implied value. Major League Baseball star Albert Pujols of the St. Louis Cardinals (Figure 8-2) takes his batting gloves and throws them into the stands. The person catching the gloves puts them up for sale on eBay and gets a bid for $1,000. Anyone can buy the same gloves at a sporting goods store for $50. The intrinsic value of these gloves is $50 and the implied value is $950. The intrinsic value plus the implied value equals the market price.

Value of gloves in sporting goods store = $50

Bid price for gloves on eBay = $1,000

Implied value = $1,000 - $50 = $950

This is the classic problem with bubbles – implied values get too high. Valuations get out of whack and investors don't realize it until the bubble pops by which time it is too late. It takes keen discipline, or a detached investment analysis to understand bubbles. Alternately, you could implant Mr. Spock's Vulcan brain as your own and understand that most speculative bubbles are "illogical".

How much would you pay for his $50 batting gloves?

Figure 8-2
Albert Pujols

Beanie Babies

Remember the Beanie Baby mania? These stuffed little animals ignited international speculation in the late 1990s. What made these $5 to $7 animals so desirable? The appeal for kids was the pleasing combination of softness and floppiness. They came with cute names like Leopard and Pinchers the Lobster. At $5 to $7, they were imminently affordable. Parents lined up early in the morning for a shot at a Baby they just had to have. The creator of the Beanie Baby, Ty Warner, devised a unique distribution model where the stuffed toys were only available through specialty or gift stores instead of the larger chains. This approach created the impression of scarcity despite the fact millions were being produced.

The Beanie Baby company would abruptly end production of one model and replace it with another. Beanie enthusiasts were stirred into a frenzy by this action since it made the discontinued Baby model more valuable. The $5-$7 toys sold for many times that in the resale market, some for as much as $600 to $3,000. A Baby selling for $3,000 had over $2,990 of implied value! An entire publishing industry emerged around Beanie Babies when the magazine *Mary Beth's Beanie World* had a circulation of 650,000 copies per month at $5.99 per.

The price of Beanie Babies in the resale market began to plateau. Ironically, the inventor of the Beanie Baby precipitated its demise by ceasing production of the toys in late 1999. Perhaps he hoped that ceasing production would spur demand. It did not. In early 2000, production of Beanie Babies resumed but they never reached their previous level of popularity. A toy some thought would help pay for their child's education fell dramatically in value. In the words of one parent, "They make great insulation if you stick them in the walls."

Why did these stuffed animals become so popular and whip the public into such frenzy (Figure 8-3)? The cycle model discussed in an earlier chapter laid the foundation for human behavior patterns. The period from 1982 until 2000 characterized a great euphoria in the investment markets. Beanie Babies went from being a stuffed toy to a full-fledged mania culminating in a speculative bubble. The Beanies reached their zenith right around the time of the first stock market top in early 2000, also known as the dot com bubble. That both bubbles popped at about the same time is another affirmation of a waning positive social cycle.

These stuffed animals whipped the public into a frenzy!

Figure 8-3
Beanie Baby

Tulip Bubble

The first recorded speculative bubble was the Tulip mania in Holland beginning in November of 1636 and ending in May of 1637 - our flower reference from earlier (Figure 8-4). The peak price of a tulip was 20 times that at the beginning of the mania. The mania reached its peak in February of 1637 and fell to its original starting point a mere three months later (Figure 8-5). At its peak, the price of a tulip was 10 times the yearly wage of a skilled craftsman.

The Tulip Bubble is a great example of pricing gone wild. The intrinsic value of a flower is its aesthetic quality. When a tulip reaches a price of ten times the yearly wage of a skilled craftsman, it's probably fair to conclude there are at least 999 parts of implied value and only 1 part intrinsic value. That's what makes bubbles so irrational. Investors are caught up in a boundless euphoria that always ends badly.

"Get your tulips here. Only 10 times what you make in a year."

Figure 8-4
Tulip Mania Depiction

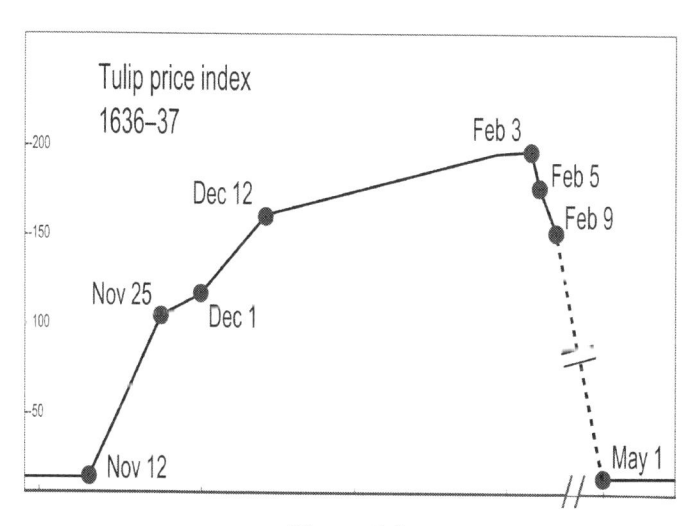

Figure 8-5
Tulip prices during the bubble

South Sea Bubble

Another famous mania was the South Sea Bubble of 1711-1720. This bubble started as an exchange of £10 million in British Government debt for stock in the South Sea Company (SSC). The government granted this company exclusive trading rights in Spanish South America. The plan was for government to give the company a perpetual annuity of some £576 thousand. The government would apply a tariff on goods brought from South America in order to pay the annuity. The holders of the government debt, now holders of South Sea Company stock, were assured of a steady stream of income in their new company. On the surface, it seemed like a fine arrangement.

The operators of the SSC projected affluence and this made investors seek more company ownership. The company engaged in a great deal of self-promotion by creating rumors to increase the price of their stock. Some lucky recipients received stock, for which they paid nothing, and later sold the stock back to the company at a profit when the price increased. This arrangement created a moral hazard for owners of stock inclusive of government officials whose interest it was to increase the stock price. Eventually, SSC's stock price climbed 10-fold (Figure 8-6). The popularity of the SSC created a speculative frenzy in other stocks as well. One company was formed *"for carrying out an undertaking of great advantage, but nobody to know what it is."*

After reaching a 10-fold increase in price, a wave of selling began. Sellers, who had earlier purchased shares with borrowed money or on credit from the SSC, saw the value of their investment dip. Purchases made on credit were at great risk for initial selling as lenders saw the value of their collateral, SSC stock, decline in value. The leveraging evident with SSC stock occurred elsewhere and soon other stocks began their decline.

The stock's fall caused failures in the banking industry, as loans made to investors for stock purchases were uncollectible. Goldsmiths, another industry extending credit for stock purchases, experienced similar calamity. The collapse of the stock's price led to financial ruin not just for banks and goldsmiths but prominent citizens as well. With investor outrage at a fever pitch, the English Parliament convened to investigate the matter. Measures were taken to restore public confidence. Eventually the Bank of England, the British version of the Federal Reserve Bank, stepped in to buy stock in the SSC. The government also decided to take legislative action to prevent such a bubble from occurring again.

Does any of this sound familiar?

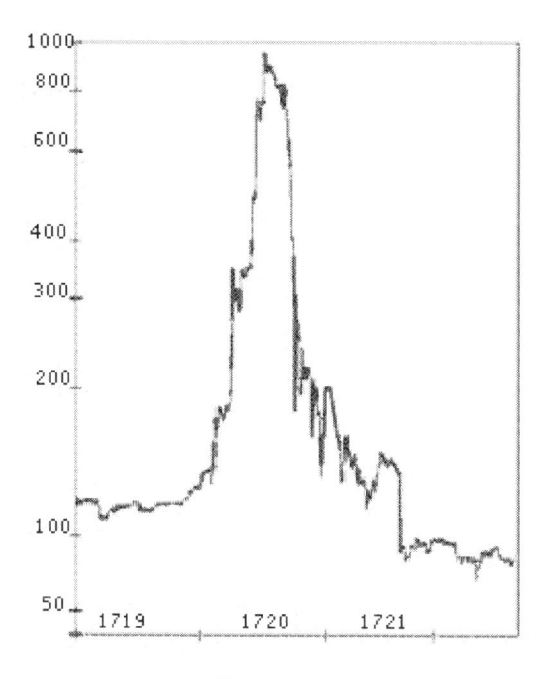

Figure 8-6
South Sea Bubble

Anatomy of a Bubble

A bubble's anatomy consists of three stages: creation, collapse, and aftermath.

Bubble Creation

1. A favorable public psychology-confidence
2. A herding instinct
3. The means to speculate with credit

Bubble Collapse

1. An investor willing to sell at a lower price
2. The default on loans and evaporation of new credit
3. Discovery of massive fraud

Aftermath

1. Collapsing prices
2. Recriminations of "guilty" parties
3. Government attempts to restore confidence

Our financial bubble began roughly in 1982, accelerated in the early 1990s, and culminated in a pop in 2007. If we dissect our bubble, we'll see how it fits the anatomy described:

Bubble Creation

- <u>Favorable public psychology</u> – increased from 1982-2000 (and possibly until 2007). We illustrated the positive mood in the cycle analysis in an earlier chapter.

- <u>Herding instinct</u> – investors piled into stocks and real estate not wanting to miss a sure thing. It did not matter if the investments were sound. Investors were climbing a wall of worry.

- <u>Means to speculate</u> – greatest credit binge in the history of the world.

Bubble Collapse

- <u>Investors selling at lower prices</u> – this occurred in stocks and real estate. When people could not afford their mortgages, it led to lower sale prices and problems with mortgage securities.

- <u>Evaporation of new credit</u> – government officials said the credit markets "seized up", less bank lending.

- <u>Discovery of massive fraud</u> – FBI discovered dozens of high-profile Ponzi schemes. There was the discovery of widespread mortgage fraud.

Aftermath

- <u>Collapsing prices</u> – falling home prices, defaults, bankruptcies, lower stock and commodity prices.

- <u>Recrimination of "guilty" parties</u> – severe public backlash erupted against leaders of banks, hedge funds, and former market wizards

- <u>Government attempts to restore confidence</u> – stimulus, more spending, new legislation.

Whether it was the South Sea Bubble or our current credit bubble, a bubble follows the same path. First, there has to be a very confident public. Credit accompanies that confidence. Once that confidence breaks, the bubble collapses and prices return to where they started. The aftermath is a painful period of recovery and assigning blame.

The problem with our present bubble is its sheer size. Our addiction to credit was unmatched in history. Credit is the Wicked Witch of the West, always trying to take something from us. This witch is very clever and often in disguise so the credit seems painless. It was very difficult for the public to recognize their rotting core - debt accumulation - since the witch made us numb to the pain.

Progression of Our Bubble

The biggest indicator of our bubble's progression is the dramatic increase in public and private debt. Our public debt reached $2.6 trillion by 1988. By 1992, this debt surged to $4 trillion. It took 8 years to reach $5.6 trillion in 2000. By 2007, the top of the bubble, the debt reached $8.7 trillion. Today our debt stands at $13.8 trillion - U.S. debt increased by more than 50% in just three years! Our debt ceiling, or legally allowed debt, is now $14 trillion. With current deficit projections extending beyond the $1 trillion range in the near future, that debt ceiling is made of paper. Even though the bubble popped, the government continues as if it has not.

How have private individuals fared during this bubble? Regrettably, individuals swallowed large pieces of debt. At the bubble's peak, the U.S. commercial banking system alone held $2.6 trillion in consumer revolving and non-revolving loans (Figure 8-7), $900 billion in individual loans and nearly $4 trillion in mortgage loans. For those scoring at home, that is a cool $7.5 trillion. Personal savings, on the other hand, fell dramatically during the bubble. While debt increased exponentially, savings experienced a decline – a fatal condition.

Since the bubble popped, a shift occurred in the private sector with savings increasing at the greatest rate since the Federal Reserve Bank of St. Louis started tracking this data in the late 1950s. Consumer revolving/non-revolving debt decreased in this same period. The reduction of credit and increase in savings are manifestations of initial deflationary conditions.

The Wicked Witch of the West has infiltrated our governments too. Rather than help the country, and in fact the world, confront the bubble's explosion, governments have coordinated their efforts to employ massive economic stimulus. The bubble ended and the party is over. The chairs are on the table and the lights are off. Government, with the help of the Wicked Witch, is trying to restart the party. Unfortunately, the partygoers have had their fill of food and drink.

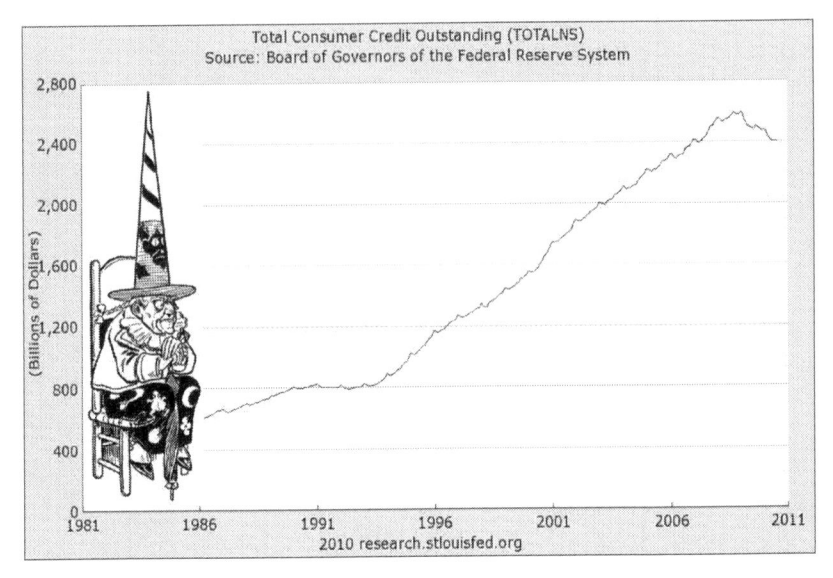

Figure 8-7
Consumer Credit

Lessons Not Learned

Speculative bubbles suffer from the persistent view that such things cannot happen to investors. Investors are smarter, they do things better, they have much more information available to them and the old rules of valuation no longer apply. Speculative bubbles are outdated. Investment or the economy in general is based on sound fundamentals, superior technology, or good governmental policy. In the end, this time is *not* different.

On the eve of the great stock market crash in September of 1929, a daily publication called *Standard Statistics* reminded their readers that buying into a bubble was inexcusable. In their estimation, there were simply too many facts available to allow investors to make unsound investments and be susceptible to hazardous speculation. The stock market crash the following month cast great doubt on the value of all those facts.

Our recent speculative bubble also suffered from the belief that globalization, technology, esoteric financial products, and the wizardry of monetary policy could help avoid any notion of hazardous speculation. While some people are coming to grips with the end of this bubble, others are trying to keep it alive.

Summary

The following are key points from this chapter:

- Bubbles or manias occur due to the innate human instinct to herd.

- The herding instinct occurs since individuals feel they don't have any better information so the public at large must know something they don't.

- Beanie Babies were an example of a mania. Though not as severe as a full-blown speculative bubble, it serves as an example of irrational behavior.

- Two of the most famous speculative bubbles were the Tulip Bubble in Holland in the 17th century and the South Sea Bubble in England in the 18th century.

- Bubbles have a general structure that includes creation, collapse, and aftermath.

- Our current bubble is massive creation of credit that directed itself into stocks, bonds, real estate, and government spending.

PART III

PREPARING OUR ESCAPE

Part III is all about what you need to do to preserve your wealth. Since any forecast has the possibility of being wrong, I offer you a layered approach to wealth preservation. Failure of any one approach will not capsize your ship. Your ship may take on water, but it will still float. Be prepared. Other ships around you may sink and you may have to take on survivors.

I will preface the contents of this section by suggesting that what I present are guidelines and reasons for taking action. The execution of these steps will require some knowledge and effort on your part. If you do not have this knowledge, seek assistance from a qualified financial advisor. Some of these approaches may have tax implications for you. Consult with a tax advisor if necessary.

I start Part III by helping you understand investor psychology. You need to know yourself and understand how to approach investing in a different manner. I spend several chapters discussing various investment vehicles and what you should do with each. I return to the topic of knowing yourself and provide a categorization of who you are as an investor and how you should construct your portfolio. Finally, I close with a chapter on planning. This planning is not just for determining your financial path but how you should prepare for dealing with some of the anticipated changes resulting from government withdrawal from parts of the economy. To quote President Kennedy, "And so my fellow Americans, ask not what your country can do for you but what you can do for your country."

Chapter 9
Investor Psychology

This chapter examines the psychology behind two bubbles where there was widespread public participation. Because there was such broad participation, the objects of the bubble were not something specific like the stock of one company or a flower. Stocks and real estate formed two of the largest, most identifiable bubbles in history.

The bursting of the dot com bubble proved only a temporary setback to the stock market. After peaking in 2000, the stock market fell for a couple of years before resuming an advance to the historic 2007 top. Why would investors bid up stocks so soon after such a historic bubble pop in 2000? Investors lack strategy for entering and exiting a market. Another component in investor behavior is how they view prices in consumer transactions versus financial transactions.

The real estate bubble is truly something to behold. At one time in the United States, the dollar value of loans for home ownership grew slowly and yet the percentage of families owning homes grew dramatically. A home loan was something that people acquired to put a roof over their head. In the last 20-30 years, however, a home morphed into an investment.

Investors have a myriad of analytical tools at their disposal. Our computing power is unparalleled and there are plenty of investment advisors to go around. Despite all this ammunition, few seemed to identify either bubble. The great central banker Alan Greenspan and the great investor Warren Buffett both admitted they could not foresee the housing meltdown. If those guys can't identify a bubble, how is an ordinary Joe going to? Maybe there is a psychological component afflicting investors of all stripes.

Stock Investment Psychology

The easiest approach for an investor is to follow the crowd. In the last two decades, stock investors perfected crowd following. Many invested in particular stocks and mutual funds because their brokers told them to, or their friends and family suggested it. Crowd investing is a very powerful force. Once someone else has success in the market your instinct is to follow. Remember, people want to belong to a group. The desire to belong to a group is a powerful emotional motivator creating a psychological dependence. A group of investors on a nice ride up in stocks provides a compelling reason to belong. Rational approaches to market investing were not in vogue in the late 1990s. How do we know this? If stock markets always followed a "rational" approach, the prices of some technology stocks would never have reached the lofty heights experienced in the dot com bubble.

There were plenty of stock valuation methods available to determine the stock market's health. The price/earnings ratio, yield, or book value should have alerted an investor that the price of some stocks was not rational. In fact, applying those measures to the entire market was an early warning system about the dot com boom in the NASDAQ. Investors and analysts discarded these time-tested measures. New paradigms emerged justifying stock prices. We heard things like "this time is different" or "New Economy". These justifications were necessary in order to override rational stock valuation methods.

During the dot com bubble, I would ask people about their exit strategy with stock investments. I often got a blank look. What would cause them to sell their stock and take their profit? For most stock investors, the idea of taking a profit is not in their DNA. Will your profits always be on paper? Do you know when to take a profit? My first law of investing says:

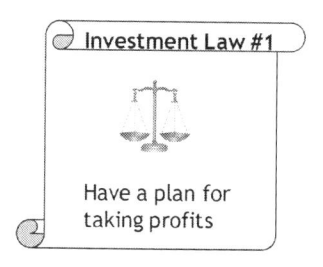

Investment Law #1

Have a plan for taking profits

One of the reasons investors do not adhere to Investment Law #1 is the difficulty most have in timing the market. Common practice is to simply buy and hold. Unfortunately, investors have a penchant for buying and selling at the wrong time. The fact this occurs confirms they have no plan for exiting with a profit. Buy and hold is a great approach as long as you are in a bull market. When the bear arrives, buy and hold will wipe you out.

A profit-taking plan is necessary if you are to make money in stocks. If you need help, seek professional advice. Have a plan and stick to the plan.

The most difficult aspect of stock investing, and perhaps investing in general, is to know when to take a loss. Take a loss? Most investors have no plan to exit a stock after it experiences losses. The most common response is to buy and hold since the market always comes back. During the Great Depression, the top of the market occurred in 1929 and the bottom came in 1932. At historic bottoms such as 1932, investors have no appetite for stocks since most held on for the plunge and are now mentally exhausted or financially ruined. Undoubtedly, 1932 was <u>the</u> year to buy stocks but the psychological damage was done.

The accompanying chart (Figure 9-1) shows the amusement park ride an average investor experienced starting in 1929. Stocks lost 90% of their value and did not achieve their 1929 levels for 25 years! Could you hold on to your stocks for an entire generation with these types of fluctuations?

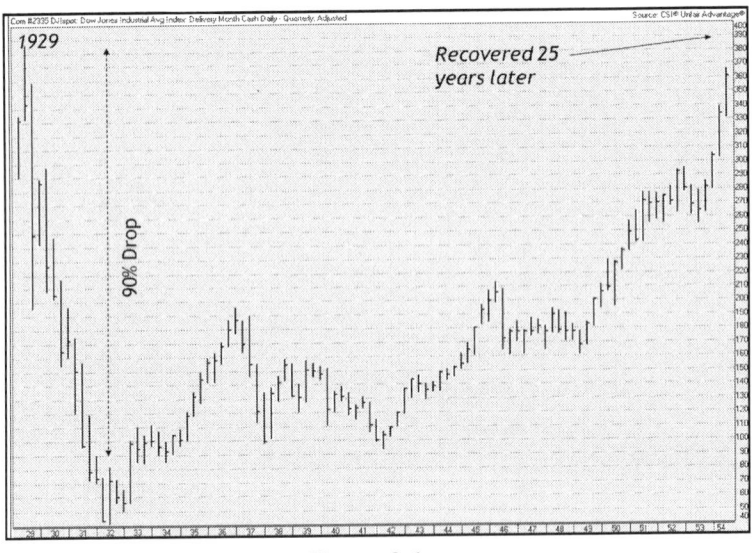

Figure 9-1
Dow Jones Industrial Average (1929-1955)

Fidelity Investments, a custodian for 401(k) accounts, reported very little movement out of stocks in early 2009 despite significant losses. We can conclude there was a level of confidence with 401(k) investors; otherwise, there would have been a massive stampede out of stocks. The public felt the market would come back. The public had no exit strategy since most investors or advisors never experienced anything but a rising market.

The psychology of not knowing when to take a loss is akin to a gambler who loses money at the table and continues to bet. In fact, the bets may increase in the hope of winning back the earlier losses. Financial advisors or pundits advocate purchasing stocks after a big drop since they are "cheaper". The musician Kenny Rogers sang, "You gotta to know when to hold up. Know when to fold up. Know when to walk away. And know when to run." These words give rise to the second investment law:

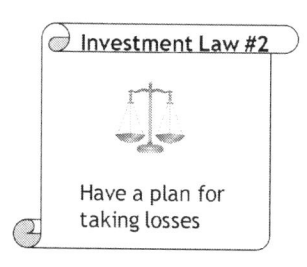

Investment Law #2

Have a plan for taking losses

Investors have a difficult time admitting when they are wrong. It is simply not in our nature to admit defeat. Imagine entering a casino and deciding ahead of time that you would lose no more than $100. Would that limit your losses? It certainly would provided you had the discipline to adhere to your decision. If you went in without a loss limit, how long would you continue gambling? I'm not trying to compare gambling with stock investing. What I'm trying to establish is how little discipline investors have with respect to investments. Not having a plan for taking losses is akin to the gambler who does not know when to leave the table. In the stock market of today, many will stay long after they should have gone home.

Real Estate Psychology

Real estate investment psychology is similar to that of stocks. Crowd following happened here too. A major reason for the real estate bubble was a public convinced that the roof over their heads was an investment – it was not and is not. Figure 9-2 shows the exponential rise in all real estate loans. From the late 1940s to the early 1970s, the line on the chart hardly rises. Yet during that period, U.S. home ownership exploded from 43% of the population to 63%. From 1980 to 2000, the slope of the line increases dramatically from less than $400 billion to $1.4 trillion. If you concluded that home ownership rates went up dramatically during this time, you would be wrong. Home ownership rates increased to 66.2% of the population.

Okay, I will give you one more chance. What do you think happened to home ownership rates between 2000 and 2008? Surely, ownership rates skyrocketed during that period. Home ownership rates were 67.8% in 2008, a mere 1.6% higher. What did we get for all the real estate debt? We got marginally higher ownership rates, more expensive homes, and much less home equity.

Consumption real estate morphed into investment real estate when borrowers and lenders assumed more risk. Lenders greatly relaxed the standards used to extend credit. Those borrowing money for a home felt confident enough to have a much smaller margin of error. All this borrowing and lending is an example of the first Economic Law (credit = confidence). Everyone was confident. Those that were already homeowners tapped their paper equity to finance consumption items such as appliances, vacations and recreational vehicles. Credit issued for a consumption item, a house, turned into credit for more consumption. For some homeowners, this was a frightening case of piling debt on top of debt. Presently there is $600 billion of this type of revolving home equity loans.

The public does not consider their home a consumption item. Real estate always goes up in value, right? They aren't making any more land, right? During the Great Depression, some homes lost 90% of their value. In 2009 losses of 90% occurred in some neighborhoods in Michigan. A 2009 report by ABC News profiled a neighborhood in Phoenix, AZ where a 2,300 sq ft. home whose original sale price was $250k in 2006 sold for $95k. This is a stunning loss of 62% for a home originally selling for a reasonable $108/sq. ft.

For those with a small margin of error, the ability to maintain house payments can vanish quickly, leading to a forced sale or even foreclosure. The place where you live is <u>not</u> an investment.

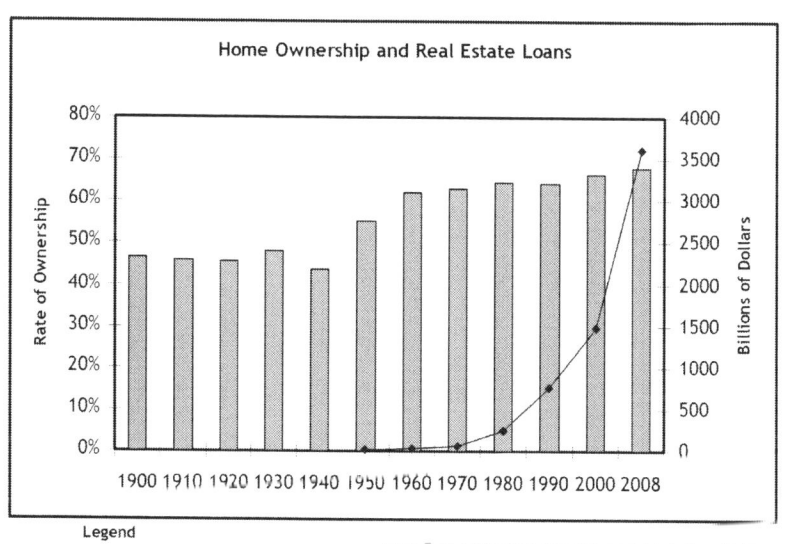

Figure 9-2
Home Ownership & Real Estate Loans

Does Emotion or Logic Rule Investor Habits?

Historical evidence shows that a typical investor earns less than a mutual fund's reported returns. These are the same funds so keen on providing investor diversification. It appears there is a predisposition to buy high and sell low and to cling to losing investments. This is a further affirmation that most investors do not adhere to Investment Law #2 – they have no plan for exiting a bad investment.

The fields of investor psychology and behavioral finance shed new light on how people make investing decisions. Something known as the Efficient Market Hypothesis (EMH) postulated that investors had the cold, rational logic of Star Trek's Mr. Spock. The opposite is more likely the case. EMH is one of the pillars of classical finance theory but as we will see, it has its flaws. Consumer finance and investor finance present two models of stark contrast. For example, consumer finance tends to follow the more predictable supply-demand curve. If the price of filet mignon were $1.99 per pound, the demand would be quite high. If the price of filet were $50 per pound, the demand would drop. This is what we would expect in consumer finance – when the price is low demand is high and when the price is high demand is low (Figure 9-3).

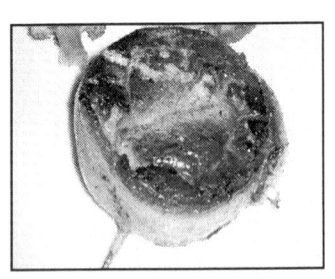

Figure 9-3
Filet Mignon

We buy less of this when the price goes sky high. With housing and other assets, higher prices did not discourage more buying.

The world of investor finance is a different matter. Consider stock prices. Prior to 2007, stock prices were rising for the preceding five-year period after the bear market of 2000-2002. Prior to 2000, the stock market was rising for a sustained period beginning in 1982. A rational analysis of both periods indicated that investors continued to pay higher prices for stocks even though dividends paid did not keep pace. That is to say, the dividend yield was historically low. By one very important measure, stocks were expensive and yet the public continued buying. We will cover this topic more in Chapter 13.

EMH suggests rational investor behavior which should lead to stock prices that are relatively stable. Any new information reaching the market would impact all investors the same way. Most of the time stocks should exhibit a sideways movement. If an impactful piece of information came out, then stocks should react strongly either up or down. The movement of prices might look like Figure 9-4. Figure 9-4 features a hypothetical company that makes athletic equipment, shoes, and apparel. Price movements of their stock reflect a rational response to events surrounding the company.

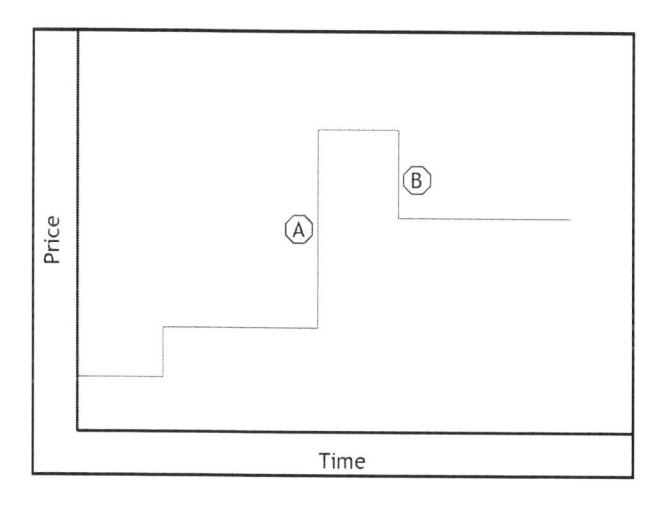

Figure 9-4
EMH Stock Price Movement

For example, the price movement reflected by the line segment "A" might be an announcement by the company that the National Football League has signed an exclusive contract with them to supply all uniforms, shoes, and footballs. Rationally, we should expect this company's fortunes to be bolstered by this contract. Conversely, line segment "B" might represent this company's loss of an exclusive contract with the National Basketball Association. Figure 9-5 illustrates stock prices from a similar company in the real world, Nike Inc.

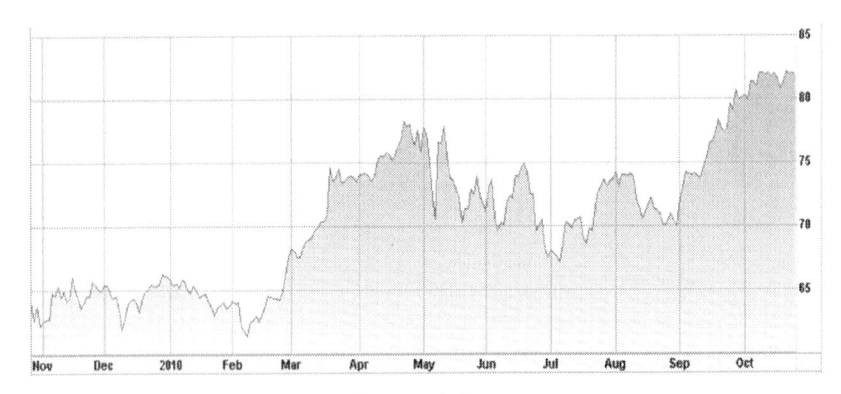

Figure 9-5
Nike Inc. Stock Prices

So what makes people behave differently with stocks or housing versus a loaf of bread? A stock is a financial asset whose valuation is more uncertain than the price of bread at a grocery store. It's fair to conclude that bread prices do not fluctuate like stock prices. Bread is an economic good to be consumed. As such, consumers have a much better idea of how to value it which is why few would pay $100 for a loaf of bread. Stocks are not economic goods to be consumed but rather they represent investments. Because stocks are investments, it is difficult to know how others will value them over time. This difficulty creates uncertainty, which is manifested in the hourly, daily, weekly, and monthly fluctuation of stock prices.

You might ask why housing prices behaved as they did. With respect to housing, the public took an economic good, the roof over their heads, and turned it into an investment. It was certainly an investment since large numbers of people wanted to sell housing in the future for a higher price. Even those with no intention of selling risked their financial welfare on the hope of a higher home price.

The uncertainty of investment valuation means we have to engage our brains to make those assessments. Investors think they are using one part of their brain, the logical pre-frontal cortex, but in reality, they use another part of their brain, the amygdala, for making investment decisions (Figure 9-6). The amygdala is all about emotion. This behavior *is* hard-wired into our biological makeup.

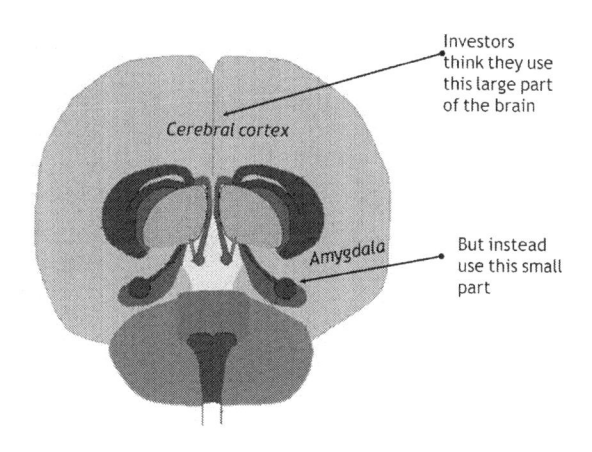

Figure 9-6
Human Brain

We have established that investors have a propensity to herd. Herding is a function of the emotional part of the brain kicking in and overriding rational thought. Herding is also an unconscious, impulsive behavior designed to increase the chances of survival in times of danger. Since rational thought is a function of gathering facts and making interpretations of those facts, having <u>few</u> facts creates legions of followers. Complicating rational thought is the fact that humans tend to organize facts around stories. The dot com bubble brought us the Internet. The story of the Internet meant the end of bricks and mortar retailers – it was to be a New Economy. A new paradigm in business was going to promulgate an explosion in commerce. It was going to be a gold rush. Companies of dubious merit were able to raise large amounts of capital or see their stock prices rise dramatically. Since "everyone" was investing in dot com stocks, it must have been a great investment, right? No, investors forgot to gather the facts.

So if investors are herding due to the small part of their brain kicking in, what does the large part of the brain do? Research shows that investors employ the large part of their brain *after* engaging in a herding action. One researcher concluded that humans are built to cover up the fact that our emotional brain influences us. If we believe we took action because of our rational brain, we probably made up a story that justified our action.

For example, the stock market crash of 1987 was blamed on overpriced stocks and institutional trading systems hitting certain stop-loss points. A stop-loss point is actually an application of Investment Law #2 where someone sells a stock at some point below its market price. One researcher found that 43% of a random sample of institutional investors experienced unusual symptoms of anxiety on the day of the crash. Why were these institutional traders anxious with their knowledge of EMH and the rational trading systems they no doubt employed? The same researcher could find no external reasons for the crash. Scholars still have a hard time explaining the causes of not only the 1987 crash but the crash of 1929 as well.

Most recently we had the "flash crash" on May 6, 2010 where the Dow Jones Industrial Average fell 1,000 points before rallying to close down 350 points. The Securities and Exchange Commission (SEC) and the Commodity Futures Trading Commission

(CFTC) issued a post-mortem on the flash crash and blamed poor trade execution by a mutual fund. There has not been much agreement on the cause of this crash despite all the data available to study. One thing we can agree on is that there was a whole bunch of herding occurring that day—there were many more sellers than buyers!

The herding instinct was firmly in play for a generation of investing that had only witnessed progressively rising stock prices. The ride to Dow 40,000 encountered a huge sinkhole after the stock market top in 2007. Investors experienced the failure of Lehman Brothers and government takeovers of Fannie Mae, Freddie Mac, and General Motors. Whereas the years prior to 2008 had the public rushing to check their investment balances, now many did not want to see them. During the plunge in stock prices, the average investor held on. If they didn't sell their stocks, somehow they would avoid the loss and the psychological destruction that comes with it. Losing money is painful though it is part of the investment process.

February of 2009 arrived with a continuation of the bear market in stocks. A public partially exhausted by the losses withdrew $25 billion from stock funds, which was the greatest monthly outflow in the previous two years. The timing of the withdrawal was poor since the market made a major low in March of 2009. Many did not take any action near the market low and remained invested. Other investors who bailed out at the worst time may never reenter the market. You also have a larger number who took no action and are feeling better about their investments.

Most investors are not equipped to deal with the cold, hard logic necessary for successful investing outcomes. Only a small percentage of investors can be logical and rational. Emotion tends to rule the day. The antidote to this emotion is to acquire the knowledge necessary to overcome the innate biological tendency to herd.

Summary

The following are the important points of this chapter:

- Investors do not behave in a rational manner when it comes to stock investing. Rational analysis would never have allowed the dot com bubble.

- Investment Law #1 suggests investors have a plan for taking a profit. If you don't have a plan, you may never have a profit.

- Investment Law #2 suggests investors have a plan for taking a loss. You might be wrong so you had better have a plan to get out.

- The public behaves differently in the area of consumer finance versus investment finance. In consumer finance, higher prices discourage buying. In investor finance, higher prices encourage buying provided there is available credit. Credit will fuel price increases.

- The Efficient Market Hypothesis (EMH) says investors will behave in a rational manner. Investors tend to engage the emotional part of their brain instead of the larger, rational portion.

- Home ownership increased dramatically in the U.S. after 1940 though home mortgage debt grew moderately. After 1980 home mortgage debt grew dramatically though home ownership percentages barely increased.

Chapter 10
Bank Investing

If you are reading this book, chances are you own one of the 7 trillion dollars in the banking system. One way or another, a bank is part of your life. Your employer transfers paychecks electronically to your bank account, or you stand in line to make a deposit. ATMs are everywhere. Many of you also have savings accounts, money market accounts, or certificates of deposit in retirement or non-retirement plans. Banking is tightly woven into the fabric of our lives.

Since the banking industry was heavily involved in massive credit creation, they will also suffer from the aftermath. The once safe banking industry has struggled with bank failures, large and small. The government entity in charge of insuring the banking industry, the Federal Deposit Insurance Corporation (FDIC), faces its own struggles with inadequate funding to meet their daunting task of insuring trillions in deposits. Banks face a multitude of challenges, some legislative, and others caused by borrowers.

The most common bank investment products include savings accounts, money market accounts, and certificates of deposit. While these certainly are not new or sophisticated investment products, they provide a small interest rate and ostensibly a return *of* your investment. We use the word "ostensibly" since the risk of not getting back your money increases daily.

Banking Risks

During the early years of the Great Depression, bank failures were widespread. From 1929 to 1933, more than 9,700 banks failed (Figure 10-1). During the years of the S&L crisis from 1985 to 1992, about 2,000 banks failed (Figure 10-2). One of President Roosevelt's first acts after his inauguration in 1933 was to declare a bank holiday. Banks closed on March 4, 1933 and did not re-open until March 13, 1933. During the middle of that holiday, Congress passed the Emergency Banking Act of 1933. The Act shuttered insolvent banks, and provided for the reorganization of banks strong enough to survive.

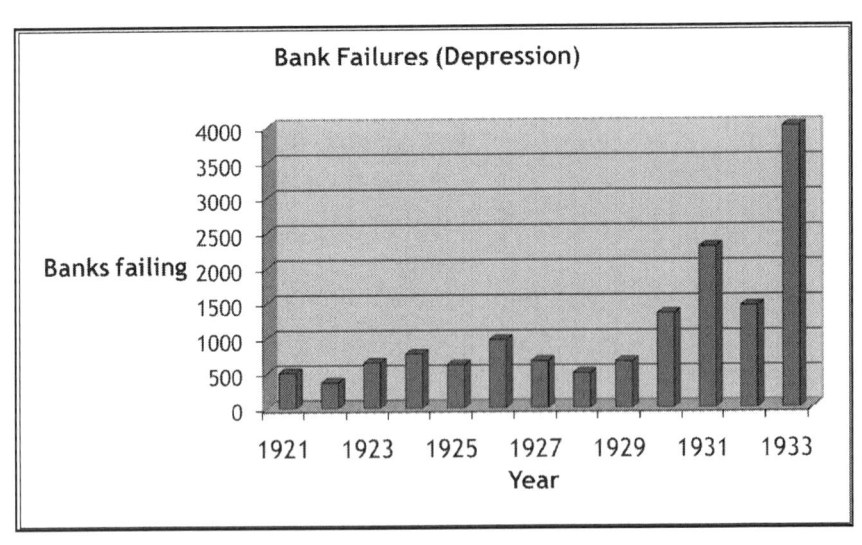

Figure 10-1
Bank Failures 1921-1933

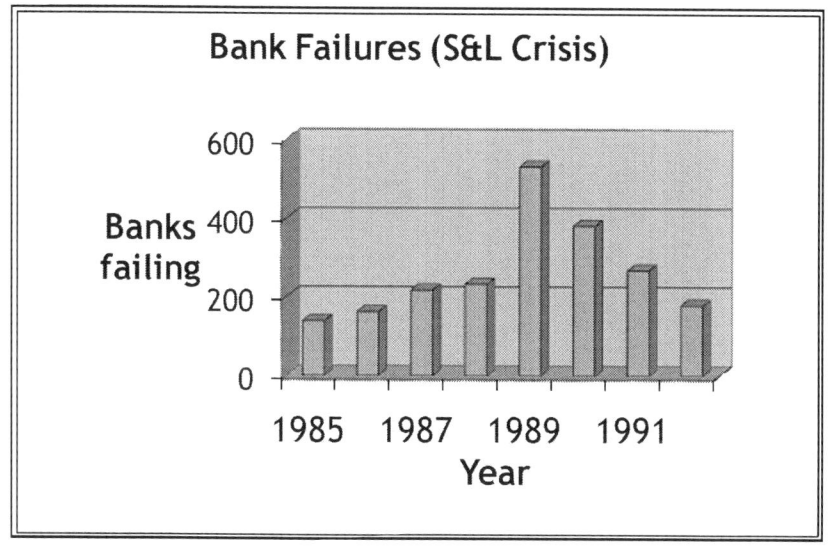

Figure 10-2
Bank Failures 1985-1992

One of the reasons banks fail is due to the nature of what a bank deposit really is. Your bank deposit is not like a warehouse receipt where you show a ticket and the warehouse returns your stored item. A bank deposit is an IOU from the bank to you. So while you legally have a claim on your deposit, that claim is predicated on the bank's ability to turn loans made with your money back into your deposit. When a bank fails, it means it cannot pay back its depositors. When depositors fear that banks cannot pay them back, a bank run ensues. This goes back to one of the most used words in this book, CONFIDENCE. Banking solvency is based on confidence.

Banks have an ever-present challenge of balancing deposits and loans. Banks accept savings (regular savings & certificates of deposit) and demand deposits (checking accounts) which can be withdrawn on short notice. They lend money at longer maturities in the form of loans to businesses or to others such as home-owners. In less stressful times, a bank has enough liquid resources to handle depositor withdrawals. Under the weight of heavier withdrawals, a bank will be forced to dip into their asset pool to satisfy depositor withdrawal. This implies selling at "fire sale" prices. If depositor withdrawal becomes systemic, many banks will be trying to sell assets at the same time in which case the market for those assets can evaporate. Assets that may be liquid under normal conditions become highly illiquid just when the banks call ill afford to have them.

The act of balancing short-term deposits with long-term lending is captured in a ratio known as the loan-to-deposit ratio. To calculate this ratio, we take a bank's total loans and divide them by their deposits.

Loan-to-deposit ratio = Loans / Deposits

A simple average of this ratio for the 50 states and territories yields 88%. Within that average, there are the extremes of 165% for North Dakota and 67% for Utah. The average ratio means that for every $100 of deposits, there is $88 in loans and $12 in what should be liquid instruments like Treasury Bills. For a state like North Dakota, it means there is $165 in loans for every $100 in deposits; yes, it is possible to have more in loans than deposits. The national average ratio of 88% is a bit deceptive, however. The "loan" portion of the ratio does not include municipal bonds or mortgage-securities that we will learn later are perhaps even more risky than a typical bank loan. Therefore, the 88% figure likely understates the ratio by a significant amount.

It is not as simple though as just having banks lend less in order to have a better loan-to-deposit ratio. There are actually banking regulations penalizing banks for not lending enough! Under a banking act passed by Congress in 1994, Federal banking authorities monitor the lending activities of interstate branch banks. If authorities determine the interstate bank does not lend enough relative to its peers in that state, those same authorities can close the branch and prohibit the interstate bank from opening new branches in that state. This is yet another example of government legislation with unintended consequences.

This chapter section presented some of the basic challenges banks face and you face as a depositor. These challenges can eventually morph into bank holidays or bank failures. Bank holidays are not unique to the U.S. In November of 2001, the government of Argentina imposed partial withdrawal restrictions on deposits. This restriction remained in place for one year. Germany had a bank holiday in 1931 and Panama had a 9-week holiday in 1988. This is just a *very small* sample of historical worldwide banking holidays and failures.

Resolving bank failures and dealing with holidays can become a long, arduous legal and legislative/governmental problem. If you want free access to your deposits, you don't want to be around a failed bank. The U.S. created an agency during the Great Depression to calm the fears of depositors and to prevent bank runs.

FDIC

The government established the FDIC in 1933 in response to thousands of bank failures occurring in the 1920s and 1930s. It is an independent agency of the Federal Government receiving no congressional appropriations. In other words, it truly operates as an insurance fund with premiums supplied by banks and thrift institutions. This point is important since it means the insurance fund is supposed to cover the losses of its insured members. The FDIC's claim to fame is that no depositor has lost a single penny in an insured account resulting from bank failure. The FDIC insures more than $7 trillion in deposits. These details are simply another way of saying the FDIC promotes confidence (Figure 10-3). Confidence is credit (Economic Law #1). The FDIC's job has gotten more difficult in recent years as the number of bank failures increased.

When depositors see this seal, they are more confident. Should they be?

Figure 10-3
FDIC Seal

In response to bank failures and to increase confidence, the FDIC increased the insurance on each account from $100k to $250k effective until 12/31/2013. If the FDIC increases its account insurance by a factor of 2.5, should we feel more secure about the FDIC's ability to cover our deposits?

According to the FDIC's web site,

> *"FDIC insurance covers all deposit accounts at insured banks and savings associations, including checking, NOW, and savings accounts, money market deposit accounts and certificates of deposit (CDs) up to the insurance limit."*

Throughout this book, I cite credit expansion and credit contraction. The FDIC contributed to the expansion of credit under the category of moral hazard. A moral hazard in the insurance industry implies that those shielded from risk behave in a less cautious manner since they know they are insured. A good example of moral hazard is intentionally leaving your old car exposed to a violent hailstorm knowing the insurance company will pay for a new vehicle. Banking has a similar but more subtle moral hazard. Depositors did not pay much attention to the lending and investment activities of their banks – they knew the FDIC had their back. Banks could take more chances making questionable loans and investments since they knew the FDIC was there to bail out depositors.

According to the FDIC's web site, there were nearly 150 failed banks in 2009 (Figure 10-4). One way the FDIC rescues or "resolves" a bank is to exchange bad assets of the failed bank for better assets the FDIC already owns. That way the assets of the bank look better and the bank remains solvent. In other cases, the failed bank is merged with a healthier one. Ultimately, any insurer must maintain a reserve fund to cover potential losses. The FDIC maintains a Deposit Insurance Fund (DIF) that must maintain a reserve ratio of 1.15%. This means that for every $100 on deposit, the DIF must hold $1.15. As with any other insurance, we expect the insurer to have adequate reserves on hand to meet losses. With recent bank failures, the FDIC does not have this level of funding.

Recognizing their inadequate funding, on September 29, 2009, the FDIC adopted a plan to return to the 1.15% reserve ratio, within 8 years! The total size of the DIF stood at $65 billion as of 6/30/2009 but only $22 billion of that was in cash and marketable securities, the better assets. The FDIC is hopeful that the other toxic stuff they acquired in saving failed banks *eventually* will have value. As part of their effort to increase their insurance fund, the FDIC adopted a measure to raise cash more quickly. Depository institutions were required to pre pay three years worth of higher premiums as of 12/30/2009. The problem with increasing the premium is that more healthy banks suffer the FDIC's expense of resolving failed institutions. Increasing premiums on healthier banks means they have less to lend. Less lending is deflationary.

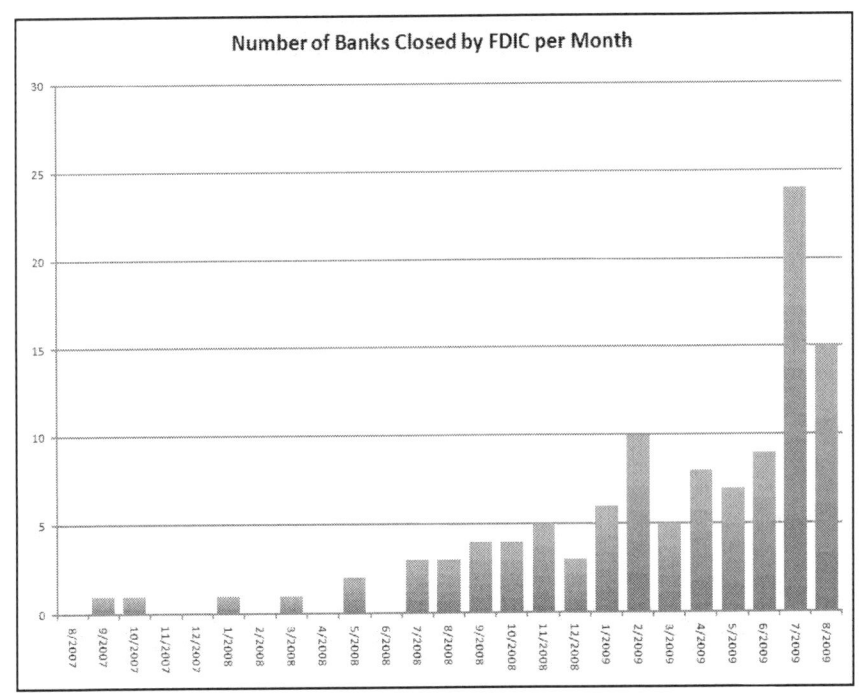

Figure 10-4
Bank Closures
Aug. 2007—Aug. 2009

Table 10-1 shows the distribution of insured deposits in the U.S. banking system. Using the figures from this table, the FDIC insures nearly $7 trillion in deposits (the FDIC web site uses $7 trillion as their figure as of June 2010). Using rough math, the DIF reserve ratio is somewhere in the neighborhood of ($65 billion/$7,000 billion) = 0.92%. If we use the more realistic figure of the FDIC's liquid assets, we arrive at ($22 billion/$7,000 billion) = 0.31%. These are rough estimates but you can certainly get the sense of how dire the FDIC's reserve fund is. The FDIC is nowhere near their required funding level.

Category	Amount (billions)
Checkable deposits	$ 813
Savings deposits	$4,880
Small time deposits	$1,090
Total	**$6,783**

Table 10-1

The funding problems for the FDIC are occurring at a time when 150 banks failed in one year. In the next 2-3 years, a number of residential loans will come up for refinancing. Since many of those loans are under water, the likelihood of orderly refinancing is slim. Banks don't want to refinance underwater loans, and homeowners are walking away from their houses. Refinancing activities will have undesirable outcomes for banks facing more loan write-offs. During the Great Depression, many multiples of 150 banks failed. Granted, the FDIC did not exist prior to 1933 but realistically, how many more bank failures can the FDIC handle at present funding levels? For the first six months of 2010, 86 banks failed, which is ahead of the pace in 2009, and this was in an economy that statistically was not in recession.

While the FDIC says they can insure the massive pool of deposits in the United States, they are nowhere close to the funding level even *they* say is required. If bank failures increase as I expect, the FDIC will have to turn to the U.S. Treasury for help. The FDIC should not have to come with hat in hand to the U.S. Treasury since their funding *should* come from premiums charged to banks. The question then becomes, how good is FDIC insurance if they have to turn to the Treasury Department? In an earlier chapter, we outlined the financial condition of the United States. Nothing in that analysis leads us to conclude the Treasury will be in a favorable position to help. For this reason, the health of your bank is now more important than ever.

Legislative Problems for Banks

Besides the FDIC, there are other reasons for you to worry about banks. Banks are saddled with far too many non-performing loans. Many of those non-performing loans eventually turn to default. When a homeowner defaults, banks have an interest in pursuing them to recover at least some of the money owed.

There are laws in certain states prohibiting banks from pursuing money owed to them due to a default on a home loan. These types of loans are non-recourse loans. If a homeowner defaults and walks away from their home, the bank's only recourse will be to take possession of the home even if the home does not cover the loan value. For many homeowners in the predicament of an underwater mortgage, walking away, while still painful, could have limited effect on the remainder of their assets. Owners who walk create another condition for banks to have their portfolios further deteriorated. Banks do not want to be in the home ownership business and now in some states, they cannot recover what is contractually theirs.

Legislators hoping to assist beleaguered homeowners created these non-recourse laws inadvertently harmful to the banking industry. The effect of these laws is deflationary since it means more failed loans and greater reluctance by banks to lend.

Kick Me Out If You Can

Aside from the legislative hurdles banks face, they have a new worry. Even for those people who have fallen into foreclosure, banks are encountering a new challenge – the homeowner who will not leave. This is a homemade, mortgage modification program. The homeowner has a zero payment and they use funds otherwise designated for the mortgage for day-to-day necessities.

Even though banks initiated foreclosure proceedings against 1.7 million households, the pace of resolution is slow. Legal challenges, foreclosure moratoriums, government pressure to modify loans, and the sheer number of foreclosures are overwhelming the nation's banks. Banks simply do not have the personnel to process this many foreclosures in a short amount of time. In January of 2008, the average borrower was delinquent for 251 days prior to their eviction. The figure as of June 2010 was 438 days. Homeowners recognize this and make the decision to stay in their house rent-free and use the mortgage payment for something else (Figure 10-5).

Bank Asset Profile

It used to be that the business of banking involved holding loans and U.S. Treasury assets. In the 1950s, banks held as much as 40% of their assets in Treasuries. The figure dropped to less than 1% in June 2009. Why does this matter? There have been no defaults in Treasuries in U.S. history. A bank investing in Treasuries had an implicit guarantee on the return of principal and interest. This is not the case with residential mortgages.

When bank asset profiles changed to greater issuance of residential mortgages, their risks increased accordingly. If residential loans soured, the bank's balance sheet would suffer more than if invested in U.S. Treasuries.

Another problem with bank assets was the percentage of loans they were making to consumers versus businesses. When banks loan money for productive and profitable ventures, loans are paid off rapidly and bank credit continues to be available. Businesses have the productive capacity to repay the loan out of profits. When banks loan to consumers, there is no productive capacity for repaying the loan. The bank relies on the ability of the individual to maintain an income stream necessary for loan payoff. Absent this income stream, the consumer must raise cash to payoff the loan or go into default.

An allocation of assets weighted towards more risky home mortgages has made insolvency a more realistic possibility for some banks. This will only add to the FDIC's misery as more banks reach the precipice of failure.

They will probably find people living in those homes.

Figure 10-5
Foreclosure Tours

Judging Bank Health

By now, you should realize the great challenges facing the banking industry. Finding the right bank is of utmost importance. While it is nice to have free checking and other amenities, the most important aspect of banking today is <u>safety</u>. There are two basic statistical measures to assess a bank's safety. One such statistic, the liquidity ratio, measures a bank's ability to handle withdrawals. A higher ratio implies greater ability to handle withdrawals. Another statistic is the equity to assets ratio. The ratio demonstrates the percentage of depositor assets covered in the event of bank asset liquidation. A larger percentage is better. While you can calculate these ratios yourself, there are independent organizations providing a broader evaluation of bank health. One such organization is Veribanc® (www.veribanc.com). For a small fee, they provide a listing of "safe" banks within a particular geography. Their publication is the Blue Bank Report. Provide Veribanc information on where you live, and they will publish a list of their top-rated institutions headquartered in your area and branches with headquarters elsewhere. They also publish a list of less highly rated institutions satisfying their "green" or 3-star criteria.

The key is to find a highly rated bank and perform monitoring on a quarterly to semi-annual basis. Banking must not be a passive activity – you must be vigilant with the health of your bank. If you doubt this last statement, look at Table 10-2 containing data from Veribanc's Blue Bank Report. The table has data for a bank region in the state of Missouri comparing 2008 and 2009.

	Number of Blue Banks Based in State	Number of Blue Banks with Branches in State
June 2008	20	11
December 2009	11	6

Table 10-2

On a parenthetical note, Missouri had unemployment levels slightly below the national average. The state also did not experience the stratospheric increases in home values, and their subsequent fall. This addresses the suspicion that this state's banks were unusually hammered by people losing their jobs and unable to pay their mortgage.

The number of highly rated banks in this state nearly dropped a staggering 50% in the course of a year. With the coming resets of Alt-A and other residential mortgages in the next 2-3 years, you can bet there will be fewer banks on this list. Pay close attention to your bank.

Forecast

Expect bank failures to increase. With banks so tilted in favor of consumption-type loans, their borrowers will struggle to repay them. Loan modification programs enacted by the government have done little to stem the tide of pending foreclosure activity. Many homeowners are walking away from their mortgage even if they can pay under the euphemism of "strategic default". In some states, banks have little recourse of pursuing the amounts owed beyond the home itself under non-recourse loan provisions.

Bank woes will result in more effects that are deflationary. With borrowers unwilling or unable to repay loans, banks will tighten their credit standards and that means a reduction in loan availability. Both the inability to pay and a reduction in potential credit are deflationary events.

Banks will continue their policy of reducing customers with credit cards. Through reduced credit lines, higher interest rates and other penalties, banks are thinning the ranks of credit card users. The reduction in lines of credit is a deflationary event.

The FDIC is also contributing to the deflationary bear. They are tightening rules on required capital ratios and imposing additional monitoring on bank activities. Both of these events reduce the amount of available credit and that is deflationary.

The FDIC may well have closed more banks in 2009. Part of the problem is the resources required to "resolve" a bank. The

FDIC simply may not have sufficient personnel to close more banks. Bank failure in and of itself is a deflationary event.

The FDIC will ask for additional funding from the U.S. Treasury in order to deal with the coming wave of bank closures. The worst thing that can occur in the banking industry is a lack of depositor trust. The Obama and future administrations will do everything in their power to assuage bank closures. That said, I hope there will be public dialogue encouraging other forms of bank insurance since, as we demonstrated earlier, the "insurance" provided by the FDIC is illusory.

Readers should not be "head faked" by the lack of publicity surrounding bank failures nor the FDIC's power to "insure" deposits. There are fewer banking institutions now so the failure of a single bank has more meaning. Investors need to focus on the core of banking now more than ever.

Investor Action

- Find a safe bank. A safe bank may not necessarily be convenient.

- Use resources such as Veribanc to find safe banks.

- Monitor your bank's health on a quarterly to semi-annual basis.

- Keep your funds in bank investments of shorter duration.

- Despite your best efforts, your chosen bank may still fail. Diversify your bank holdings by finding more than one bank.

- Do not use a bank safe deposit box to store something you might need in the event of a bank closure, like cash. In the event of a bank closure or failure you may not be able to access the contents of the box for weeks or months.

Summary

The following are key points in the chapter:

- Banks are suffering from the aftermath of the credit bubble.

- The FDIC, the entity charged with insuring the banking industry, is woefully underfunded. They cannot possibly insure all of the nation's deposits with their present funding. A trip to the U.S. Treasury to ask for help is in their future.

- Banks are encountering legislative problems as well. Non-recourse loans prohibit banks from recovering money lost in a foreclosure. The banks simply get what they can from the home sale regardless of what is owed on the loan.

- Companies like Veribanc® provide independent analysis of banking health. Even companies like Veribanc reflect the deteriorating condition in the banking industry by having fewer banks appear on their "Blue Ribbon" report.

Chapter 11
Real Estate Investing

Residential real estate is not an investment. Though that may sound at odds with conventional belief, I hope to paint a different picture. Residential real estate was casualty number one of the great credit boom. When people think of the economic crisis, they think of real estate. That is not surprising since an estimated 27% of all homeowners with a mortgage in the first quarter of 2009 owed more than their home was worth. Worse yet, of that 27%, half had a mortgage that was 20% higher than the value of their property. The residential real estate market is in the first stage of a two-pronged failure. Stage 1 was the sub-prime mortgage meltdown. The next stage will be the wave of foreclosures derived from Alt-A (aka "liar's loans") and other loans considered above sub-prime. The size of this loan pool is equivalent to the sub-prime wave. Figure 11-1 shows the progression of these loan resets. Many of these loans will emerge from their low teaser rates and resettle on higher interest rates. Compounding the issue are continued job losses placing further stress on debt payments. Perhaps the biggest challenge facing loan resettlement will be the inability to refinance based on homes being "under water".

There is a fundamental problem with considering real estate as an investment. Residential real estate, where you live, is the roof over your head. The place you live is not an asset with great liquidity. Historically, homeowners did not purchase the roof over their head for profit selling. That we experienced such a state in recent years was merely an expression of the real estate bubble. Selling a home typically involves moving to another one. Sales cycles can be long and a third party, the bank, usually has a say in the outcome. Compared to other investments, real estate presents many basic problems.

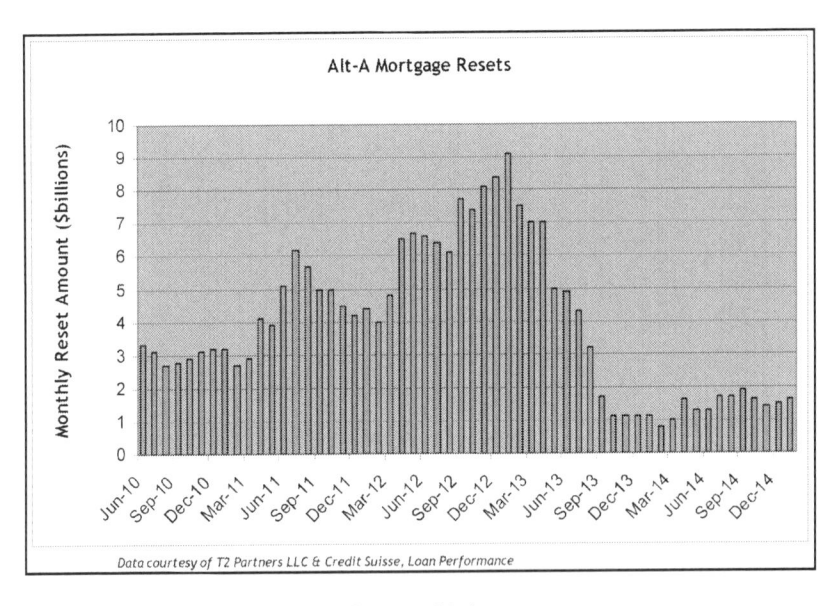

Figure 11-1
Alt-A Mortgage Resets

The Stressed American Consumer

How stressed is the American consumer and what is their ability to pay a mortgage? A MetLife study found that 45% of Americans, if they lost their job, have one month of savings before they are unable to meet financial obligations. A disturbing 19% indicated that a 2-week loss of income creates the same problem. Even more shocking was the 59% of respondents who felt they were living paycheck to paycheck.

There is plenty of stress paying the mortgage right now. At of the end of 2009, a full 14% of all mortgages for 1-4 family dwellings was either delinquent or in foreclosure. Just think of what will happen if there is more job loss or when the Alt-A loans start to reset.

But wait, won't loan modification programs stem the tide of foreclosures? Figure 11-2 shows the subsequent delinquency rate for homeowners granted loan modifications. These homeowners defaulted already and received a break from their lender to make the loan work. There are four curves in Figure 11-2 showing what happens to the re-default rate when the lender reduces the payment by the stated percentage. The 0 line means there was no reduction in monthly payment while the > 50 line means the lender reduced the monthly payment by at least 50%. For those homeowners receiving a 50% or more reduction in their monthly payment, a full 50% were delinquent again after 12 months. The delinquency rate approaches 80% for those receiving a small break in their payment. This chart illustrates how little price support exists in the housing market. If homeowners with modifications continue to default, what will happen when economic conditions worsen?

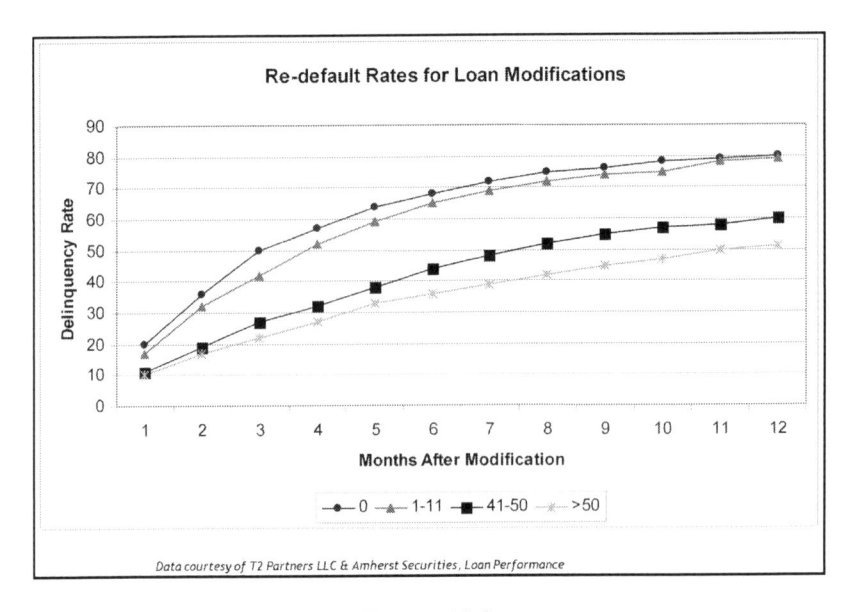

Figure 11-2
Re-default rates for modified loans

Under Water

The term "under water" has a different meaning in our lexicon today. It probably has less to do with your adventure at the lake and more to do with the state of your home mortgage. Being under water refers to a homeowner who has a larger mortgage than the market value of his or her home. Homeowners facing this condition can:

- Continue making payments until the end of the loan term.

- Engage in a "strategic default". They are able to make payments on the home but decide it is not worth it given its value. They simply walk away.

The coming wave of home loan resets features homeowners who locked in at a low rate of interest a few years ago with the hope of an easy refinance. Refinancing was no problem until the real estate market tanked. Suppose a mortgage of $150,000 sits on a home whose value is now $120,000. What lenders are willing to refinance this home? Conversely, how many homeowners would rather walk away from such a situation? It makes little sense for a new lender or the homeowner to enter into this arrangement. How many banks would lend you more than your home's value when you first moved in? Therein lies the emerging problem with lower collateral values. Banks don't want to give out a loan for more than the collateral value but if they don't, they will own a bunch of homes. That's what lenders face with under water properties.

The next wave of loan resets will result in more foreclosures, short sales and lower prices (Figure 11-3). Additionally, the banking effect of lower prices and foreclosures will be a reduction in the amount of credit, which is deflationary.

"...next wave of loan resets will result in more foreclosures, short sales and lower prices."

Figure 11-3
Foreclosed Home

Federal Government to the Rescue

The only support for real estate is the Federal Government and the Fed. The Obama administration offered tax credits and encouraged loan modification programs to provide a floor for real estate owners. The Fed lent their support by purchasing mortgage securities to the tune of $1.25 trillion. The Fed's action moved toxic assets from commercial banks' books to their own. The Fed is a bank too so there is dissension in their ranks about taking on ugly assets. The acquisition of these assets allowed banks to have healthier balance sheets so they could lend. Unfortunately, banks have only partially cooperated.

The residential mortgage market we see today is a government-sponsored affair. Fully 90% of residential loans originate with a government-sponsored enterprise (GSE) like Fannie Mae, Freddie Mac, Ginnie Mae, and the Federal Home Loan Banks. Long-term, government-led efforts in residential mortgages are leading to the demise of the private mortgage industry. GSEs welcome risks private banks shun. Fannie Mae and Freddie Mac are allowing refinancing of mortgages whose owners have a negative equity of 25% - the unsound credit practices of the previous bubble live to see another day. Government wizards continue to pull levers and push buttons but these efforts are futile.

This leaves the Federal Government and the Fed, as the last lenders and guarantors in the economy (Figure 11-4). When confidence in their ability to lend and guarantee evaporates, spending discipline is shortly around the corner. Spending discipline means less credit and deflation.

Cartoosh's View

© 1-10-2009 Cartoosh.com

Figure 11-4
Government as Guarantor

Innocent Bystanders

Here are two examples of what can happen to unsuspecting homeowners in the great housing crash. In both cases, the homeowners had no problem fielding the monthly mortgage. The situation around them created their own personal devastation.

In the first case, a family from New Jersey purchased a condominium in Florida for $430,000 in 2005, the top of the housing bubble. With a mortgage of $336,000, their life savings went towards the living unit. As it happened, they were the only residents of the condominium tower of 32 stories. What do you think the value of their "investment" is now in a vacant condominium tower? There will likely be more stories of vacant or nearly vacant residential areas in those regions of the country most affected by the housing bubble.

What happens when a whole subdivision comes into a distressed market? One unfinished Atlanta subdivision is home to just a dozen families in a development earmarked for 400 houses. It takes just one seller and one buyer agreeing to a lower price for the market to fall. In the case of this zombie subdivision, no selling or foreclosure needed to take place. In fact, all the homeowners in that subdivision may be current on their mortgage. These homeowners are victims of another economic effect. A tremendous supply glut, estimated at nearly 10 years in suburban Atlanta, and an unfinished, exterior development they expected (no swimming pools, no walking paths, no clubhouses) is devastating the owners in this subdivision. They will be unable to sell their homes, if there is even a market for them, for anywhere near their original purchase price.

Figure 11-5
Miami Beach

On a personal note, I recently stayed in a beachfront hotel on Miami Beach (Figure 11-5) that was a converted condominium tower that did not sell as expected. It sat next to another mostly vacant condominium tower. Property not pictured in Figure 11-5.

Real Estate Risk

If one is inclined to purchase a home in the current environment, there needs to be the recognition that a lower price is likely in its future. The degree of decline will be a function of local market dynamics and the size of that market's upward move in the previous real estate bubble.

Where is the bottom in the housing market? Figure 11-6 offers readers a chart of median housing prices since 1974. I estimate somewhere around 1996-1997 as the bubble launch point for residential real estate. So regardless of where you may live, use the median price from 1996-1997 as a starting point for a potential bottom. This method allows for regional differences. The preceding points notwithstanding, there is real estate in some parts of the country, Michigan for example, where prices have already declined 90% from their peak. This is clearly an extreme case but it illustrates what is possible in a bear market. Speculative bubbles often retrace their entire move. The only debate is where the speculative bubble started. If it started in 1996-1997, prices can fall 40% from where they are presently. Chapter 4 provided ample evidence of a generational speculative bubble beginning in 1982. Using 1982 as the starting point, the potential fall in prices is closer to 60%. These figures are averages.

Real estate in your area may fall less. Understanding how important location is in real estate, I emphasize that these are averages. That said, it is difficult to conceive a scenario where prices can remain firm anywhere.

Secondary residential real estate refers to property purchased for rent or leisure usage. Investors should consider this type of real estate as very risky in the current environment since it is highly likely to decline further in value. Owners of this type of real estate don't have the same attachment to their properties like they do for the main roof over their head. When push comes to shove, owners will jettison this type of real estate first.

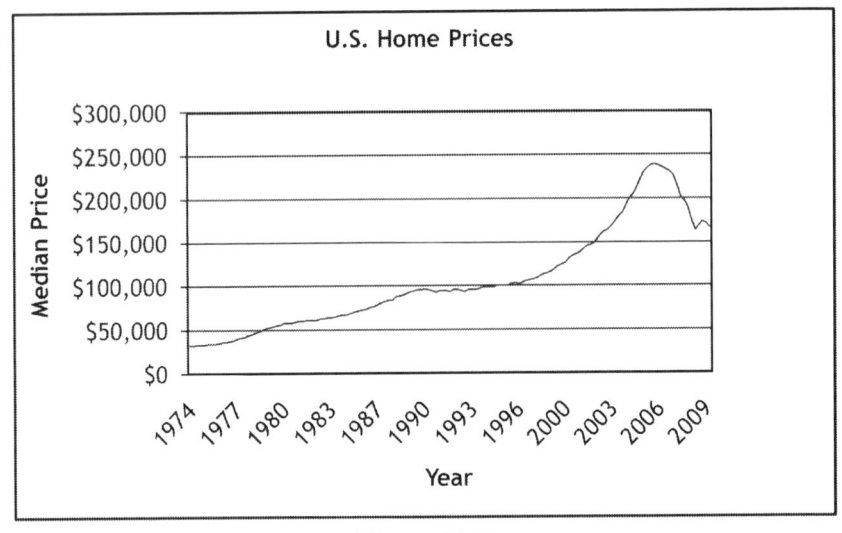

Figure 11-6
U.S. Housing Prices

Commercial Real Estate

Commercial real estate (CRE) values are in their own quagmire dropping 40 to 45 percent from their peak. Office building vacancies are rising as employers return space to property owners. According to real estate research firm Reis Inc., strip mall vacancies are at an 18-year high, and large malls are at their emptiest in a decade. The increase in vacancies is not a surprise given the unstable unemployment rate. Moreover, green initiatives and an overall relaxation of the business culture are encouraging more employees to telecommute. CRE has not been in the public's crosshairs in comparison to residential real estate. Politically, the demise of CRE is less concerning when compared to having millions of homeowners under water on their mortgages or even worse, having to abandon their homes. Economically, the prospect of a residential real estate collapse may appear to have more impact, but CRE matters as well.

Markets tend to adapt to conditions and the struggling CRE market is no exception. An excellent example of adaptation is the emergence of pop-up stores and temporary retail outlets. These stores allow a merchant to establish a temporary bricks and mortar presence without committing to a multi-year lease. At one time, pop-ups had the connotation of a shady operation - no longer. A number of big-name retailers are in the pop-up business including Toys "R" Us, American Eagle, Gucci, and The Gap. For property owners, the temporary retail outlet is not ideal but having three weeks of rent is better than no rent. Additionally, having a retailer occupying the property gives a "lived-in" look that makes the property potentially more appealing for another suitor.

Unlike home loans, commercial loans tend to be of a shorter term (average of five to seven years). If the CRE market top is also in 2005, there is the expectation that a wave of mortgages, estimated at $2 trillion, written at that time will mature beginning in 2010. According to a report by Deutsche Bank, many of these properties will not qualify for refinancing. The absence of refinancing will mean more bank-owned properties on the market, depressing prices. Refinancing challenges should lead to widespread defaults. CRE owners are more likely to walk away from their properties compared to homeowners. Typically, the owner of the property is a business rather than an individual and that business may not have the same emotional attachment to the property as a homeowner would – and we see less emotional attachment now from homeowners. Given that many CRE mortgages have a balloon payment at the end of the term, it is very unlikely that much equity exists in these properties with 55% - 60% of CRE mortgages being under water.

There is also less financing power available now. After the S&L crisis of the 1980s, Wall Street created the commercial mortgage-backed security (CMBS) as a way to bundle large pools of mortgages for investors. The CMBS represented a claim on the cash flows from mortgage bundles sold like a security. According to the Securities Industry and Financial Markets Organization, the mortgage security market, which includes CMBS and residential mortgages, is valued at $9 trillion. There are fewer CMBS issued now due to the overall problems in the real estate market, so it is much harder to raise refinance dollars.

Commercial banks will be unable to jump in with both feet when all this refinance activity comes forward. The Federal Government will be asked to provide some type of short-term finance guarantee, as the FHA has done for the residential market, in order to provide some hope - and hope is all that it could be - for a return to a stable prices. Given what I noted about the financial condition of government, it's unrealistic to expect much help. There is much more political will for rescuing homeowners than there is for the CRE market. There are more votes with potentially displaced homeowners than there are with disgruntled CRE investors.

Forecast

Real estate will continue to have its problems. According to Deutsche Bank, there are approximately 51.6 million mortgages in the U.S. Twenty-seven percent (27%) of those mortgages were under water at the end of the first quarter 2009. They estimate the 27% figure will rise to nearly 50% by the end of 2011. With unemployment numbers increasing and a wave of Alt-A loans coming due in the next year, it is not hard to envision that figure. Moreover, U.S. households have little margin for error in their personal finances. The average U.S. household simply cannot withstand more than a short period without income. This condition merely sets the stage for a continuation of the housing slump for the following reasons:

a) A wave of mortgage resets is on the way. Many mortgages will require refinancing with future estimates of 50% of all mortgage holders having loan amounts greater than the value of their properties. How many banks, or for that matter homeowners, will refinance under those conditions?

b) Banks are sitting on properties that are at or near foreclosure. This is the "shadow" inventory.

c) Homeowners are willing to walk away from their properties despite being able to maintain payments. They see their homes as a cash drain in an increasingly uncertain environment.

d) Banks have problems on the commercial side with plunging collateral values. This will have adverse consequences for lending.

e) Government will have to withdraw the support they have given to the housing market. The current deficit picture and the bond market will dictate this. The Federal Reserve has seen their portfolio of assets deteriorate significantly now that they hold toxic sludge acquired from banks. They have little desire to continue holding this sludge.

f) Residential real estate should have a lower value in the future. Consider that once a bottom forms, the psychological destruction present at the bottom will take time to repair. Not until that repair occurs will prices have a foundation for increase. Real estate will collapse further for the same reason it increased in a bubble-like fashion. What abundant credit fuels, a lack of credit starves. Real estate prices will starve for years.

Another area of real estate, the mega-skyscrapers, will see their fortunes change. It will be many years before we see projects undertaken like the Burj Khalifa, formerly the Burj Dubai, or the Trump Tower in Chicago. The Burj Khalifa is the tallest man-made structure ever built. After opening this year, the Burj Khalifa has seen its rents drop 36% and its condo unit prices drop 33%. Consider both of these structures part of the speculative euphoria that has now died and which should remain dormant for perhaps an entire generation.

Investor Action

- Stay away from real estate. There are simply too many problems in this sector.

- Do not consider the roof over your head an investment. It is not. It is a consumption item.

- The same comments for residential real estate apply to the commercial sector. This sector does not have the emotional attachment that a home does so it is even easier for an owner to walk away.

- Deflation will hit real estate with particular ferocity. Remember that Economic Law #3 states that inflation precedes deflation. There is not an asset more inflated than real estate.

- Consider renting.

- There is little reason to entertain a home equity loan or line of credit.

- Even if you are a well-heeled investor, consider that any property purchased for investment purposes may well be worth less in the future.

- Accumulate cash now for the real estate bargains in the future.

Summary

The following are key points in this chapter:

- The typical American family has very little room for error in their finances. Short bouts of unemployment will strain their budgets and their ability to pay the mortgage. This comment applies even to those making more than $100k per year.

- Billions in mortgages will have their interest rates reset in the next few years. Those homeowners will find it difficult to refinance if their home is under water.

- Commercial real estate (CRE) has its refinancing day of reckoning just ahead as well. CRE loans are of much shorter duration and many loans originated in 2005. There are $2 trillion in property refinancing beginning in 2010. This sector will face the same challenges as the residential sector since many properties are under water.

- Housing prices have further to fall. On *average*, the fall could be at least 40% from current levels. This number is subject to variability based on geography.

- Government efforts in the crisis will only delay but not resolve the real estate problems.

Chapter 12
Bond Investing

Government debt discussed in this chapter will refer primarily to obligations of the Federal Government of the United States and state and municipal issues. I will also discuss other government obligations of shorter duration like Treasury Bills. Investment bonds allow you to loan money to companies or governments for a pre-defined amount of time. The institution pays you periodic interest and then returns the money borrowed at a future date. The price of a bond is inversely related to its interest rate. If interest rates are low, then bond prices are high and vice versa.

The emerging concern for investors in bonds is the return of money, the principal, originally lent. There is always a tradeoff between the interest paid on a bond and the bond's riskiness. A higher interest rate implies greater risk. This is one reason why historically, interest rates on high quality government-issued bonds paid the lowest rate of interest. Readers are encouraged to review Appendix C for a description of how bonds and other debt obligations work.

Federal Government Borrowing

Governments borrow money when their tax revenues are unable to meet expenses. They also borrow to roll over old debt coming due. The U.S. Government (USG) borrows money through the sale of Treasury Bonds, Notes, and Bills.

Chapter 7 discussed the creditworthiness of the United States and outlined the financial condition of the government. The challenge for the debt market is whether it can continue to absorb current levels of government borrowing. The source of this funding must come from domestic or overseas investors. Does the market have the stomach for enormous lending at historically low interest rates? Since the USG has been a good credit risk historically, investors still have a great deal of confidence in the return of their principal. I will even recommend investing in U.S. Treasuries, albeit for _very_ short time periods. It's one thing to roll credit over every 90 days, like a T-bill, and another to roll it over in ten to thirty year increments. Lending at longer terms will become more challenging for the USG. One investor that can _always_ lend to the government no matter the time horizon is the Fed.

The fiction of the Fed and the USG is the notion that all this lending comes with a legitimate treasure chest at hand – no financial wizard can do this. The degree to which the Fed can purchase debt is limited. Investors can become spooked if they see the Fed buying large amounts of USG debt with money created out of thin air. This could cause a demand for higher interest rates. Higher interest rates exacerbate the financial condition of the USG since now more of the budget must go to service debt. Since the Fed is a private bank, even they could have concerns over acquiring poor quality debt.

States Borrow Too

States and municipalities have borrowing needs and issue bonds as well. Unlike the Federal Government, they cannot run deficits, so their budgeting process is more stringent. Recent shortfalls in tax revenue are hurting state governments. The Nelson A. Rockefeller Institute on Government published a report outlining the health of state governments. The report showed that in the first quarter of 2009, state tax revenue declined 11.7%, marking the sharpest decline in 46 years of data. Tax revenue declined in a staggering 47 states. The decline in personal income tax was an unprecedented 17.5%. These were the continuation of trends beginning in 2005.

While *local* tax collections remained steady, much of this is due to the relatively stable nature of property taxes. Sharply declining property values will attack this stable base very soon. If you think the first quarter 2009 data was an anomaly, the April-May 2009 data showed a drop of 20% in total tax revenue. This period is a critical one for state governments after residents file income tax returns. The state budget picture is worsening. Even if no further degradation in revenue occurs, states are facing future budget shortfalls of at least $50 billion.

Despite the deterioration in state finances, investors still show great affinity for municipal bonds. U.S. investors have taken the plunge with billions invested in tax-exempt municipal bond issues. During the investment euphoria, these bonds were perceived to be a great deal. During the ever-evolving state debt crisis, these bonds will present extreme risk for unsuspecting investors. In addition to the tax base deterioration, municipalities are burdened with derivatives and pension fund obligations that carry greater peril. Some state pension funds have taken the approach of assuming greater risk in order to make up for the shortfall in their funding level. This is moving from the cauldron straight to the fire. Since the beginning of 2010, 35 municipal bond issues totaling $1.5 billion have experienced failure, meaning they did not make all payments, on time and in full, as promised. This failure could encompass such events as bankruptcy, a moratorium on payments or some other inability to pay.

I'm not entirely certain states and municipalities can react fast enough to their budget crises. Government is usually behind a trend and the recession is no exception. After the historic stock market top of late 2007, U.S. private sector, non-farm payrolls peaked and started dropping, indicating a sharp increase in the nation's unemployment rate. What do you think happened to state and municipal payrolls? If you guessed they continued to increase, you are becoming a better student on how government operates. This is another example of government not reflecting economic reality. In fact, there are 10 states where 16% or more of the population works for government.

Remember what I said about government creating a problem, attempting to solve it and creating another? In an effort to assist state governments with their potential funding efforts, the American Recovery and Reinvestment Act (aka Obama stimulus) created a special class of bonds called Build America Bonds. These are taxable, as opposed to tax-exempt, municipal bonds carrying special tax credits or subsidies for the bond issuer or bondholder. The intent of the program is to reduce the cost of financing for states and local governments by having Uncle Sam help out the state or bond investors through tax policy or subsidy. The program places yet another debt burden on the Federal Government since they will have to borrow money just to pay the tax credit or subsidy. Someone is still borrowing money; in this case, it is Uncle Sam. To date, $115 billion in these bonds have been issued, so the pile of debt gets deeper for the states and Uncle Sam. The program also shines the spotlight of concern on the very municipal bond issues needing financing. If it truly were a *safe* municipal bond offering, why would it need help from Uncle Sam?

A story in the *Wall Street Journal* illustrates the fate of state governments quite well. The controller of the city of Harrisburg, Pennsylvania, the state capital, suggested the city might have to declare Chapter 9 bankruptcy. This seldom-used portion of bankruptcy law gives municipalities protection from creditors while they sort out a plan to pay off debt. Municipalities invoking Chapter 9 face tremendous challenges floating future bond issues. If they don't issue bonds, they can raise taxes. Raising taxes presents a challenge since that might not be enough to cover their obligations and could drive residents elsewhere.

Harrisburg took the first step towards bankruptcy by skipping a $3.29 million municipal bond payment in September 2010. While municipal bond defaults are still small compared to investment grade corporate bonds, there is a growing fear that it will become easier for states and municipalities to default especially if there is a bond insurer available to cover the payment. We will discuss bond insurance in the next section.

Many states are teetering on a financial precipice. Teetering states make poor debtors. In time investors will realize how particularly dangerous municipal and state bond issues truly are.

Bond Insurance

Earlier we discussed how interest rates imply how risky a bond is - the higher the relative interest rate, the riskier the bond. A lower relative interest rate implies a less risky bond. If there is a high demand for a bond, the issuer does not have to pay as high an interest rate. Low demand for a bond could mean the issuer has to increase the interest rate to attract investors. There is another metric that assesses the riskiness of a bond and that is the credit default swap.

Credit default swaps (CDS) received much notoriety during the early stages of the economic crisis when issuers of debt bet against the debt defaulting. CDS provide important information regarding how investors perceive the likelihood of a bond's default. A CDS is an insurance contract of sorts though it is not subject to the same regulations governing typical insurance contracts like casualty and life.

Here's how a CDS works (Figure 12-1):

1. An Insurance Buyer owns a bond (Item Insured) and wants to purchase protection in the event the bond defaults.

2. An Insurance Seller agrees to provide insurance in exchange for a Premium.

3. The Premium or spread is what the Insurance Seller charges for the protection.

4. If no default occurs, the Insurance Buyer pays the Insurance Seller quarterly payments until the bond matures.

5. If default occurs, the Insurance Seller pays the par value of the bond to Insurance Buyer. The Insurance Buyer delivers the defaulted bond to the Insurance Seller.

Note: The entity issuing the Item Insured (a government or a company) is not part of this transaction.

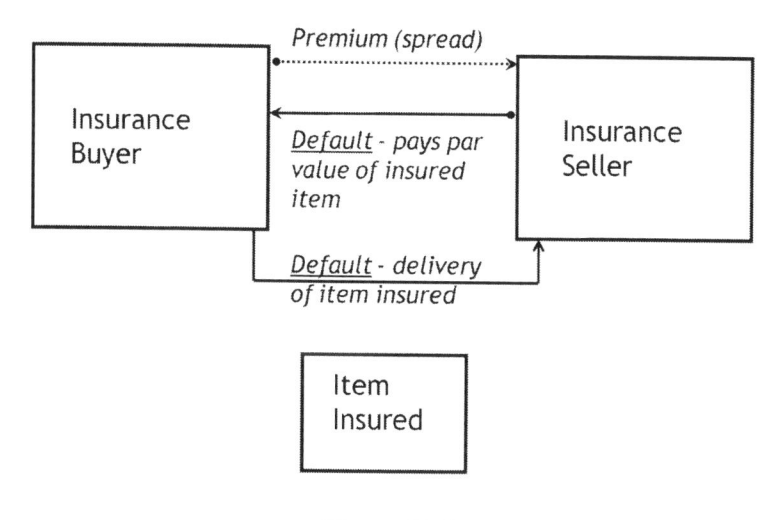

Figure 12-1
How a CDS works

To understand the dynamics of credit default swaps let's look at a couple of examples. In our first example, we will go back to Emily's lemonade stand. It has been a particularly hot summer and Emily's sales have been quite successful. She wants to expand her operation by purchasing a refrigerated cart. This cart will help her store more lemonade and keep it cooler. Her problem is she does not have the $1,000 for the cart. Appreciating her entrepreneurial spirit, you loan her the $1,000 by writing a 2-year IOU and giving her a check. You give Emily two years to pay back the loan with $50 in interest payable each year. You have concerns about her ability to pay back the loan, and the loss of $1,000 would dent your pocketbook.

Your friend Jared is confident Emily will continue to do a great lemonade business and proposes to insure your loan. He offers to insure the $1,000 loan for annual payments from you of $25. If Emily is able to pay off her loan, you will have paid Jared a total of $50 (2 years at $25 per year). If she is unable to pay her loan, Jared will pay you $1,000, and you will deliver the IOU to Jared.

In this example, Emily is not a party to the transaction between you and Jared though her IOU is the item insured. Furthermore, Jared is not limited to writing these insurance contracts with just you. Other kids in the neighborhood see an opportunity to get in on the action. Some of them think Emily will fail to pay back the IOU. Jared can write insurance contracts with other kids. The other kids pay Jared $25 annually for the contract and Jared is still obligated to reimburse these kids $1,000 if Emily fails to pay her IOU. If enough kids approach Jared and request these insurance contracts, Jared can increase the amount the kids pay him. The other kids in the neighborhood, based on their perception of Emily's ability to pay, determine the premium on the insurance contract.

For our second example, we will use sovereign debt, or loans to government entities of nations. Table 12-1 illustrates CDS rates for sovereign debt on June 30, 2010.

Country	CDS spread
Greece	912 bp
Japan	96 bp
U.S.	39 bp

Table 12-1

For the U.S., it costs 39 basis points to insure government debt for a period of 5 years.

Definition: it cost $39,000 per year ($195,000 for 5 years) to insure $10 million of US Treasury debt for 5 years. Greece, in the news in 2010 for their government debt woes required $912,000 per year ($4.56 million for 5 years) to insure $10 million of their debt. Clearly, investors feared Greek debt default many times more than a U.S. default.

Using the sovereign debt table, let's step through a CDS operation. Suppose you owned U.S. Government debt (bond) and wanted default protection. You would pay an Insurance Seller $39,000 per year. At the end of five years, if the U.S. bond did not default, the Insurance Seller is $195,000 ($39,000 x 5 years) richer and you are poorer by the same amount. If the U.S. bond defaulted during the five-year period, the Insurance Seller would owe you $10 million, and you would deliver the bond to the Insurance Seller.

If you owned Greek debt instead, your premiums would be much higher ($912,000 per year) and the Insurance Seller would still be responsible for $10 million in the event of default.

There seems to be a paradox here. Is U.S. debt that much better than Greece's? The financial condition of the United States Government is poor. The debt of the U.S. is in the $13+ trillion range and there are some $63 trillion in unfunded liabilities. I demonstrated the U.S. to be a questionable credit risk by virtue of the derived FICO score and questionable scores by debt rating agencies. Despite the evidence of a precarious financial condition, U.S. debt seems to be pristine. When in doubt, we turn to our first Economic Law that says CREDIT = CONFIDENCE. Investors and ratings agencies do not consider the overwhelming weight of evidence and still have *confidence* in the USG. As long as this confidence remains, the interest rate on this debt will be low and so will the CDS rate. But how long will confidence remain high?

Investing in Long-term Bonds and Funds

Because investor confidence is so high in USG bonds and interest rates are historically low, there is little upside potential in bond investing. Interest rates cannot theoretically go below zero.

Interest rates approaching zero present another problem for the operators of bond funds since they need to make money off the bonds in order to cover their management fees.

Bonds and bond funds provide two vehicles for investors to participate in debt issuance. Bond funds also carry the name of "income funds". They are called income funds since they pay interest on the pool of bonds they own. Individual bonds and funds range from those with "junk" status to those of the highest quality. In that continuum, a large number of bond issues exist. The selection of bonds/funds within that continuum is of absolute importance. Challenging economic times create more problems for lower rated issues.

Rating agencies like Standard & Poors, Fitch, and Moody's evaluate bonds and provide ratings or grades. These agencies are not infallible as witnessed by questionable ratings given to issuers nearing bankruptcy and their overwhelming assignment of favorable ratings to mortgage-backed securities. Standard & Poors uses a letter grade system much like that in academics. Table 12-2 illustrates their rating system.

The key point to remember about a bond is the ability of the issuer to pay interest and eventually the principal. During economic crises, this ability diminishes for less worthy issuers and investors demand higher interest rates. Bond prices fall as interest rates rise. Junk bonds/funds or those of lowest quality are not recommended for any investor. Their likelihood of default is high during our economic crisis.

We should view medium and high quality bonds with similar skepticism. A number of bonds, including municipals fall in this category. I expect long-term interest rates to increase due to decreased confidence. Since bond prices fall when interest rates increase (Appendix C), it is hard to imagine medium and high quality bonds escaping a price fall. For this reason, I cannot recommend any bond or bund fund.

Rating	Description
AAA, AA	High quality, investment grade
AA, BBB	Medium quality, investment grade
BB, B, CCC, CC, C	Junk, not investment grade
D	In default

Table 12-2

Investing in Money Market Funds & T-Bills

A money market fund is an open-ended mutual fund investing in commercial paper, government treasury debt, government agency debt (Fannie Mae, Freddie Mac), certificates of deposit and other liquid investments (Figure 12-2). The fund attempts to maintain a share price of $1 and pays money market rates of interest. The rate of interest paid can fluctuate based on market conditions. Consider the term "money market" to represent the universe of short-term debt instruments.

Money market funds are a *relatively* safe place for your investment funds during a period of rising interest rates. Since they pay the prevailing rate of interest, their interest rate should adjust accordingly. I suggest the funds are relatively safe but consider that the government does not insure these funds and the funds essentially hold portfolios of debt. If any component of the money market fund were to find itself in bankruptcy, it stops paying interest on its debt. Your investment in that component of the fund may be compromised or extinguished.

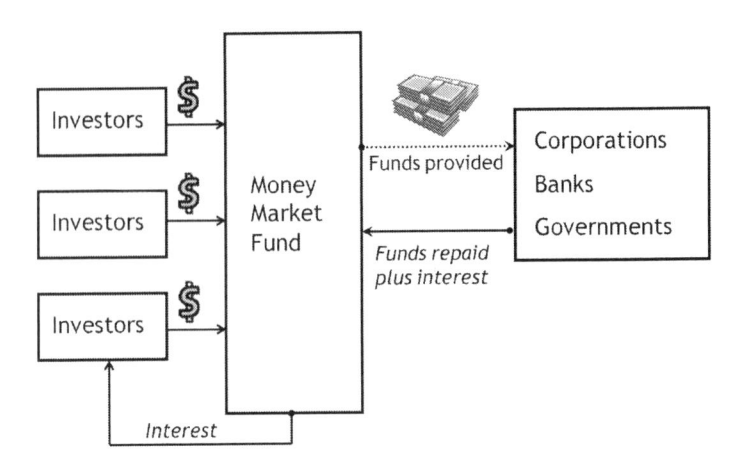

Figure 12-2
Money Market

The composition of the money market fund is the most important consideration. Investors believe government agency debt is just like any other government debt – it is not. Government agency debt is littered with real estate loans subject to homeowners' ability to pay mortgages. While agency debt brings higher interest rates (good for the fund), there is also higher risk. Mortgage insurers such as Fannie Mae and Freddie Mac will suffer along with the rest of the real estate market so holding their debt should bring you no comfort. Some funds seek to pay a higher rate of interest but the only way they can accomplish this is through the assumption of greater risk. Assuming greater risk during a period of increasing defaults will have adverse consequences for ostensibly safe money market funds.

The best option for a money market fund is to find one with the safest short-term debt available. That debt is the U.S. Treasury Bill. Treasury Bills offer protection against rising interest rates. The Treasury Bill market is large, very liquid and represents the shortest loan you can make to Uncle Sam. Investors can purchase Treasury Bills directly through an auction or through mutual funds holding Treasury only debt. Mutual funds like Dreyfus 100% Treasury Money Market (DUSXX) and American Century Capital Preservation (CPFXX) are examples of these funds. Your broker can assist with identifying funds that are 100% Treasury only. Other fund mixes introduce risk to the investor.

Holding Treasury Bills through a fund offers the convenience of having this debt rolled over for you by the fund manager. The government does not insure these funds; however, they are the safest government debt. They are insured against fraud or theft but consider that insurance companies will be just as vulnerable to default with their own investments. Money market funds use custodial banks for their holdings. The custodial bank is responsible for safeguarding the fund's financial assets. If something were to happen to the custodial bank, the fund's holdings might be frozen until the bank gets resolved. In Chapter 10, we discussed the problems banks face and the FDIC's challenges in insuring deposits. You might feel comfortable with your money market account until you find out the custodial bank has failed.

Purchasing T-bills directly from the government places you more directly in contact with your investment. There is no middleman. You will have the added burden of managing your portfolio since you will have to be mindful of rolling over your debt. The government has a web site available for the direct purchases of Treasury debt called TreasuryDirect (www.treasurydirect.gov).

TreasuryDirect is a financial services website allowing you to purchase debt directly from the U.S Treasury. As an alternative to having your funds with an online broker and then purchasing Treasury debt, this site serves as that online broker so to speak. Your purchases are limited, however, to obligations of the USG.

Treasury Bills or Treasury only funds pay a very negligible rate of interest at this time. Investors scoffing at these rates should consider the return OF their principal more than the return ON their principal. When interest rates rise, these short-term obligations will be rewarded. Government will have no choice but to pay higher interest rates on these debt instruments and the fact they have a short life allows you to capture interest rate increases very quickly. You won't be locked into a fixed interest rate for years as you would with a Treasury Bond or Treasury Note.

There is still some risk investing in Treasury Bills. A Federal Government default is not out of the question. I spent a whole chapter discussing the creditworthiness of the U.S. Government so you should have a good sense of the dangers of $13+ trillion in funded debt and the $63 trillion in unfunded liabilities. Despite this overhang of debt, the Treasury Bill is currently the safest U.S.-based interest bearing instrument. The very short-term nature of this debt provides some layer of security. For most borrowers and the USG is no exception, short-term borrowing usually takes precedence over longer-term needs. Our investment strategy is to have layers of defenses. The Treasury Bill is one of those layers.

Certificate of Indebtedness (C of I)

TreasuryDirect offers a product known as a Certificate of Indebtedness (C of I). This product earns no interest and is a source of funds for purchasing eligible interest-bearing Treasury debt. Consider it a place to park funds prior to the purchase of Treasury debt. For readers of this book, the C of I can serve as a place to hold funds for the purchase of <u>Treasury Bills</u>. There are other debt instruments on the TreasuryDirect site that I do not recommend; focus on T-bills. TreasuryDirect also offers the convenience of easy transfer from your bank account. Transferring money directly into a C of I is limited to $1,000 per iteration. This restriction is likely to avoid the appearance of competition with the banking industry. It is also possible to have an unlimited amount of money in a C of I.

Forecast

My long-term forecast on bonds is for the eventual fall of prices. The fall will not occur in one step. In the early stages of the credit crisis, there will be a "flight to quality". This flight describes the movement towards investments perceived to be the safest. Since the first stage of the bear market in stocks, investors have rushed into bonds to the tune of hundreds of billions of dollars. U.S. Treasury Bonds and Notes in particular staged dramatic price increases. Municipal bonds have also seen their share of new investment. The stock market scared investors into bond funds as part of this flight to quality. Investors will regret this headlong rush when lower rated bond issuers have problems paying back their loans. The stampede towards municipal bonds is particularly worrisome when so many states and localities are encountering frightening budget problems.

The demand for debt obligations has been driven to extreme highs and their corresponding rate of interest to extreme lows. The shortest-term obligation, a Treasury Bill, paid just above 0% interest for much of 2010. This means investors are willing to lend the government money for 3-month terms for barely any interest. As I mentioned earlier, such low interest rates are problematic for money market funds relying on the income from investments to provide their management fee. Longer-term interest rates are also remarkably low. It is a paradox that given the financial condition of the U.S. Government, investors would be so eager to lend to the government for anything other than a short time.

Lower rated or junk bonds will be most at risk in the early stages of the crisis. A measure of that risk is the difference in interest paid between a bond of perceived low quality and one of high quality. I call the difference a bond quality spread. When the spread is small, overall market confidence is high – investors see very little investment risk between the highest and lowest quality bonds. When the spread is large, market confidence is low – investors see more investment risk between the highest and lowest quality bonds. This spread will continue to widen implying a loss of confidence in the lower rated issues.

Investor Action

- Invest in Treasury Bills directly or through Treasury-only money market funds.

- A Certificate of Indebtedness (C of I) is another vehicle for parking funds used towards the purchase of Treasury Bills. The C of I is set up through a Treasury Direct account. Use a C of I as a form of near-cash.

- Do not invest in long-term government notes and bonds. This includes Treasury Bonds, Notes, EE bonds, E bonds, and I bonds.

- Do not invest in municipal bonds.

- Do not invest in mutual funds with long-term government notes or bonds as part of the portfolio. Do not invest in mutual funds with municipal bonds in their portfolio.

- Do not invest in hybrid funds, which are a mixture of stocks and bonds.

Summary

The following are the important points in this chapter:

- Interest rates on bonds move opposite to their price. As interest rates move up, bond prices move down. As interest rates move down, bond prices move up.

- Interest rates *should* not fall below 0%. Bond prices are near historical highs (interest rate lows) meaning their upside potential is limited.

- The strong recommendation given by ratings agencies belies the actual financial condition of the United States. The financial condition is poor yet investors show confidence in U.S. debt by accepting historically low rates of interest.

Chapter 13
Stock Investing

Stocks and stock mutual funds are two of the most popular investment vehicles for individuals. The popularity of mutual funds exploded to where now there is a fund for every conceivable type of market sector. Despite the dot com stock collapse during 2000-2002, investors rushed back into stocks and mutual funds to propel stock indices to new highs in 2007. There are 87 million individual investors owning mutual funds. Sixty-six (66%) percent of them own more than half of their financial assets in mutual funds. The carnage of 2008 did not deter them either. In 2009, investors added $196 billion in individual stocks and $308 billion in stock mutual funds. The total mutual fund market in the U.S. was $11.1 trillion with 44% held in stock mutual funds. With roughly $5 trillion in assets, stock mutual funds provide a great way for investors to participate in company ownership. Much like other asset classes discussed in this book, this one also experienced generational euphoria after the stock market low of 1982. A number of factors will conspire to deflate the euphoric bubble in stocks once again.

The Case for a Bear Market

A multi-generational bear market in stocks will propel the indices to levels unforeseen by most. This is a difficult forecast for investors to digest since stocks and mutual funds are part of the investment fabric today whether we are talking about retail bricks and mortar brokerage accounts, online accounts, 401(k) plans, or pensions. There will come a time when stocks of great companies will fetch a fraction of their value today. Some stocks might survive the onslaught of falling prices, but picking them will be tricky. My forecast is based on the overall performance of the stock market and not individual issues.

Stock investment psychology continues to exhibit *some* signs of confidence. In Chapter 9, we suggested that emotion tends to rule investor habits. The brain's limbic system governs emotions and even though the public does not view themselves as emotional with their investment decisions, scientific research suggests otherwise. Emotion appears to reside with the buy and hold script followed for many years. Once this emotion changes, stocks will fall further and more dramatically.

To build a bearish case for the stock market, I will revisit the discussion on cycles from Chapter 4 and introduce statistical measures like the dividend yield, P/E ratio, and sentiment indicators. I will use cycles and statistical measures to show that our stock market looks like it is much closer to a historic top than a bottom. None of the indicators by themselves say the market is closer to a top than a bottom, but taken together they provide evidence of a market with much downside potential.

Growth of Stock Industry

Before I build the case for a bear market, let's briefly examine how the stock market grew from the depths of the 1982 bottom. At the last major stock market bottom in 1982, American households were not that interested in owning stocks. The growth of the stock industry was aided by the creation of IRA accounts (1974) and 401(k) plans (1980). IRA accounts came during the stock market bottom of 1974 and 401(k) plans arrived just before the major stock market bottom of 1982. Stock ownership comprised barely 12% of all household financial assets in 1982 where now 2/3 of investors have half their financial assets in mutual funds. Stocks litter IRA and 401(k) accounts, the most precious of savings vehicles. Fifty-four percent (54%) of households own stock mutual funds and 37% own individual stocks in their IRA accounts. This does not tell the whole IRA story. Another 27% own hybrid funds and 34% own annuities both of which have stocks in their portfolios. The 401(k) picture is more tilted towards stocks.

As illustrated in Chapter 9, buy and hold is an integral part of investment philosophy. Even with the stock market drop in 2008, investors are not conditioned to accept a persistently declining market. It is entirely possible for our stock market not to eclipse a previous high for a period of 25 years - a generation. This happened from 1929 to 1954.

In order to combat the eventual dips occurring in the market, investors were encouraged to diversify. Diversification implies that some of the stocks selected might be losers so you should pick a broad range of them since you will undoubtedly have winners in that group. The problem with diversification is uninformed people rely on word of mouth, their friends, co-workers, internet chat rooms or their advisers to provide "better" information. Near stock market tops, that herd is wrong and the diversification effort fails.

The multi-generational bear will create a more hostile environment for stocks and the interest level will wane. At the next bear market bottom, the public will not want to talk about stocks and the industry will be at a nadir once again.

Cycle Model

The model of Chapter 4 presented the confluence several cycles that either ended or are about to end. These cycles are of various lengths making their confluence even more important. The K-Wave cycle shows every indication of transitioning to the "Winter" period. Elliott Wave analysis shows the end of a Supercycle (1932-2000) and a Grand Supercycle (1784-2000). The Millennium Wave shows the end of the Millennium cycle, Grand Supercycle (1789-2000) and the Supercycle (1932-2000). Both Elliott Wave and Millennium Wave analysis also show the end of a smaller cycle from 1982-2000. I want to emphasize that the cycles need not finish exactly in the year 2000; this is an approximation.

In Chapter 4 I also discussed an important cycle called the Saeculum, which is a length of time roughly equal to a human lifetime, progressing through four generations or seasons (youth, rising adulthood, midlife, and old age). Each one of these generations comes of age during different points in the Saeculum. Society reflects those generations' thoughts, hopes, and aspirations. Those thoughts, hopes, and aspirations show up in economic and investor behavior. Positive feelings in society, influenced by the Boomers, contributed to the investment euphoria, propelling the stock market to historic highs. The stock market's rise would not have been possible without these feelings of euphoria and without an abundance of credit. As I have stated numerous times in this book, credit = confidence, so it is difficult to imagine such investment euphoria without abundant confidence.

It is possible to have a cheap stock market and a dearth of buyers if there is no confidence. Likewise, it is possible to have an expensive stock market and buyers storming the doors to get at stocks – this is characteristic of confident, euphoric feelings. Investors are notoriously poor with timing their moods. One way to gauge mood is to observe news stories. During the period from 1982 to 1984, as the stock market rose more than 50%, the ratio of negative stories to positive stories on the Big Three networks (ABC, CBS, and NBC) was 4.9 to 1. What do you think the ratio of negative stories to positive stories was in 1986-1987 when the stock market rose 25%? If you guessed it was lower than 4.9, you would be wrong. The ratio actually in-creased to 7 to 1. Public mood takes time to recover from a low in the market and then stays euphoric long after the market makes its high. Our current market is no exception.

Chapter 9 on investor psychology discussed how and why people invest. Investor behavior is different from consumer be-havior. Higher prices tend to discourage buying in consumer products while higher prices in financial products do not deter buying especially if there is credit available. Feelings of euphoria and rapid increases in debt are characteristics of Wave III of the K-Wave. Likewise, Wave B of Elliott Waves emphasizes a con-tinuation of the euphoria and a denial of what lies ahead. In-stinctively, an individual investor may suspect what lies ahead but is unwilling to step out on their own since at that point they are not following someone else.

Investing follows a pattern of herding. In the absence of bet-ter information, people will follow what others are doing. With financial assets, there was a great deal of herding; all my friends bought this stock so it must be a good investment.

The most important thing to remember about the stock mar-ket is that it is all about people. As long as people feel good about the market, they will buy. If they don't feel good, they will stop buying or sell. People are also responsible for changes in trend. These trend changes tend to occur in cyclic patterns. We notice cycles in areas like women's hemlines, music or the weather. The shorter the cycle the easier it is to identify. Length-ier cycles, particularly those that are generational, saecular, or even longer are difficult to identify since your entire lifetime is spent within a much larger cycle. Trends change when a steadily increasing number of people change their mind. Recall the example I gave in Chapter 4 regarding teens and their athletic shoes. All it took was a few teens to start a new trend when they wanted low-tops instead of high-tops.

The same thing will occur with the stock market. The catalyst for the trend change will be any number of things for different people. We cannot ignore the end of a major credit cycle. Easy credit allowed a great deal of speculation and the stock market was no exception. Once a credit boom breaks down due to debt saturation, the stock market cannot be far behind. The influence exerted by the Boomer generation and the trends they created has ended and now society must deal with the great economic challenges presented by their influence.

The stock market made important tops in 2000 and 2007. The housing market peaked around 2005. Whether we use the year 2000, 2005 or 2007 as the official end to these cycles, it is important to recognize the profound changes occurring in the financial markets and the economy. All cycles point to an economy and stock market in old age.

Outside of cycle analysis, it is difficult to imagine a vibrant stock market with the rash of economic problems facing us. I don't need cycle analysis to interpret the financial problems for individuals and governments. Since the stock market is an expression of economic optimism and pessimism, it is difficult to envision a scenario where you have the economy in a down cycle and the stock market in an up cycle.

Dividend Yield

The dividend yield of stocks is one of the statistical measures I will show to compare the present stock market to historical tops and bottoms. There is a very clear pattern in the historical data that can tell us if we are near a stock market top or bottom based on looking at the dividend yield.

Dividend yield = Dividend Paid / Stock Price

The dividend yield is the dividend paid by a company divided by its stock price. Company earnings not retained go to shareholders in the form of a dividend and represent income on the stock investment. Consider the dividend a profit distribution for shareholders. The average dividend yield of a stock index like the S&P 500 tells you how companies are rewarding investors on a broad scale. Historically, the average dividend yield is in the neighborhood of 5-6% (Table 13-1). At the last major stock bottom in 1982, the dividend yield was near 6%. At the historic stock market bottom of 1932 it was near 14%. The average dividend yield of the S&P 500 is currently below 2% and there are well over 100 stocks in the index, out of 500, that pay *no* dividends. The current dividend yield shows a market closer to a top than a bottom since the current yield is actually lower than the historic tops of 1929 and 2007.

What is significant about the dividend yield? When the dividend yield is low or non-existent, companies have less concern about attracting investors since those same investors are all in with stocks. When there is less interest in stocks, companies can attract investors by increasing the dividend. Other investments compete with stocks. If those other investments provide a greater yield, stocks must do something to compensate. A higher dividend yield is that compensation.

The current dividend yield is not close to the historical average. To get to a dividend yield comparable to the 1982 bottom, stocks would have to drop to 1/3 of their present value if dividends stayed constant. To match the dividend yield of the 1932 bottom, you are looking at a stocks falling to 1/7 of their present value. I anticipate a multi-generational bear market, which implies dividend yields near the experience of 1932.

Dividend yields below 2% imply that we are nowhere near a bottom. By historical standards, the stock market is expensive and investors are getting a low return for their investment. Investors accept low returns since a psychological shift occurred after 1982 that geared people to focus on capital gains instead of dividends. Investors reap capital gains when they buy a stock and then sell it for profit. Owning stock is not a risk-free proposition. You are turning over your hard-earned money to a company who you hope will offer a reward, a dividend, for your investment. In the best case, you receive a dividend and then sell the stock for a capital gain. The buy and hold mentality with which investors became accustomed does not encourage selling. As I mentioned in Chapter 9, most people have no idea when to take a profit. Without selling a stock, you will never have a capital gain.

As we move forward through our economic problems, investors will become more cash conscious implying they will place more emphasis on dividends rather than some prospect for capital gains. I wonder how many investors will want to continue holding stocks that pay *no* dividends like the 20% plus in the S&P index right now. The economic stresses of deflation will alter how people view stock investment.

Date	Dividend Yield	Significance
1932	14%	Historic stock bottom
1982	6%	Major stock bottom
2010	<2%	TBD
2007	2.1%	Historic stock top
1929	2.9%	Historic stock top

Table 13-1

Price Earnings Ratio

Another statistical measure that has historic significance is the Price/Earnings or P/E ratio. Like the dividend yield, there are distinct ranges of values that occurred near stock market tops or bottoms.

The P/E ratio is the price of a stock (P) divided by the net income or earnings (E) on a per share basis. The ratio is a financial metric designed to show how much investors are paying for each unit of earnings. We can also look at the P/E ratio of a broader population of stocks like the S&P 500.

Using historical data, the average value for this ratio is between 15 and 16. While the ratio has fallen since the 2009 high, it remains in the mid-20s range as of this writing. The major stock market lows in Table 13-2 have P/E ratios that are 1/3 to 1/4 their present value. With current P/E ratios this high, this is another metric indicating a market closer to a top than a bottom.

Some analysts felt this ratio lost meaning in 2009 when the P/E ratio of the S&P soared to 122. Since earnings fell so dramatically that year, it caused the ratio to soar and for some analysts it meant the ratio was no longer relevant. Analysts further suggested the ratio would lose meaning if earnings went negative. I respectfully disagree. In the years of data compiled a P/E ratio of 122 stands out. The mere fact the market reached a P/E ratio of 122 should tell you something was awry in the price of stocks. A ratio of 122 meant that stocks were 8 times above historical P/E values! Analysts who for years trusted statistical measures like the P/E ratio suddenly found a justification for why the measure was no longer valid. This is typical behavior near market tops.

P/E ratio = Stock Price / Earnings per share

Date	P/E Ratio	Significance
12/07	22.2	Near major stock market top
12/99	30.5	Near major stock market top
9/82	8.8	Major stock market low
12/74	7.7	Major stock market low
9/32	5.5	Historic stock market low
2010	Mid 20s	TBD
Historical	15-16	Average value

Table 13-2

Payout Ratio

This ratio is not a statistical measure that provides a historical comparison to stock market tops or bottoms. Discussing the payout ratio provides reinforcement to my earlier points about the dividend yield and the P/E ratio. The payout ratio tells you how reliable the dividends payouts are, given how much money companies are making. The payout ratio tracks dividends as a percent of earnings. The ratio is the percentage of a company's profits paid to shareholders in the form of a dividend.

Payout ratio = Dividends/Earnings

Companies can keep their earnings, pay out earnings to stockholders or some combination of the two. The part of earnings they keep are the retained earnings while the part they pay out to stockholders are the dividends. Most companies opt for a combination of earnings retention and payout. Less mature companies tend to retain their earnings and not pay out much in the way of dividends. Companies with dependable earnings streams tend to pay out more in dividends. Table 13-3 illustrates payout ratios per decade in the S&P 500.

Decade	Payout Ratio
1930s	90%
1940s	59%
1950s	54%
1960s	56%
1970s	45%
1980s	48%
1990s	47%
2000s	32%
Average	54.3%

Table 13-3

The payout ratio has been trending down since the 1930s. The stock market registered an historic low in 1932 during a time investors had little appetite for stocks. One way to rekindle investor interest is to pay a high dividend. In an earlier section we showed the dividend yield reaching 14% in 1932 and the payout ratio table (Table 13-3) tells us that companies were doing all they could to pay dividends since 90% of their earnings went right back to shareholders. At the depths of the Great Depression, this was what companies had to do. Notice how the payout ratio eventually moderated to a level around 50% from the 1940s to the 1990s. This seems like a reasonable distribution – companies split the profits evenly with their shareholders. The decade of the 2000s brought greatly reduced payout ratios. Companies were paying less in dividends and keeping more of the profits for themselves. Investors simply did not demand the same level of dividends as in the past since they were chasing capital gains.

In May 2009, the payout ratio of the S&P 500 index reached 317%. What did this mean? It meant that for every $3.17 in dividends a company paid, it had only $1 in earnings. How can companies pay more in dividends than they earn? While a company *could* pay dividends from other sources (cash held, selling of assets, etc), this would not be a sustainable plan. A company could pay 100% of its earnings in the form of dividends but then no other earnings exist for the company to use for internal operations. A figure of 317% was not sustainable meaning one of two things must happen:

    a) Earnings must more than TRIPLE just to bring the index below 100%.

    b) Dividends will be slashed dramatically.

Companies did report greater earnings in 2009 and thus far, the earnings picture in 2010 looks decent so that helps the earnings scenario from above. The dividend yield has gone down from 2009 until the writing of this book meaning that stock prices have increased, dividends have gone down, or some combination of the two. Stock prices did increase from March 2009 to May 2010 and there are over 100 companies in the S&P that pay no dividends. The combination of an earnings increase and lower dividend helped lower the payout ratio. In the past 30 years, whenever the payout ratio in the S&P 500 index spiked above 100% it quickly came down to 50% or lower.

Two salient points come to mind in this discussion. First, the trend in payout ratios has been down for several decades. This trend is a function of an investor psychology focused more on making the big capital gain in a stock rather than using a stock as an income source. Second, the recent outlier value in the payout ratio (317%) says something about the patient – the fever spiked and came down. What caused the fever? Clearly, the ratio had to come down and we have seen evidence with the increase in earnings and the reduction in dividends. But why did the payout ratio get that high in the first place? To dismiss the high ratio as an anomaly is to miss the point. The payout ratio got too high because companies continued to pay dividends as if they were making the same earnings as before.

I mentioned at the beginning of this section that the payout ratio discussion was not one to pinpoint stock market highs and lows but rather to reinforce the discussion on dividend yield and P/E ratio. The sudden spike in the payout ratio meant that companies had to reduce dividends and consequently the dividend yield of their stock went down. Low dividend yields are signals of stock market tops versus bottoms.

The Earnings Myth

This chapter talks about earnings with respect to the P/E ratio and a Payout ratio. In both cases, earnings are the denominator in a fraction. How important are earnings themselves? If companies are making good earnings, shouldn't this be good for the stock market? There is a pervasive feeling that earnings drive stock prices.

Here are some of the problems with using earnings as a predictor of stock prices. Reported earnings are a reflection of what happened in the previous quarter. The positive relationship between earnings and stock prices does not always hold. During the 1973-1974 bear market earnings rose while the S&P 500 declined nearly 50%. Earnings were *historically* woeful in March 2009 right at the important bear market bottom from which stocks rose more than 50%! As of this writing, earnings are good once again and yet the stock market lags.

To get around the issue of using previous quarter earnings as a predictor, analysts use projected or forward-looking earnings. Projected earnings often tend reflect analyst bias towards optimism or pessimism that makes market forecasting even more inaccurate. Near stock market bottoms, earnings forecasts are too pessimistic while at stock market tops, they are too optimistic. While there are times when earnings do track with stock prices, there are other, significant times when they do not.

Sentiment Indicators

Sentiment indicators are "contrarian" in nature. By contrarian, I mean they are contrary to conventional thinking. For example, when a certain threshold of people follows a trend, there are fewer new entrants to that trend. If 98% of the people own cell phones, the market can only expand by an additional 2%. Likewise, if 98% of a market is bullish, it leaves few new market entrants that are potentially bullish. If overwhelming majorities of people are doing the same thing, it leaves few new people to join the fray.

One sentiment indicator is the percentage of cash held in stock mutual fund portfolios. Cash held in mutual funds is money not invested. The contrary thought here is that low levels of cash mean the mutual fund industry is mostly invested so less money is available for new stock purchases. Historically, mutual funds tend to hold small amounts of cash near stock market tops and large amounts of cash near bottoms. Table 13-4 lists historical milestones in the stock market and the amount of cash held by stock mutual funds.

The percentage of cash currently held by stock mutual funds is quite low (near 3%) on a historical basis implying we are closer to a top than a bottom in the market. If my forecast is correct and this is a multi-generational bear market, expect stock mutual funds to hold more than 12% cash in their coffers at the bottom.

Investors Intelligence is a research organization providing analysis of trends in stocks and other financial instruments. Two of the statistics they track serve as contrarian indicators as well. The bullish percentage index (BPI) is a reading of the number of buy signals received from all the stocks on the New York Stock Exchange (NYSE) as a percentage of all stocks on the exchange. If there are 2800 stocks on the exchange, then 1400 having a buy signal indicates a BPI of 50%. This is a contrary indicator since the greater the bullish behavior in a market, the fewer new buyers exist. Recent history showed the BPI hovering around 80% for a good portion of 2009 and 2010. By comparison, the BPI was about 10 points lower at the important stock market high of 2007. As of this writing, the BPI has fallen though it remains well above the most recent stock market low of 2009. This statistic can experience a fair amount of oscillation so we have to keep that in perspective. The important point is to consider the amount of time the market was so bullish.

Another important contrarian indicator from Investor's Intelligence is the percentage of investment advisors that are bullish. Typical percentages near stock market tops are 50% and above. We have hovered at or above this range for an extended period. When investment advisors are that bullish, it is a sign that fewer new advisors are likely to join the bullish fray.

Date	Cash Holdings	Significance
3/10	< 4%	Bear market rally high
8/07	3.5%	Prior to major market top
3/00	4%	Major market high
9/82	Near 12%	Major market low
12/74	11-12%	Major market low

Table 13-4

The Myth of Corporate Health

There is a myth currently circulating about how healthy U.S. corporations are. U.S. companies are supposedly sitting on massive amounts of cash ready for injection into the struggling economy. Earnings are said to be quite robust and investors should benefit through higher dividends. Companies somehow got healthy by becoming more productive and trimming their payrolls. But where did all this cash come from? If we go back to our discussion on money and credit from Chapter 1, I should probably ask, "Where did all this credit come from?"

According to data from the Federal Reserve, nonfinancial firms acquired another $289 billion in debt in the first quarter of 2010 extending their total domestic debt to $7.2 trillion, the highest level on record. Since the first quarter of 2007, nonfinancial firms acquired another $1.1 trillion in debt. That is an astounding increase considering the economic shock in 2008. Consider also that this debt is from nonfinancial companies, the same ones considered healthier than the moribund banking and financial industries. The gross domestic debts of nonfinancial corporations are roughly half of the country's GDP, making it a post-war record. Even after fighting WWII, the figure was 20%.

The balance sheets of U.S. corporations don't look as good as advertised. The liability side of the ledger looks quite compromised. Discarding all the cycle and statistical analysis of this chapter, do you feel energized about investing in stocks with this much corporate debt?

Forecast

This chapter presents a case for a bear market in stocks. Various statistical measures illustrate a market much closer to a top than a bottom. Contrary sentiment indicators also seem to indicate little upside potential is available in the stock market. The extent of the bear market cannot be understated. A confluence of several important cycles of various lengths should exert strong downward pressure on the stock market. As a multi-generational bear market, it will plumb depths that have been witnessed by few, if any, alive today (Figure 13-1).

The progression to a final bear market bottom will not be a straight move down. Bear markets exhibit very strong rallies as we saw from March 2009 to May 2010. Psychologically, the rallies serve to create final positive sentiments on the path to eventual oblivion. Rallies will succeed in fooling investors by presenting mere interruptions to the eventual outcome.

Don't get in this bear's way!

Figure 13-1
Kodiak bear

Investor Action

- Stay away from stocks in general. This includes individual stocks, stock mutual funds, stock index funds, and diversified funds.

- Some stocks may retain or increase their price. Picking individual stocks will be very difficult unless you or your advisor has very specific expertise in a stock.

Summary

The following are key points in this chapter:

- Stocks were relatively unimportant to investors at the start of the great bull market in 1982.

- Several statistical measures including the dividend yield, P/E ratio and the payout ratio are at levels historically associated with stock market tops rather than bottoms.

- Sentiment indicators reaffirm the public's continued strong interest in stocks. Sentiment that strong leaves little opportunity for more stock gains.

- The U.S. corporate sector is not as healthy as perceived due to extensive debt accumulation. Much like individuals, companies were not immune to the euphoria of the credit cycle.

Chapter 14
Retirement Accounts

IRA and 401(k) accounts allow individuals to decouple themselves from rapidly evaporating company pensions and the stressed Social Security system. Private employers offer defined contribution plans like 401(k) to alleviate themselves of future pension burdens of defined benefit plans. For employees, it is a fair alternative since many companies offer a matching amount to employee contributions. Another benefit is contributions are made with pre-tax dollars and accounts grow tax-free until withdrawal.

The 401(k) plans tend to be restrictive in that account options are limited to perceived "safe" investments. Options have evolved to include lifecycle plans that allocate between stocks and bonds depending on the number of years until retirement. The theory here is younger workers should hold a larger portfolio of stocks and older workers hold a larger portfolio of bonds. The breadth of investment options in 401(k) accounts is limited.

IRAs offer more investment choices particularly if your plan is self-directed. For some, IRAs provide a tax deduction.

Facts and Stats

About 4 of 10 U.S. households (46 million) were owners of IRAs as of mid-2009. Thirty-seven (37) million owned traditional IRAs and 17 million owned Roth IRAs, which were introduced in 1998. Another 10 million households owned employer-sponsored IRAs (SIMPLE, SEP, SAR-SEP). In commercial banks alone, there are about $600 billion in IRA accounts.

The average IRA household head had a median age of 52 and held $30,000 in IRAs. Growth in IRA accounts has come from investment gains and rollovers from employer-sponsored plans. Only 15% of households actually contributed to an IRA in 2008. Fifty-four percent (54%) of IRA households own stock mutual funds, 37% own stocks outright, 27% own hybrid funds, 32% own bond funds, and 17% own bonds outright (Figure 14-1).

Employer-sponsored defined contribution plans have grown in popularity as more companies are opting for this type of retirement plan versus a defined benefit plan. These primarily comprise 401(k) plans but also include 403(b), 457, and Keogh accounts. These defined contribution plans have $4.1 trillion invested in them with the lion's share ($2.8 trillion) in 401(k) plans (Figure 14-2). For investors in their twenties, 401(k) plans have 38% invested in stock funds, 8% in company stock, and 28% in balanced and lifecycle funds, which also invest in stocks. Participants in their sixties were weighted less towards stocks and stock funds. Fifty-three (53%) of participants in their twenties have more than 80% of their investments in stocks or stock funds.

I outline these details so you can see how important these savings plans are to the long-term financial health of individuals. If Social Security won't be available exactly as people expect, private retirement savings take on added importance. With so much invested in these plans, a reduction in their value has significant, future deflationary impacts. If my forecast is accurate, private retirement plans should experience a reduction in value even greater than the 30-40% declines of 2008.

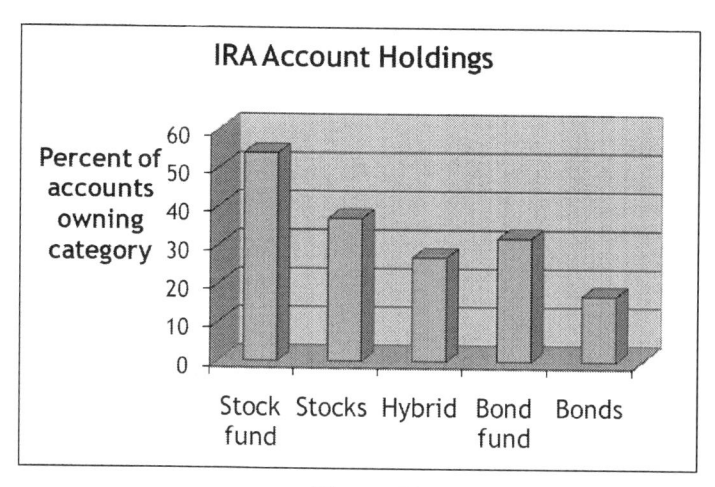

Figure 14-1
IRA Account Distribution

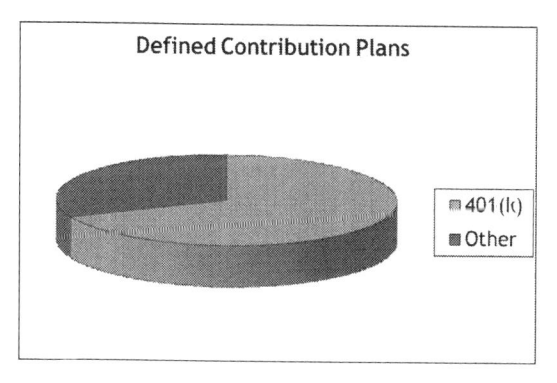

Figure 14-2
Defined Contribution Plan Distribution

What Should I Do With My IRA or 401(k)?

What the government gives, the government can take away. IRAs and 401(k) accounts are sheltered investments, but the government gets to make the rules. I outlined the awful condition of U.S. Government finances in an earlier chapter. Despite the ugly financial state, the markets continue to behave as if there is no problem. Watch out. When the market changes its mind, government may not be so benevolent in their treatment of these accounts; the rules may change. During Argentina's debt crisis, the government seized money from private pensions so it could pay its bills.

It would not be beyond the realm of possibility for someone to suggest using private savings to rescue the government for the good of the nation. One such option might be a restriction on investment options in these accounts to Treasury debt only, particularly long-term debt. Restricting investment to Treasury debt would instantly provide the U.S. Treasury with a large funding source. If the restriction allowed only long-term debt, it would give the government more time to sort out its finances. There might even be a proposal to disallow Treasury sales within IRA or 401(k) accounts. There is no question that such a proposal would face unparalleled political challenges. We are in unchartered waters with our country's debt condition and all options will be on the table. Desperate times could bring demagoguery adversely affecting private retirement accounts. This is not a prediction but at least we have to consider this a possibility.

The early warning signs of a further deterioration of government finances will occur when interest rates on longer-term bonds start to increase. Remember, even the government's own projections indicate all Federal revenues going to entitlement programs and debt service in the year 2020. Those projections came before the recently passed health care legislation and do not consider higher interest rates. We are in an extremely low interest rate environment right now. Problems will occur well before 2020. Remember that 77 years ago government declared private gold ownership illegal due to a national financial emergency. The financial condition now is much worse.

If conditions deteriorate enough, you may want to consider pulling out of 401(k) and IRA plans even considering penalties. If you find yourself unemployed, taking a distribution, even before the age of 59 ½ might not be as painful since you should be in a lower tax bracket. Consult with your tax advisor on these matters. The point is to be prepared for a liquidation of these plans if conditions warrant. If you are not prepared, you may be subject to new rules on your retirement accounts that you won't like. Government leaders will have to be very creative to address future debt issues, especially when interest rates rise. A patriotic appeal is not out of the question.

While you do have money in these plans, do not invest in stock or bond funds. Also, do not invest in lifecycle funds since these have an asset distribution of stocks and bonds. The longer until your retirement, the more the lifecycle fund invests in stocks. Place your holdings in the safest money market fund or guaranteed investment contract (GIC) fund. The safety of the money market fund will depend on the percentage of U.S. short-term Treasuries held. The safety of the GIC is contingent upon the company providing that guaranteed income, perhaps an insurance company. There is still risk in these latter two options though you lessen it.

What Should I Do With My Annuities?

Annuities comfort investors since they provide a steady stream of income at some predefined future time. Some insurance companies providing annuities offer a minimum return. If the stock market goes south, the insurance company is supposed to provide a minimum level of income. There is no magic potion here. Insurance companies use standard investments like stocks, bonds, and real estate – all things I do not recommend. An insurance company can go bust in which case your annuity could go with it. The most important point is to do your homework with your insurance companies. Understand how they invest their own money for funding annuities. Be wary of annuities promising a minimum return. When the deflationary grip takes hold of the economy, the minimum return may not be what you anticipate.

There are insurance raters who can provide an evaluation of the health of your company. Their analysis methods will likely not consider a deflationary environment and they are more conventional in their views of stocks, bonds, and real estate. Annuities are another area where investors need to do their homework. Given what I anticipate from the investments made with annuity contracts, it is difficult to recommend them.

Investor Action

- I strongly recommend safe money market investments for IRA and 401(k) accounts particularly those weighted towards short-term U.S. Treasury instruments like Treasury Bills or associated funds.

- Be prepared to take a distribution from an IRA and 401(k) plan if conditions warrant. An early warning signal may be a legislator discussing the use of these plans due to a national financial emergency. This recommendation may not apply to everyone reading this book so consult with your financial advisor.

- If you must have money in annuities, pick one with the least exposure to stocks, bonds, and real estate. Do not invest in annuities otherwise.

Summary

The following are the key points in this chapter:

- IRA and 401(k) accounts are prevalent in the United States. Most accounts are heavily weighted towards stocks or stock funds.
- IRA and 401(k) accounts are subject to government rules. Government rules may change as government finances become more strapped.
- Annuities are only as safe as their own investments. Most annuities are weighted towards stocks, bonds, and real estate.

Chapter 15
Money Investing

I started this book by talking about money. Money originally was akin to our definition of wealth. Gold and silver coins circulated as money. In the absence of coins, paper certificates that were exchangeable for coins were money. Only government actions slowly eroded the value of money to the point where a paper certificate no longer represented anything of value. The result was government telling us what money was worth.

When government tells us the value of money, it leads to money devaluation. Easily devalued money also leads to easy credit. In our economy's case, easy credit meant excessive credit. The result of the excessive credit will be a deflation of similar degree. The deflation or reduction of credit means the remaining money will be worth more. Precious metals occupy an important place in a wealth preservation plan. The progression of our current financial mess will be deflation due to credit destruction. At the end of this process, we may well have inflation or an entirely new currency. Gold, silver and cash provide hedges against various outcomes.

Precious Metals

Precious metals, by virtue of their association with wealth, represent real money. Rather than be concerned about the "price" of gold or silver, it is more important to consider their outright ownership. I recommend ownership of non-numismatic gold and silver coins. By non-numismatic I mean coins that do not have an implied value. Numismatic coins are collectible coins that have intrinsic value (the pure gold content) and implied value (the collectible part). A numismatic coin features rarity, condition and its precious metal content.

The types of coins you should own include those minted by the U.S. Treasury (gold and silver Eagles, Buffalos) or other sovereign coins (Figure 15-1). Other sovereign coins include the Canadian Maple Leaf or the South African Krugerrand. All of these coins have a specific gold or silver content meaning the value of the coins is mostly intrinsic. Each of these coins also has a face value. The face value is what the issuing government says it is worth and bears no relationship to the actual coin value. For example, a one-ounce 2010 U.S. gold Eagle coin says it is worth $50. Its actual value is something north of $1,300 based on current gold prices. I can state with confidence that a $50 gold Eagle will never be $50 unless we are using real money in our economy again.

Another good idea is to maintain a stock of silver coins (pre-1965). These silver coins were circulating currency at one point and have a small amount of actual silver. For well-heeled investors, gold or silver bars are also an excellent option. These bars are available in 400-ounce sizes. This size has the added benefit of being used by central banks and is recognized by commodity exchanges like the COMEX (Commercial Exchange of New York).

A great challenge with gold is its storage. One place NOT to store gold is in a safety deposit box at a bank. Some of the problems we mentioned regarding bank failures will affect access to bank vaults. Even if the bank failure is resolved in an elegant manner, it could be weeks, months or years before you are able to access your possessions. Bank failures can be legal and governmental affairs so don't count on quick and easy access to your safety deposit box. I recommend you locate a secure storage facility where you have access to your possessions and one not adversely impacted by financial calamities.

You might ask why someone would want to accumulate gold or silver now if deflation is ahead. Won't gold and silver go down in dollar price during a deflation? They will go down in dollar price but there are other considerations here. You should not assume that gold will always be freely available. Recall that in 1933, President Roosevelt outlawed gold ownership for U.S. citizens. It was not until 1975 that citizens could own gold once again. The threat of gold confiscation would make its dollar price skyrocket and make it harder to acquire. Gold confiscation might only occur in the United States but not in other countries. That would make those countries more attractive, which is something an American government would not want.

At some point, the public will demand honest money backed by something more tangible than what they have today, which is nothing. The backing for that money will likely be a precious metal like gold, which historically served this purpose. This is part of our eventual escape from the Financial Land of Oz. We slowly got away from having real money and we will rediscover its virtues.

At the end of the deflationary cycle, governments could get desperate and ignite inflation through actual money printing. The media and public tend to use the term "printing money" incorrectly. When people say "printing money", it really means creating credit or facilitating the creation of credit. Credit must be lent into existence so without willing borrowers and lenders credit facilitation means little. When I use the term "printing money" with respect to government desperation, I literally mean the creation of paper notes (Federal Reserve Notes). The creation of paper notes would be highly inflationary as illustrated in several examples in history. If this occurs, gold will have significant value.

U.S. Buffalo   Canadian Maple Leaf

Gold Bullion Bar

U.S. Gold Eagle

Figure 15-1
Precious Metals Examples

Gold and Silver Exchange Traded Funds

Exchange traded funds (ETF) will be covered in more detail in the next chapter but it is appropriate to mention two popular ETFs. GLD and SLV are two popular ETFs that are not good substitutes for owning actual metal. Here are some of the problems from the GLD prospectus:

- ☐ The fund is not responsible for the fineness or quality of the gold.

- ☐ Inspection of the gold held by the custodian is limited.

- ☐ The gold held by the custodian is not segregated. In the event of custodian insolvency, there may be problems identifying ETF gold from other gold held.

There are other concerns with these funds. These types of funds operate on a fractional reserve basis meaning that they are unlikely to own metal in amounts equivalent to their stated holdings. These funds represent a promise to pay metal and are not products that provide direct ownership of metal. Remember, a promise to pay is simply an IOU. During the anticipated credit contraction, IOUs are at risk. This is counterparty risk since you are dependent upon the fund issuer's ability to meet all of its obligations.

Don't confuse these ETFs with ownership of real gold held under your name. There simply is no substitute for holding precious metals under your immediate possession or in a storage facility with your name attached to the account.

GoldMoney

GoldMoney allows individuals to purchase precious metals held in an account in your name. Gold, silver and platinum bullion is stored securely in vaults in London, Zurich and Hong Kong. Your gold, silver and platinum are insured against theft from the vault. An independent third party safeguards the metal ensuring that gold, silver, and platinum are only removed from the vaults at the direction of GoldMoney customers. A Big Four accounting firm audits GoldMoney's procedures on a semi-annual basis and provides audits on the precious metal inventory in the vaults and metal circulating electronically in GoldMoney's system.

Unlike exchange-traded fund products like GLD and SLV, your ownership of the gold is not dependent on a fund's ability to obtain and redeem metal when you want to sell it. You already have it. If you do want to take physical possession of the gold, you have the option of 100 gram, kilogram, and 400 oz standard bars. Another benefit is the ability to exchange between the three precious metals or exchange currencies (German and U.S residents do not have the currency exchange option).

The feature that is quite evolutionary about GoldMoney accounts is their ability to function as a payment system. Since you own physical metal, you have the ability to pay others in units called goldgrams, silver ounces, and platinum grams. GoldMoney customers can settle transactions with other Goldmoney customers immediately and transaction costs are a fraction of the cost of a standard bank transfer. For example a goldgram payment valued at $50,000 costs $3.83. Even a $50 goldgram payment costs $0.50. The ability to function as a payment system with real wealth standing behind the unit of money allows GoldMoney to behave like legitimate wealth-based money. The operators of GoldMoney are not artificially creating more units of money since every goldgram/silver ounce/platinum gram is backed by physical metal.

Cash

I began this book talking about money and I will end this chapter on the subject of money. This time we will talk about cash money. By cash money, I mean the green pieces of paper that say Federal Reserve Note in your wallet or purse. During a deflation, cash is king. Cash is king because credit collapses. We can see the effect of credit collapse by witnessing housing prices. We also see declining stock prices. We will see credit collapse further when bond prices fall. We will also see banks failing. All of these events are deflationary. Demand for credit is inversely related to the demand for cash. When credit is freely available, the public holds less cash. When credit is not as available, people hold more cash.

It might seem strange to think of cash as a wealth preservation vehicle. The money that remains during a deflation has more value since it is no longer competing with the same amount of outstanding credit for goods and services. Even if that money is fiat money or money by government decree, people will accept it as long as there is confidence that it will continue to have exchange value.

In the event of bank failure, you will no longer be able to withdraw cash. ATMs could shutter. A bank holiday may be declared. Where will you get cash? In such an environment, people will be eager to sell assets in order to raise cash. It will be difficult to trade a watch for groceries. It might be difficult to trade a one-ounce gold coin for groceries.

You should keep cash on hand and in a safe place. This cash will serve two purposes. First, it will provide some protection against banking system failure or holiday and it should increase in purchasing power in a deflationary depression. Secondly, it may be the only medium of exchange available for common transactions. The amount of cash on hand is a matter of personal preference, storage considerations and overall wealth. At a minimum, I recommend 6 months worth of typical expenses as a cash store. These expenses consist of things for which you typically pay with cash or a debit card now or other items necessary for day-to-day living. Figure 15-2 is the largest circulating Federal Reserve Note denomination.

Figure 15-2
"Benjamin"

Investor Action

- Own non-numismatic precious metal coins such as the U.S. Eagle, Canadian Maple Leaf, and the South African Krugerrand.

- Establish a GoldMoney account. This account can serve as a depository for precious metals and a payment system.

- Own cash for protection against bank failure and deflation.

- Gold and silver exchange traded funds like GLD and SLV are not good substitutes for owning actual gold.

Summary

The following are the key points in this chapter:

- Precious metals represent true, honest money.
- The term "printing money" is often used improperly. No actual money printing occurs. What occurs is credit creation.
- The paper currencies we use are not honest money. Governments tell us what the money is worth. That said, paper currencies will continue to be accepted as a medium of exchange until a currency revolution occurs.

Chapter 16
Alternative Investments

This chapter introduces alternative investments. I call these "alternative" since they are outside of what typical investors employ in their portfolios. As might be expected, these investments are risky so they are not for everyone. The investments profiled in this chapter can help you capitalize on the anticipated bear market in stocks since their performance is inversely related to the market. When the market goes down, these investments go up and vice versa.

ETF & Inverse Funds

An Exchange Traded Fund (ETF) is an investment vehicle tracking an index, bought and sold like a stock, aggregating all of the stocks comprising the index. Since it is a stock-like product, it is bought and sold during trading hours and requires a broker for transactions. An ETF tracking the S&P 500 uses the stocks comprising that index as its holdings. An inverse index ETF attempts to mirror the opposite performance of an index such as the S&P 500 (Figure 16-1). Some inverse index ETFs mirror the opposite performance of an index with two or three times leverage meaning when the index decreases in value, the ETF increases at 2 or 3 times the fall in the index value. Conversely, the leverage can work against you; when the index increases in value the ETF decreases at 2 or 3 times the increase in the index value. The advantage on the up side is very powerful just as it is quite powerful on the down side.

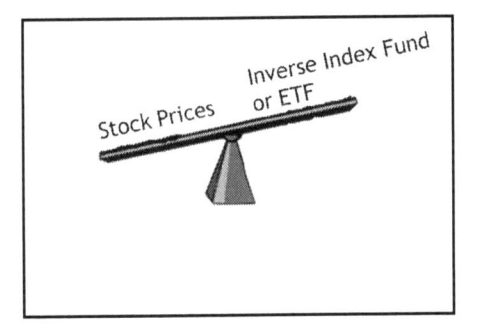

Figure 16-1
Inverse Fund Performance

A mutual fund is an open-ended fund (no set limit in time or size of fund), run by an investment company raising money from shareholders for investment in specific assets. The assets selected are in accordance with fund objectives. A mutual fund shareholder becomes a partial owner of all the assets in that fund. The fund has a Net Asset Value (NAV) for each share determined once per day. Some index funds have a NAV available more than once per day. An *inverse* index fund attempts to mirror the opposite performance of an index such as the S&P 500. When the S&P 500 decreases in value, these funds increase in value and vice versa (Figure 16-1).

Examples of inverse index ETFs include issues from Pro-Funds and Direxion. Examples of inverse index funds include those by Rydex Funds and Federated Funds. These funds track indices inversely and some do so at twice the rate. For example, if the S&P 500 index falls by one percent, the Rydex fund whose symbol is RYTPX increases by two percent. An increase of one percent in the S&P 500 causes the fund to fall by two percent. Table 16-1 provides a listing of some ETFs and inverse funds and their intended performance.

Fund Family	Name	Symbol	Objective
Federated	Prudent Bear	BEARX	Inverse performance of S&P 500
Rydex	Inverse S&P 500	RYURX	Inverse performance of S&P 500
Rydex	Inverse S&P 500 2x Strategy	RYTPX	2x Inverse performance of S&P 500
Leuthold	Grizzly Short Fund	GRZZX	Inverse performance of S&P 500
ProShares	Short Dow 30	DOG	Inverse performance of Dow 30
ProShares	Short S&P 500	SH	Inverse performance of S&P 500
ProShares	Ultrashort S&P 500	SDS	2x Inverse performance of S&P 500
Direxion	Daily Large Cap Bear 3x Shares	BGZ	3x Inverse performance of Russell 1000

Table 16-1
Inverse Fund & ETF Listing

This is not an exhaustive list of ETFs or funds moving inversely to the market. Others follow or relate inversely to the NASDAQ. There are funds moving with or inversely to the U.S. Dollar. Another class of funds follows or moves inversely to the bond market. Still other funds move inversely to the real estate market. Rydex Funds probably has the most robust offering of inverse funds and ETFs. My intent is to provide you investment alternatives that perform during a multi-generational bear market and the anticipated deflation.

While the intent of the inverse funds is to mimic the inverse performance of the tracked index, there is no guarantee this will occur. Fund managers may adopt a different posture in order to limit losses. For the ETF, some issues do not have the same level of liquidity implying the volume of trading is thinner. The risk with thinner volume is bid-ask spreads that are wider meaning your entry price could be higher than expected. For example, on 7/2/2009 the bid-ask price range for the ProShares Short Dow 30 was 61 bid and 82 ask.

Funds with two and three times leverage magnify gains but also magnify losses. This is a factor you need to consider if you are unable to stomach daily fluctuations. Inverse funds and inverse ETFs also suffer from something known as beta slippage. These funds and ETFs track the particular market based on percent change. Volatile markets experience greater slippage.

Here is an example of beta slippage. You invest in an inverse ETF tracking the Dow Jones Industrial Average (DJIA). The inverse ETF will move opposite to the Dow. The Dow falls from 10,000 to 9,000 in one day, a decline of 10% - good for your position. If you purchased the inverse ETF for $100, it should rise to $110 - an increase of 10%. The Dow then climbs from 9,000 back to 10,000 on the next day, an increase of 11.11%. The ETF will fall by 11.11%, from $110 down to $97.78. Even though you are back where you started in the Dow, at 10,000, your ETF value went from $100 to $97.78, a loss of 2.22%. Table 16-2 provides an illustration of this example.

The problem of beta slippage magnifies if the fund has 2x leverage. In this case, after day one when the Dow lost 10%, your fund would gain 20% - the ETF price would be $120. After day two when the Dow went back to 10,000 your loss would be

22.22%. Your new ETF value would be $93.34. Once again, even though the Dow Jones Industrial Average is back where it started, your loss is 6.66%. Table 16-3 illustrates the effect of 2x leverage and beta slippage.

DJIA	Change in DJIA	Change in ETF	ETF Value
10,000	N/A	N/A	100
9,000	-10%	+10%	110
10,000	+11.11%	-11.11%	97.78

Table 16-2

There are also other risks with these vehicles including counterparty risk, leverage risk and liquidity risk. Many of these funds utilize the futures markets or other derivatives to synthesize their positions. Counterparty risk refers to the inability of a party in a transaction to meet its obligation. Leverage risk exists when a fund or ETF is exposed to a greater loss than the amount invested. Liquidity risk refers to the inability of a fund or ETF to exit a position. Problems in the futures markets with trade execution or counterparty solvency could well complicate the value of these investments. In a fast moving downward market, though favorable for the fund itself, some of these problems may arise.

DJIA	Change in DJIA	Change in ETF	ETF Value
10,000	N/A	N/A	100
9,000	-10%	+20%	120
10,000	+11.11%	-22.22%	93.34

Table 16-3

Inverse funds are not for all investors. They require more vigilance particularly in volatile markets. You should only allocate risk investment funds to these options.

Investor Action

- Inverse index funds are well-suited for <u>risk</u> capital.
- Limit your exposure to inverse index funds and ETFs.
- Trading in index funds or ETFs requires a constantly vigilant approach. You will need someone or a system identifying changes in market trend on a day-to-day or weekly basis.

Summary

The following are key points from this chapter:

- There are classes of investments that can perform well in strong bear markets in stocks.
- Such investments include inverse index mutual funds and exchange traded funds (ETF).
- These types of funds are not recommended for most investors.
- A number of risks exist with these investments.

Chapter 17
Investor Types & Model Portfolios

Given the current economic conditions, how can you position your assets to survive or even prosper in the future? This chapter includes a spectrum of approaches depending on your risk tolerance. It is important to consider the concept of risk tolerance with respect to investment strategies. During the speculative bubble, investors lost an understanding of investment risk. Diversified portfolios further clouded investment risk and lulled investors into a state of complacency.

The ABCs of Investors

Someone who *invests* is different from someone who *trades*. Traders do not mind being in and out of investment positions on a frequent basis. The extreme form of a trader is a "day" trader or someone who is actively in the market opening and closing positions daily. Traders may also speculate in commodity futures or option instruments. Traders are constantly in and out of markets based on signals given by their trading systems using technical or fundamental analysis. If trader describes who you are, this chapter does not address your needs.

An investor is someone who is not constantly in and out of the market. An investor would rather place money somewhere and not have to bother with checking their portfolio values on a daily basis. Within the realm of investors, there are different risk tolerances. Some investors may be comfortable in the occasional role of a trader.

The three investor types include:

Type A

This investor is **A**ggressive with a high degree of risk tolerance. The higher tolerance opens a broad array of investment opportunities not otherwise recommended for others. A Type A is comfortable investing in managed funds with higher risk profiles such as hedge funds. Managed funds have explicit requirements surrounding minimum individual net worth. Type A investors are not necessarily "traders" but need to be more involved in managing their portfolio. Type A investors may even have some experience trading commodity futures for their own account.

Type B

This investor is **B**alanced. They don't seek risk but are comfortable with some exposure. A Type B is open to the idea of a professional managing their portfolio in higher risk investments but not necessarily those with minimum net worth requirements. They do not have money in hedge funds nor have they traded commodity futures for their own account. They do not need to be actively involved in managing their portfolio.

Type C

This investor is **C**onservative. They seek little risk. I am careful not to use the term "no risk" since any investment, even doing nothing, is subject to risk. This investor class wants to make an investment decision and only follow its progress periodically. This investor is most comfortable in what they perceive as straightforward investments.

The categorization presents a simple, yet well-defined approach to investor profiles. Moving from Type A to Type C defines less risk tolerance and a more detached approach to investing. While a high-risk tolerance "A" investor is more engaged in the investment process, a "C" investor wants low risk and detachment. It is important that you are honest and place yourself within the proper investor type. Most investors fall in the "C" and "B" categories with "C" containing the lion's share.

What Happened to Diversification?

During our speculative bubble, many investors were unwittingly lured into risk. I make similar comments for many investment professionals. As markets became frothier and investment vehicles made more complex, individuals and professionals improperly evaluated risk. In fact, a great deal of academic justification emerged seeking to create the appearance of less risk.

Many investment houses convinced themselves that armies of PhD mathematicians and scientists could model away any risk in credit-based securities. A black swan event (Figure 17-1) became nothing more than an academic matter. In his book *Black Swan*, Nassim Taleb noted how banks, trading firms and others became vulnerable to black swan events (high impact, low probability) and were exposed to losses not predicted by their models. The black swan event for this economy was the predictable end of the credit bubble.

Black Swan events are of low probability , but high impact.

Figure 17-1
Black Swan

Long ago, the idea that investors could not beat the market as a whole, meaning the S&P 500 or the Dow, led to the creation of index funds. The funds replicated the basket of stocks in the index and ostensibly lessened investor risk. The idea was that an investor could place money in an index fund and watch the money grow as the stock market rose. The dramatic fall of index funds caught investors off guard.

In addition to investing in index funds, many professional investment advisers created portfolios for their clients that were "diversified". How were these portfolios diversified? Diversified meant the creation of investment portfolios in asset classes such as stocks and bonds. The stock asset class considered small cap, mid cap and large cap stocks or specialty areas like technology or real estate. "Cap" refers to the market capitalization or the outstanding value of all stock in the company. There were foreign stocks and further subclasses such as emerging markets. Fixed income/bond investments including long to short-term obligations of companies, local government, state government, or Federal government were typically part of the portfolio. Recall what I said about the mutual fund industry and its growth. There was a mutual fund for every conceivable type of investment. That mutual fund breadth facilitated the creation of ostensibly diversified portfolios.

The theory held that as long as a diversified bundle of stocks comprised the portfolio, you were less likely to lose money overall. The addition of fixed income investments would further lessen risk. Unfortunately, when the investment bubble euphoria ended it affected most stocks and the riskier end of fixed income investments. Despite the collapse, many continue to chant the mantra of diversified portfolios. If conservative diversified portfolios minimized investor risk, why did many perform so poorly? The reason is due to their actual lack of diversification. Diversification existed within an admittedly large asset class. However, there was never any consideration of this asset class experiencing a secular decline.

Figure 17-2 shows the composition of an actual professionally managed portfolio as of 9/1/10. The portfolio uses designations from an investment advisor and are not official names. The term "Balanced" does not necessarily imply diversification. At first glance, the portfolio looks diversified given distribution into 12 areas. The low cash percentage (1%) illustrates a contrarian sentiment indicator of a market closer to a top than at a bottom. When professionally managed cash levels are this low, it means there is little new cash to enter the market for purchasing.

CASH EQUIVALENTS	1.00%
BALANCED	51.00%
LARGE CAP STOCKS	8.00%
MID / SMALL CAP STOCKS	7.00%
INTERNATIONAL STOCK	4.00%
WORLD STOCK	1.00%
HEDGE FUNDS	0.50%
LONG / INTERMEDIATE TERM FIXED	16.50%
HIGH YIELD FIXED INCOME	0.50%
INTERNATIONAL FIXED INCOME	1.00%
MULTI-SECTOR FIXED INCOME	9.00%
SPECIALITY SECTOR	0.50%

Figure 17-2
A Professionally Diversified Portfolio

Examining the portfolio a little deeper reveals the specific holdings within each designation. The following are key words used in the descriptions of the investment categories in Figure 17-2 (I will add commentary on what the descriptions imply):

Capital growth, small, mid-cap companies – Usage of the word "growth" implies investments in stocks. In this case, they are small to medium-sized companies.

REIT and real estate investments – Real estate investment trusts (REIT) manage portfolios of real estate.

40% high-yield, 30% USG & investment grade, 15% emerging, 15% developed market – "High-yield" implies higher risk. These are bond investments.

Non-investment grade bonds – These are high-yield investments with high risk.

Fixed income securities, mortgage-backed securities, GSE securities w/no support – GSE securities come from Government Sponsored Enterprises like Fannie Mae.

This portfolio contains investments in risky areas like stocks, real estate, and lower grade bonds. In order to provide true diversification, you have to create a spectrum of categories that are truly non-correlated. We can't declare a portfolio diversified because of investment in a variety of stocks, bonds and real estate. All of these areas should experience a continuation of a bear market that started in 2007 for stocks and 2005 for real estate. Bonds have absorbed some of the lost euphoria and have yet to experience the same bear, particularly at the investment grade and higher level. There are periods where safety is the primary consideration. For all types of investors, this is one such period.

Where to Invest

The investment profiles, regardless of investor Type, focus on the return OF principal more than the return ON principal. The recommendations made are based on the investment type as a whole – the entire real estate market or the entire stock market. There could well be real estate values that increase in selected areas. Individual stocks may be higher than they are now. Unless you have very specific knowledge in those areas, do not delve into them. These recommendations are at a macro level based on the forecasted economic and financial conditions ahead.

Table 17-1 lists various investment classes and suggested portfolio inclusion. I map each investment to each investor type defined earlier (A, B, C).

Investment	A	B	C
Real Estate	N	N	N
Domestic stocks & stock funds	N	N	N
Foreign stocks and stock funds	N	N	N
Junk or high-yield bonds	N	N	N
Corporate bonds & bond funds	N	N	N
Hybrid funds (stock & bond mix)	N	N	N
U.S Treasury bonds and notes	N	N	N
Municipal bonds	N	N	N
Government agency bonds (Fannie Mae etc.)	N	N	N
Collectible items	N	N	N
Annuities	N	N	N
U.S. Treasury Bills	Y	Y	Y
Foreign govt. short-term obligations [1]	Y	N	N
Certificates of Indebtedness	Y	Y	Y
Cash (paper bills)	Y	Y	Y
U.S. Treasury money market funds	Y	Y	Y
Bank Products [2]	Y	Y	Y
Foreign Bank Accounts [3]	Y	N	N
Inverse Index Mutual Funds	Y	Y	N
Inverse Index ETF	Y	Y	N
Precious metals (physical)	Y	Y	Y
Goldmoney account	Y	Y	N

Table 17-1

(1): This topic is beyond the scope of this book. Using mutual funds could dilute the effectiveness of this investment. I recommend direct investment in short-term sovereign debt of financially stable countries. Please be aware of IRS reporting requirements.

(2): Subject to safe bank identification

(3): This topic is beyond the scope of this book. The investment could be a USD or foreign currency account in a foreign, financially stable country. Please be aware of IRS reporting requirements.

Suggested Allocations

For each investor type, a suggested allocation percentage is included in Table 17-2. Readers should consider their own personal situation and what is appropriate. The amounts noted do not include funds required for typical expenses. The percentages noted in the table are investment amounts only. I cannot stress enough how important it is to find a safe bank since a minimum of 30% of your investment funds will reside there. These allocations are not static since market conditions may dictate movement in the various asset classes.

Type	Cash/Bank Products	Short-term Obligations	Precious Metals	Inverse Investments
A	30%	40%	10%	20%
B	30%	50%	10%	10%
C	40%	50%	10%	0%

Table 17-2

Chapter 18
Planning For The Future

The next few years will present societal as well as financial challenges – the financial challenges will lead to the social challenges. How we respond to those challenges will determine our future.

Be prepared for much public debate on what the government should do. The political parties will be battling it out presenting the "best" economic plan for recovery. There will also be much blame thrown around too. The Democrats will blame the Republicans for inheriting a mess and the Republicans will blame the Democrats for foolish expansion of government. Upstart political movements will blame both of the major parties for getting us into the economic quagmire. This is precisely when we will be the most vulnerable.

Understand this. Nothing government proposes will suddenly make things better. Historically, all credit expansions and speculative bubbles end the same way – back where they started. The balloon has to deflate or pop. Those looking for government salvation will be sorely disappointed. Individually and collectively, we must plan a future with less reliance on government and more reliance on self and community. This chapter discusses some of the steps we need to take to develop the plan.

Plan for Conservation

The years ahead will be a time of conservation. The profligacy of the past will be quelled by the realization our collective lifestyle exceeded our capacity to maintain it. The lifestyle only existed because of debt. For this step to be successful, avoid new debt. Pay off old debt if you are able. A greater emphasis on savings is necessary. The additional savings are necessary since we will not be able to count on the same level of government services. To rely on government promises is to risk your personal welfare. Think of saving before you think of spending.

Do Not Rely on Government Promises

The Federal Government formed a covenant with its taxpayers by making promises to take care of them in old age (Social Security), to take care of them if they are sick (Medicare), and to take care of them if they did not have the means (Medicaid). Unfortunately, the government does not have the capacity to do all of this as promised. States are in a similar predicament in terms of some of the services they offer and their pensions. Expect any benefit you receive from government, including pensions, to be less than you anticipated. Plan accordingly.

Plan for Greater Community Support

Since there will be many people not prepared for economic strife, communities will have to support them. Prepare yourself to volunteer in your community. There will be people needing assistance. The emphasis here is on community volunteerism since the support is best supplied locally. While the thought of providing assistance to others during a financially tumultuous period sounds foreign to some, the alternative will be a group of people becoming more desperate for their own survival. Consider that right now, 40+ million receive food stamps. Food pantries, animal shelters, and other support agencies have witnessed sharp increases in the demand for their services and we are barely into our economic challenges.

Beyond providing assistance to the needy, communities should strive to improve schools, transportation, public safety, and youth programs. This improvement will only occur through community integration. By this, I mean a dampening of ethnic boundaries and local, public discourse and organization. There won't be any funding for these projects in a traditional sense, so other means will have to be found.

Demand Greater Political Responsibility

A major problem in the recently ended speculative period is the public's acceptance of political-speak for responsible governance. We must hold our elected representatives responsible for proper fiscal governance. We cannot afford to have our elected officials spend incomprehensible amounts of money for programs of questionable value. The Federal budget must truly prioritize what is important to the nation. The budget should accommodate only those things that the Federal Government can uniquely do. Remember what I said the fundamental role of government is. Government's size is now well beyond the paramcters necessary for this fundamental role.

Reducing the size of government will involve curtailing their services. Some of these reductions will be quite painful. This is why it is so important to begin the process of organizing community support as noted earlier. Government must undertake no massive projects during this time. Government must return to its boundaries that served the nation well for so many years, through periods of growth and development. If we do not return government to its previous boundaries, financial catastrophe will be the result.

Invest in Youth

The generation born during the period paralleling the recent speculative boom (roughly 1982-2007) will have known only great prosperity albeit an illusory prosperity built on debt. The older segment of this generation is entering young adulthood during the crisis. Much of this generation remains in school. Youth investment relates to the community emphasis noted earlier. Schools will require more support from their communities both in time and in money. While the Federal Government will provide some support, more of it will be local. This will be no time to relax educational standards since the youth will be the foundation of the subsequent recovery. For those born earlier in this generation coming to adulthood, a greater emphasis is required in civic affairs.

Prepare the Elderly for More Self-sufficiency

The benefits paid in Social Security will outstrip taxes collected. Social Security is really a payments transfer program – current workers take care of retired workers. It's not as if the government invests the money of the Social Security trust fund. The Social Security trust fund is a great misnomer since there was a broken trust leaving only government IOUs. Society will have to redefine the concept of entitlement. Social Security recipients may be asked to undergo means testing and those qualifying might see reduced benefits. The retirement age might be raised. There could simply be fewer benefits across the board.

In keeping with the earlier plan of conservatism, we should place more emphasis on private or employer savings plans with the focus on more saving now. It would not be a surprise to see compulsory savings with an option for the savings to be in a private plan. The goal should be to unburden public retirement plans. With respect to private savings plans, many companies have no retirement plan and those that do have moved decisively towards defined contribution as opposed to defined benefit plans.

Don't Allow Government to Pick Winners & Losers

Government frequently gets involved in picking winners and losers in the economy. Typically, this means favoring one industry over another or one technology over another with favorable tax policies or direct government credit. This needs to stop. The market will be the best arbiter of deciding which industries will be successful and which should be allowed to fade. Future tax policies should encourage savings and investment versus consumption. Since the years ahead should emphasize conservation, it will be difficult to achieve these goals with tax policies favoring consumption. This type of taxation will not be popular since current policies are geared to consuming.

Changing tax policies means decoupling legislators from special interests. It also means legislators will require great political will since groups of people will be offended by a tax change that takes a benefit away.

Return to Sound Money

The money system of the United States and the entire world is a fiat system. Nothing backs the edifice of currency and credit. At one point in time, gold or silver provided the backing for money. Without such backing, credit and currency systems can be inflated at will. In this book, I demonstrated what happened to monetary systems inflated by fiat currencies. If world currencies survive the aftermath of the financial crisis, governments should base them on tangible wealth and not what government says they are worth. If currencies do not survive intact, new currencies should be based on tangible wealth. To create new currencies that are mere substitutes of old issues is pointless.

Own Wealth

I defined wealth as a material item produced by human effort having exchange value. Many things may represent wealth. Precious metals afford the owner wealth, liquidity and portability. The investor profile tells you how much precious metal you should own. While the percentage allocation may change over time, you should always own wealth.

The anticipated bout of deflation in asset values should affect the dollar or currency price of precious metals. While this will make the currency price of precious metals cheaper, it is important to own precious metals now while they are freely available. At the end of the deflationary cycle, it will be important to own more if government attempts reflationary measures at the bottom of the credit cycle. Such reflationary measures include anything from more Fed purchases of U.S. debt to outright printing of Federal Reserve Notes (cash).

Cash on Hand

During a deflation, cash is king. As the supply of credit diminishes, the remaining dollars become more valuable. Think of it this way, reduced demand or supply of credit increases the demand for cash. If something was worth $100 in an abundant credit environment, it may be worth $80 in a reduced credit environment. This deflation makes $100 held in cash more valuable since it can purchase the same item for $80.

When I say, "cash on hand" I mean that literally. Plan to have cash in your physical possession for the deflationary reason mentioned earlier and in the event of a bank holiday declaration. President Roosevelt declared a bank holiday during the Great Depression during which time banks were closed for business. The amount of cash held is a personal choice. I suggest having cash to sustain your family for a 6-month period. By this, I mean cash for items like food, gasoline and other immediate expenses. During a bank holiday, you will be unable to withdraw from an ATM and credit/debit card usage may cease as well. A bank holiday would be a very different event now than during the Great Depression when there was less reliance on credit.

Get Out of Stocks

In addition to the liquidation of stocks from non-retirement plans, take steps to eliminate stocks from your 401(k) and IRA accounts. Some 401(k) plans offer greater control over investment options through a supplemental brokerage account. With the brokerage option, there should be the opportunity to purchase Treasury Bills. It is unlikely that wealth options such as direct purchases of precious metals will be available. There will be a time to purchase stocks at the end of this bear market. At such time, there will be tremendous, once in a generation values.

Company Pension Plans

Many retirees rely on defined benefit pension plans provided by their former employer. Others hope to rely on such defined benefit plans. As a whole, these plans are woefully under-funded. These plans invest in stocks, bonds, and real estate, which are all vehicles that I generally do not recommend at this time. To make up for their funding shortfall, some plans have invested in more speculative vehicles to close the funding gap. These plans lost money in the early stages of the financial crisis and have not regained their proper funding level. As the crisis continues to develop, these plans will be hit hard again.

Do not assume that you will receive all of your defined bene-fit. Consider also that some of these plans could fold.

Loans and Debt

This book has spent time cautioning you about lending money to risky debt issuers. As credit continues to shrink, so will your chances of recovering money from those risky issuers. Now would be a great time to collect on any outstanding debt owed to you. If you own government or other corporate debt, liquidate it and get the cash. If you have personal loans owed to you, evaluate the ability of that person to return your money and act accordingly.

Your personal goal should be to become debt-free. First in the debt elimination category should be your home. I can think of few situations worse than eviction from your home. If you own your home outright, the bank can't kick you out.

Collectibles

We spent time discussing the concept of intrinsic value versus implied value. Collectibles are the epitome of items with large amounts of implied value. If you own collectibles, chances are strong that their price is at or near a peak. The values of collectible items are products of a strong and euphoric credit cycle. When that cycle ends, the value of collectibles will drop. Save your capital and wait for prices of collectibles to fall. I realize there will be readers holding collectibles for sentimental value. If this is the case, just understand your sentimental collectible will be worth less in the future.

Be Prepared to Barter

Consider that many people will not have access to credit, will not have savings, and will not have cash. For those people, bartering presents a great alternative to participate in economic transactions. While this is far from an ideal way to get things done, it may be the only way. You should be prepared to exchange services or goods in this manner.

Take Care of Your Health

The U.S. has set itself up for a dangerous future in health care. The obesity rate in the country will have far-reaching consequences. Since we anticipate a curtailment of public health benefits, additional demand for health services from an unhealthy population will come at the worst time. We know that an overweight population has the potential to suffer a range of maladies ranging from diabetes to hypertension. Begin taking measures to improve your health now so you are not dependent on public health benefits that may be unavailable. If health care costs or coverage is not an issue for you, take steps to improve your health anyway. If the forecast is incorrect about the curtailment of public health services, the advice given is still sound. The crisis and its aftermath will require great energy and focus. If you are unhealthy, you will hamper your ability to do this for yourself and family.

Epilogue

Meaningful change often does not occur without some cataclysmic or profound event. Think of how many times people change their lives after a near-death experience. The profound events in our economic and financial history hardly caused a seismic shock. The accumulation of these events created a massive fault line capable of wreaking unimaginable havoc in our economy. You have two challenges. First, get your own house in order so you don't have to rely on the Wizard. Second, be prepared to help others and construct the narrative for our new economic future. You know when they tell you during the pre-flight briefing to secure your mask first and then the child's? Put your mask on and make sure it does not come off. You will likely have to help others put on theirs.

The Wizard of Oz metaphor helps describe the journey and hopeful escape from our financial quagmire. Now that we are in the Land of Oz, many are on the road to the Emerald City to have the powerful Wizard save them. By all accounts, this Wizard is quite impressive and powerful. The Wizard operates behind a curtain, and we take it for granted that he has control. Our dog Toto is not impressed by the Wizard and barks at the curtain. The name Toto comes from the Latin "toto" which means "all, entirety, wholeness, completeness". Readers that know Spanish will recognize the word "todo" or those knowing

French will recognize the word "tout" as also meaning "all" or "everything". Toto represents the public. The public needs to understand what the Wizard is capable of doing. I want Toto to pull back the curtain. Pulling back this curtain and executing a plan will require you to use your mind, your heart, and your courage. Much like the Scarecrow, the Tin Man, and the Cowardly Lion, you have all these traits within you. It is imperative that you use these traits now.

The name Dorothy comes from two Greek words, "doron" and "theos". Doron is a word meaning "gift or present". Doron can also mean "money cast into the treasury in support of a temple or the poor". The word theos represents divinity or God. Combined, these words form the name Dorothy, whose name means "a gift from God". Dorothy represents the ability we all have within us to see through this crisis. This is a crisis of debt and credit. In the Wizard of Oz, Dorothy used water, a cleanser, to melt the Wicked Witch of the West, who represents the evils of unmitigated credit. You will have to do the same thing at both the public and private level. We will have to cleanse ourselves of debt and the process will be painful. If we don't, we will be on an endless journey to the Emerald City with the Wicked Witch of the West constantly on our tail.

I know you have heard the expression, "Knowledge is power". Let me suggest to you that *power* is the *knowledge* of how to discern and use information. The problem today is not a paucity of information but rather a deluge of it. Our challenge is separating the wheat from the chaff. We have a great responsibility to understand the issues at hand. It will simply be impossible to make informed decisions without this knowledge.

Your economic health and that of the country are intertwined. I really cannot see one being healthy while the other suffers. That said you need to organize your own affairs before the nation as a whole can be healthy again. When too many rely on government for their economic well-being, it burdens economic growth. We cannot have a recovery until we have *real* economic growth, not some debt-based version of it.

One thing we all have to admit is there are no ready-made solutions to our problems. In the Wizard of Oz, the Wizard tells Dorothy he is a good man but a bad Wizard. Our government and central bank try to do right by their constituents but they are bad Wizards. Their attempts to do the right things often lead to problems. Then they try to do more things to remediate what they did wrong.

Government leaders, the Fed, and many economists urge spending more money we don't have just to kick start the economy. Yet the question few of them can answer is why the stimulation to the tune of trillions has not worked. They are groping for answers even coming up with euphemisms like a "jobless recovery". That expression is an absurdity. Anyone can build a case of an economic recovery by talking about improved GDP figures. From 1929 to 1933, there were several quarters of higher GDP but that did not help us escape the Great Depression. Our government measures economic activity based on GDP, but I showed earlier in this book how debt can help that figure along. If GDP is going up but debt is going up faster, is that progress?

Government is doing all it can to stave off a depression. Yes, it is okay to use that word. You won't hear that term coming out of government's mouth because politicians fear what that would mean on election day. We contribute to their avoidance of that term since we only want to hear good news. Politicians are coin-operated so we have to quit feeding them figuratively and literally. Until we demand accountability from our elected leaders at all levels, nothing will be done. It is up to us to change the culture of accountability.

What lies ahead for us as an economy and what can we expect individually? I am quite convinced that a sizeable economic contraction is in front of us. As an economy, we created a bunch of credit and reached the saturation point. From here, we deflate the balloon. Despite government or Fed actions, they cannot do enough to prevent the contraction. This will be the point when the Wizard is exposed. Individuals cannot help the anti-deflation fight either. All you hear is consumers are responsible for an overwhelming majority of economic activity and that all we need to do is to get the consumer spending again. Well, many consumers see what is happening and are putting the brakes on spending.

In a system that relies on credit to feed itself, less spending means less credit. Less credit means reduced business activity. Reduced business activity means fewer employees. Unemployment means increased problems paying the mortgage and less spending. Mortgage foreclosures mean more real estate hits the market. The real estate oversupply causes banks to restrict loans or perhaps fail altogether. All of these things are deflationary. Deflation is the inflation process in reverse.

Think of how much inflation is built into everyone's economic planning. Most thought their home equity was additional wealth. That wealth might be part of someone's long-term financial planning. At some future point, they could sell the house for a profit and live off the capital gains. What if there are no capital gains? Think about retirement portfolios. We have data indicating many do not save for retirement on their own. Those that do save I'm sure are banking on having a decent nest egg after their hard working years. If their investments go down in value, they will not have time to recover. Remember, the stock market top of 1929 was not eclipsed for an entire generation (25 years). Bonds are presumed to be safer investments but that is predicated on the bond issuer's ability to pay back the principal and make interest payments. Many bond issues are at high risk of defaulting and there will be little left for an investor when that happens.

If there is less credit available and the value of people's investments goes down, there is less purchasing power chasing goods and services in the economy. Less purchasing power means prices cannot remain at the same levels. This is one of the reasons I think our future is one of deflation. Inflation is part of everyone's personal and macro economic planning. Nobody is considering an environment where the opposite could happen.

Government is trying hard to fight this trend but they cannot add real wealth to the economy since they don't produce goods and services. They can take money and spend it but that is all. Deflation will be painful especially since no one ever considered it a possibility. At the end of the deflationary process, we will have massive amounts of defaults and people so saddled with debt that they will be unable to spend as they did in the past. Default means the destruction of credit. The next round of economic recovery, and there will be recovery, will be more thoughtful and tempered.

What we have to remember is our economy does not suffer from a shortage of productive capacity. The problem is not an absence of capacity, but too much high-priced capacity. That price refers to both goods and wages.

If allowed to proceed on its own course, at the end of the deflation we will still have productive capacity. Absent a destructive war, factories will remain in place and buildings will be standing. Technological innovation can continue. The land will still yield crops. There may be different owners of the factory, the buildings, the land, and the technology but they will still exist. This is by no means a doomsday scenario, unless we allow it to progress to that level.

Some will argue that the crisis was a failure of capitalism. Capitalism did not fail us. While the definition of capitalism may be debated, capitalism involves decisions made by private individuals in a market. The Wizards have done plenty to interfere in the market. The combination of that interference and cyclic human tendencies laid the seeds for our crisis.

The many economic hardships facing us will hopefully bring more discussion around the issue of what we call money and its backing. If we play the same game again of having money without some backing, we will end up in the same place. We need honest money.

Any forecast is subject to error. Some of the scenarios described in this book may not come to fruition. I do want you to consider that the probability of my forecasts coming to fruition is increasing daily, so we cannot stick our heads in the sand. In this case, it is much better to prepare than to lament. The preparatory steps outlined will create a greater level of self-sufficiency that has been missing for some time. The risk of being incorrect with the forecast might mean opportunity cost but at least you will be prepared for a rainy day. Right now, the weather service is issuing hurricane warnings.

As the U.S. economy moves through this turbulent period in our history, there will be an opportunity to redefine the nation. This redefinition need only reflect those values and policies that allowed the nation to achieve its once proud economic prominence. The changes necessary are only achievable with the spirit of cooperation and community bonding. Courage to meet problems head-on and self-sufficiency are principles that built America and made it great.

If cooperation and bonding does not occur, it creates an opportunity for demagoguery that history has shown can have devastating consequences. A financial house divided cannot stand.

Don't let your educational process end with this book. Make it the beginning. Ask questions. Get involved. Hold elected leaders accountable. Participate in town hall meetings or other forums. Write letters to the editor. Get involved in civic affairs. Don't be a bystander.

Appendices

Appendix A
Inflation Example

Barter Economy

It is difficult to understand inflation in a multi-trillion dollar economy. A small and developing mini-economy sheds more light on the topic. In the first iteration of this economy, people barter for everything. The only method of conducting economic transactions is by trading one's production for another's. Our mini-economy consists of the following persons:

i. Person "A" produces apples

ii. Person "B" produces bananas

iii. Person "C" produces corn

iv. Person "S" provides labor to produce any crop

The Wealth Exchange Table (Table A-1) defines the barter arrangements between people.

- One (1) apple is exchanged for three (3) bananas.

- One (1) apple is exchanged for 1/3 bushel of corn or 3 apples are exchanged for one bushel of corn

- One (1) banana is exchanged for 1/3 of an apple or 3 bananas are exchanged for 1 apple.

- One (1) banana is exchanged for 1/9 of bushel of corn or 9 bananas are exchanged for 1 bushel of corn.

- One unit of labor is exchangeable for 3 apples, 9 bananas, and 1 bushel of corn.

	Apples (qty)	Bananas (qty)	Corn (bushel)	Labor (hrs)
Apples	N/A	3	1/3	1/3
Bananas	1/3	N/A	1/9	1/9
Corn	3	9	N/A	1
Labor	3	9	1	N/A

Table A-1

The relationships could change in this economy. For example, a shortage of bananas could arise due to acts of nature. The result might be a 1:1 exchange of apples to bananas for a period while the shortage existed. This is in contrast to the normal ratio of 3 bananas to 1 apple.

What happens when one person desires to consume more than they are capable of exchanging? Person B (producer of bananas) wishes to consume more corn but does not have enough bananas with which to pay Person C (producer of corn). Person B requests a corn loan from Person C. Person C gives Person B an additional bushel of corn as a loan payable in one month. For this transaction, C wants more than the 9 bananas (see Wealth Exchange Table) that is the typical exchange. Person C wants 12 bananas.

How does B pay back C for the extra bushel of corn? The payment is via additional bananas that B produces (surplus) in the future. Person B has <u>rented</u> the surplus corn from C and the

<u>rental fee</u> is the surplus banana production in the future. Person B has exchanged present consumption (corn) for future production (bananas). C has deferred consuming corn *now* in exchange for a greater number of bananas in the *future*. C gains 3 more bananas than the regular exchange rate (9 bananas for 1 bushel of corn) by demanding 12 bananas in the future. Table A-2 summarizes this transaction.

Person	Consumed Now	Given Now	Paid in Future	Received in Future
B	1 bushel corn	Nothing	12 bananas	N/A
C	N/A	1 bushel of corn	N/A	12 bananas

Table A-2

In this mini-economy, anyone wishing to consume more *now* must save their production in the future in order to pay back what they consumed. This point is vital to understand.

Person B could not have consumed the extra corn without saving bananas in the future with which to pay back Person C.

The items in the Wealth Exchange System table are wealth since human effort produces them, or in the case of labor, it is human effort [1]. The items also have exchange value. There is no inherent inflation in this mini-economy. The only way to increase your wealth in this mini-economy is to produce more, consume less, or some combination thereof. Individual wealth increases with surplus production. Let me repeat this, "Individual wealth increases with surplus production."

(1) *Some may not consider labor as wealth but rather a factor of production. For the purposes of this example, we will consider labor as wealth.*

Wealth Money

A new Person enters the economy, Person "G", and produces gold coins of different weights. All Persons in the mini-economy agree to relationships between their product and the gold coin. These gold coins represent a medium of exchange, a unit of account, and a store of wealth. Why are these gold coins money? They are definitely a medium of exchange since all Persons (A,B, C, S, G) will use them. They are a unit of account since we indicated the coins have different sizes and values. They are a store of wealth since it is a material item produced by human effort.

The relationship between the perishable products and labor retain the same values to one another, only now the gold coin is the money representing the value.

The Wealth Exchange table retains the same relationships between the crops and the labor. For example, (1) apple formerly was exchanged for (3) bananas. This is the same as saying (30) apples equals (90) bananas (multiply the quantities by 30).

	Apples (qty)	Bananas (qty)	Corn (bushel)	Labor (hrs)
Gold Coin (oz)	30	90	10	10

Table A-3

The new Wealth Exchange System table clearly indicates that 1 oz of the gold coin equals either 30 apples or 90 bananas – meaning 30 apples = 90 bananas (Table A-3).

Now, there is a more convenient means of exchange, the gold coins. The gold coins provide a reference to every item in this mini-economy. Inflation is not present in this economy even after the introduction of the gold coins. Why? Because the coins are real wealth.

As before, a shortage of bananas will result in fewer bananas exchangeable for an ounce of gold. The price increase is temporary and is a result of acts of nature – not money inflation. If production of bananas is permanently impaired, then the relationship between gold and bananas will change. The "price" of bananas increased but it was not because the value of the money decreased.

Consider the last sentence carefully. The new medium of exchange does not cause inflation by itself. Acts of nature or other events are capable of creating upward price changes. A new method of producing bananas could introduce more efficiencies making banana production more abundant. Such efficiencies should drive the price of bananas down, which is a good thing.

What if the supply of gold coins increased and everything else held constant? In this case, each ounce of gold coin purchases fewer apples, bananas and corn since the supply of coins increased relative to the other items. While one may consider this gold coin inflation, there had to be additional effort expended in order to increase the supply of coins or perhaps coin production became more efficient. The coins still represent wealth even if produced in greater quantities. The greater quantities of coins simply mean more of them are required to purchase the apples, bananas, corn, and labor.

Devalued Money

What happens if Person "P" appears and convinces the people that a barter system is not practical and that the supply of gold coins is not sufficient to grow their mini-economy? A law is passed requiring paper notes be used in the transactions. Person

P creates paper notes that say *"Good as One Ounce of Gold"*.

The rest of the people in the mini-economy accept paper notes and treat it just like a one-ounce gold coin. It requires <u>little</u> <u>effort</u> to produce this paper, compared to gold coins or anything else. Person P can produce paper notes at will. When P brought this paper into the mini-economy, it became easy for P to acquire gold, apples, bananas, corn and labor. Soon the producers of the crops and the providers of the labor find that there are fewer items available since Person P is acquiring them. This causes them to demand more paper for their own products since they need more paper to buy the other things in the economy.

The people in the economy begin to request loans from Person P since they find themselves short of paper notes. Person P loans paper notes and requests the same value of paper notes plus interest in return. The paper notes only come into existence by Person P printing them. The interest payments on the loans require more paper notes to be printed. The amount of paper notes in circulation begins to increase even more.

While this is occurring, the gold coins fall out of circulation since the participants in the economy begin to recognize their wealth is superior relative to the paper notes. Even though people were told the paper note and the gold coins were worth the same, instinctively they knew otherwise. Rather than exchanging a single paper note for a gold coin, the people demand 100 paper notes now for the gold coin. People begin to say that the "price" of the gold coin has gone up since originally, it was exchanged 1:1 with the paper note and now it is 100:1 paper to gold.

The effect of paper note introduction was inflation. Prior to paper note introduction, prices were stable. Only acts of nature or increases in efficiency disrupted pricing. Now, prices increased merely with the introduction of paper notes. It is not merely that the notes were made of paper. What is important is that nobody believed the paper was a good as one ounce of gold.

Paper vs. Gold Coins

Did the act of having paper in the mini-economy by itself cause inflation? No. If a fixed amount of paper existed in the economy relative to a fixed amount of gold coin, the paper would be a certificate or receipt for the gold. Person P did not introduce the paper notes as a receipt for the gold. P simply indicated that anyone who had the paper note commanded the same purchasing power as gold. Once more paper got introduced into the economy, it allowed the paper holder to buy more apples, bananas, and corn.

It would be no different if the producer of apples suddenly found a way to grow apples at will. They could exchange their infinite supply of apples for more corn, bananas, labor or gold coins. This is an exaggeration since people can only eat and store so many apples. Since the paper <u>was</u> the medium of exchange, everyone needed it and paper is not perishable like apples.

Mini-economy Example Recap

Initially, the economy functioned using only barter. Relationships of one product to another were established. No inflation, as we know it, existed. The barter economy was cumbersome and at times impractical since many of the goods produced were perishable.

Gold coins introduced a new level of economic functionality. The gold coins satisfied the definition of money and people exchanged their goods for coins. Changes in price resulted from acts of nature or by increases in efficiency. The former increased prices and the latter reduced them.

The introduction of paper notes, *declared equivalent to gold coins*, had an immediate inflationary effect on the economy. Suddenly all prices went up. People accepted the notes since they assumed they were as good as gold. Initial confidence in the paper was not an issue. Over time, gold coins vanished from circulation (Gresham's Law). The price of the gold coin itself went from a 1:1 relationship with paper notes to 100:1 (paper notes to gold coin). Loans, requiring payment in notes for the principal and interest emerged. The interest to pay the loans originated with Person P who was the only source of notes.

Appendix B
Bubble Dramatization

The following is a brief dramatization intended to illustrate how a bubble or mania might develop.

A company produces bobble head dolls of St. Louis Cardinals pitcher Todd Smith. The company produces them for $2.00 and sells them for $4.00. The company calls these dolls "Todalions". Initially, the dolls are available at local retail outlets and sales are commensurate for what you might expect a player of Mr. Smith's ilk to command. To spur sales of the Todalions, the Cardinals have a Todalion bobble head doll night at Busch Stadium. The team distributes twenty-five thousand dolls on a warm summer night and children comment to their parents how cute the bobble head dolls look with the lion caricature of Mr. Smith's face. The retail price of the doll remains at $4.00.

Then something interesting happens. Mr. Smith creates a Twitter and Facebook page for the Todalion. Soon, children and teens are flocking to Facebook and Twitter for daily updates on the Todalion. Cell phone text traffic increases dramatically whenever there is an update on these social media sites. The company producing the Todalions experiences increased demand for its product. Understanding economics, the company doubles the price of the doll.

A Cardinal broadcast appears on the ESPN Sunday night game with Mr. Smith pitching and the announcers mention the sudden Todalion doll craze. The game receives international attention and now orders for the dolls come from overseas. Enterprising youngsters, who earlier bought extra dolls, auction their supply on eBay. Miraculously, dolls are fetching as much as $20.

The producing company's marketing department develops a limited edition Todalion. The limited edition version sells in stores for $50. Soon, these models appear in eBay with sales of $100 commonplace. All the while, Mr. Smith's successes on the field multiply. He challenges the major league baseball record for consecutive scoreless innings. This feat receives even more national and international attention. A famous British entrepreneur, Sir Richard Smythe decides he wants to take a few Todalions in orbit around our planet. When returning from his space adventure, Sir Richard auctions these Todalions for a record $1,000 each with the proceeds going to charity.

As luck would have it, Mr. Smith did not break the pitching record, hurt his arm and did not recover from ligament transplantation surgery. The Cardinals replaced him in the rotation with another promising youngster. Without the constant media exposure, interest in the Todalion waned. Parents began to question the price of the doll. eBay auctions were no longer lucrative. The St. Louis teen community, which had so thoroughly embraced the Todalions, focused on the next edition of Guitar Hero. From a peak of $1,000, the Todalion now sat unsold on retail shelves until its production ceased. Those who had bought Todalions for "investment" purposes tried in vain to dump them. Eventually, a Chinese distributor offered $0.50 for each Todalion.

Appendix C
Understanding Bonds

A bond is an interest-bearing debt instrument that obligates the issuer to pay the bondholder specific amounts of money at set intervals in return for the principal loaned to the issuer. At the end of the bond period, its maturity, the bond issuer pays the bondholder the original principal lent. The amount originally borrowed is the par value and the end of the bond's term is its maturity. A bond pays interest until maturity at which time the entire principal is paid back.

How is a bond's interest rate determined? Creditworthiness of the bond issuer and demand for the bond determines the interest rate. Creditworthiness is the bond issuer's ability to pay the interest and return the principal. The less creditworthy the bond issuer, the greater the amount of interest paid. This is an application of Economic Law #1 in the sense that diminished confidence implies a higher rate of interest. The bond issuer must be able to pay interest on a periodic basis AND the principal at maturity.

The other factor determining a bond's interest rate is the demand for the bond. If demand for a bond is high, there is less need for the bond issuer to pay a higher rate of interest. The credit risk is still a factor but if demand is high, the issuer can pay a smaller rate of interest since the bond is attracting enough demand. Ultimately, the goal for the bond issuer is to raise funds. If the issuer can raise funds with a lower interest rate, then he or she will reduce their interest costs.

Table C-1 provides hypothetical examples of bond issues. All bond issuers in this example are requesting $1,000,000.

Bond Issuer	Term (yrs)	Interest Rate	Annual Interest Payment	Credit Risk
New Widget Company	10	12%	$120,000	High
Anytown, USA	10	6%	$60,000	Medium to Low
U.S. Government	10	4%	$40,000	Low

Table C-1

In Table C-1, the issuer with the highest perceived risk, New Widget Company, must pay the highest interest rate. When issued, the par value of the bond is $1,000,000, meaning the bond issuer wants $1,000,000. Suppose you purchase a bond from New Widget Company. The $1 million bond will pay $120,000 in interest per year for 10 years. After holding the bond for a very short time, you consider selling. You have to think about a few things prior to selling, however.

The prevailing level of interest rates affects sale prices of bonds. If prevailing interest rates have increased, investors demand a higher rate of interest on bonds. Another factor is the perceived credit risk of the bond issuer. If the credit risk has increased, investors will also demand a higher rate of interest. The par value of your bond ($1 million) and the annual interest payment ($120,000) stay the same. At the end of ten years, New Widget Company still owes you $1 million and they must still pay you $120,000 per year in interest. You as the seller of the bond must adjust the price for interest rate increases and supply/demand considerations.

When you finally decide to sell your New Widget bond, the offer price comes in at $800,000, which is lower than your $1 million par value. In your case, we can conclude the interest rate went up since the offer price on your bond is less than $1 million. The higher interest rate could be the result of higher prevailing interest rates or some perception of a higher credit risk for New Widget Company.

Conversely, if the price for the New Widget bond was $1.2 million, we can infer lower prevailing interest rates or New Widget is a better credit risk. Bond prices and implied interest rates have an inverse relationship – when one goes up, the other goes down. Understand, <u>nothing</u> has changed contractually in the original bond issue. The bond will still pay $1,000,000 at maturity and $120,000 each year. What has changed is what an investor is willing to pay for the bond.

Actual bond pricing is a bit more complicated. The price of a bond is the sum of the present values of all expected interest payments plus the present value of the initial bond price at maturity. I won't delve into the actual formula for the purposes of this discussion. What is important to remember is bond prices and interest rates are inversely related.

U.S. Treasury Bonds and Notes have similar characteristics as just described. Treasury Bonds are long-term debt instruments with maturities of 10 years or longer. The maturity is the term length described earlier. Treasury Notes are intermediate term debt instruments with maturities from one to 10 years.

Understanding Treasury Bills

Treasury Bills are debt instruments of the U.S. Government operating in a different manner than Treasury Bonds or Notes. Treasury Bills (T-bills) are short-term debt instruments with maturities of one year or less. T-bills are sold at a discount from face value. For example, a $10,000 T-bill might sell for $9,900 with a maturity of one year. The purchaser of the T-bill lends the U.S. Government $9,9000 and receives $10,000 one year later. The par value in this transaction is $10,000 and the T-Bill sells at a discount of $100.

T-bills are one of the most liquid debt instruments and should represent the lowest short-term interest rate. The issuer of the T-bill is considered to be the most credit-worthy, the U.S. Government. Since the maturity of T-Bills is so short, 91 days in the shortest case, government has to service this debt more frequently. The combination of short maturity, liquidity, and perceived creditworthiness, makes this debt instrument ideal in times of credit uncertainty.

Appendix D
Economic & Investment Laws

Economic Laws

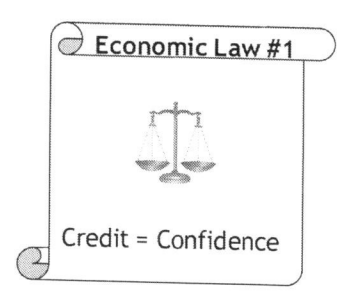

Economic Law #1

Credit = Confidence

Without confidence there is no credit. A credit transaction requires a lender having the confidence of repayment, with interest, from the debtor. Manifestations of extremes of confidence are evident with excessive credit creation. Excessive credit creation leads to inflation which many identify as a rise in "prices".

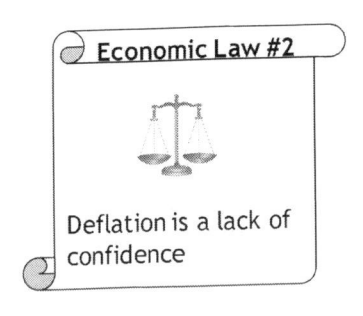

Economic Law #2

Deflation is a lack of confidence

Conversely, deflation implies an absence of confidence, which means less credit. Less credit results from fewer loan originations, loan defaults, or loan payoff. Any of these three conditions reduces the amount of outstanding credit. The reduction of credit is fatal to a credit-based economy.

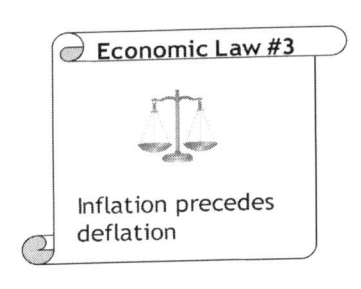

Economic Law #3

Inflation precedes deflation

Deflation cannot occur without a preceding inflation. The greater the size of the inflation, the greater the ensuing deflation.

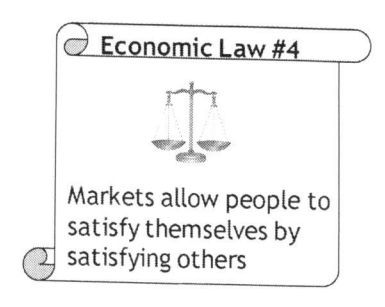

Economies are expressions of what people do. Participants in an economy act on their own behalf (what is best for them) in a manner that meets the satisfaction of others acting on *their* own behalf. The collective action of all of these participants is the Market. Therefore, the Market is a collection of many people acting on their own behalf for the benefit of others.

Investment Laws

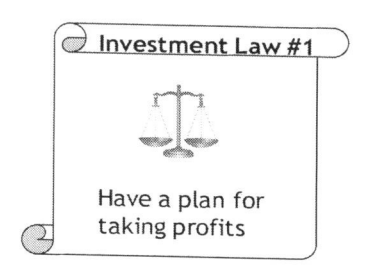

Most investors have no plan for taking a profit on an investment. For example, after gaining in an investment position and then experiencing a fall in the initial profit, when does the typical investor exit the position? Successful long-term investing requires systematic profit extraction.

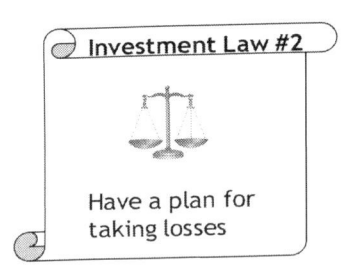

Investment Law #2

Have a plan for
taking losses

Perhaps the most difficult aspect of investing is to admit failure. Investments fail. The sooner this recognition occurs, the quicker an investor can cut their losses and move to other profitable ventures. Investors often cling to the <u>hope</u> that their investment losses will return to at least a break-even point. During a prolonged decline, this approach is fatal.

List of Figures & Credits

LIST OF FIGURES

Chapter 1

Figure	Credit
1-1	Image in public domain from Wikimedia Commons
1-2	Image by Alice Mosquera from Costa Rica Museum of Money
1-3	Image by Alice Mosquera from Costa Rica Museum of Money
1-4	Image in public domain from Wikimedia Commons
1-5	Image by Jim Mosquera. Data courtesy of New York Herald.
1-6	Image in public domain from Wikimedia Commons
1-7	Image in public domain from Wikimedia Commons
1-8	Image in public domain from Wikimedia Commons
1-9	Image in public domain from Wikimedia Commons
1-10	Image in public domain from Wikimedia Commons
1-11	Federal Reserve Bank of St. Louis: Economic Data - FRED
1-12	Federal Reserve Bank of St. Louis: Economic Data - FRED
1-13	Federal Reserve Bank of St. Louis: Economic Data - FRED
1-14	Image in public domain from Wikimedia Commons

Chapter 2

Figure	Credit
2-1	Image in public domain from Wikimedia Commons
2-2	Image by Alice Mosquera
2-3	Image in public domain from Wikimedia Commons

Chapter 3

Figure	Credit
3-1	Image in public domain from Wikimedia Commons
3-2	Federal Reserve Bank of St. Louis: Economic Data - FRED
3-3	Federal Reserve Bank of St. Louis: Economic Data - FRED
3-4	Image by Jim Mosquera (data from Federal Reserve Bank of Cleveland)
3-5	Federal Reserve Bank of St. Louis: Economic Data - FRED
3-6	Federal Reserve Bank of St. Louis: Economic Data - FRED
3-7	Image in public domain from Wikimedia Commons
3-8	Image in public domain from Wikimedia Commons
3-9	Image in public domain from Wikimedia Commons
3-10	Image by Alice Mosquera

LIST OF FIGURES

Chapter 4

Figure	Credit
4-1	Image by Nevit Dilmen
4-2	Image by Jim Mosquera
4-3	Image by Jim Mosquera
4-4	Image by Jim Mosquera
4-5	Image by Jim Mosquera
4-6	Image by Jim Mosquera
4-7	Image by Jim Mosquera
4-8	Image in public domain from Wikimedia Commons
4-9	Image by Patriot Room
4-10	Federal Reserve Bank of St. Louis: Economic Data - FRED

Chapter 5

Figure	Credit
5-1	Image in public domain from Wikimedia Commons
5-2	Image by Jim Mosquera
5-3	Image in public domain from Wikimedia Commons
5-4	Image by Ester Inbar
5-5	Image uploaded to Wikimedia Commons by "Russell" User: Adinrboltz
5-6	Image in public domain from Wikimedia Commons
5-7	Image by Jim Mosquera with contribution by Ariel Gold (fish image)

Chapter 6

Figure	Credit
6-1	Image by Jim Mosquera
6-2	Image by Jim Mosquera w/other content from public domain
6-3	Image by Ivo Shandor
6-4	Image by Christopher Ziemnowicz
6-5	Image in public domain from Wikimedia Commons
6-6	Image from Ludwig von Mises Institute
6-7	Image in public domain from Wikimedia Commons
6-8	Image by Jim Mosquera

Chapter 7

Figure	Credit
7-1	Image by Jim Mosquera
7-2	Image in public domain by White House photographer Pete Souza
7-3	Image in public domain from Wikimedia Commons
7-4	Image in public domain from Wikimedia Commons
7-5	Image by Jesper Balle
7-6	Image in public domain from Wikimedia Commons

Chapter 8

Figure	Credit
8-1	Image by John O'Neill
8-2	Image in public domain from Wikimedia Commons (uploaded by shgmom_Barbara)
8-3	Image by Alice Mosquera
8-4	Image in public domain from Wikimedia Commons
8-5	Image by Jay Henry
8-6	Image in public domain from Wikimedia Commons
8-7	Federal Reserve Bank of St. Louis: Economic Data - FRED & Jim Mosquera using image from public domain

Chapter 9

Figure	Credit
9-1	Image from CSI software with modification by Jim Mosquera
9-2	Image by Jim Mosquera
9-3	Image in public domain from Wikimedia Commons by user Tarale
9-4	Image by Jim Mosquera
9-5	Image from E*Trade with modification by Jim Mosquera
9-6	Image by Jim Mosquera

Chapter 10

Figure	Credit
10-1	Image by Jim Mosquera (data from FDIC)
10-2	Image by Jim Mosquera (data from FDIC)
10-3	Image in public domain from Wikimedia Commons
10-4	Image in public domain from Wikimedia Commons
10-5	Image by Cory Doctorow

Chapter 11

Figure	Credit
11-1	Image by Jim Mosquera
11-2	Image by Jim Mosquera
11-3	Image by Brendel
11-4	Image by Scott Cartoosh
11-5	Image Marc Averette
11-6	Image by Jim Mosquera (data courtesy of Federal Reserve Bank and Bureau of Labor Statistics

Chapter 12

Figure	Credit
12-1	Image by Jim Mosquera
12-2	Image by Jim Mosquera

LIST OF FIGURES

Chapter 13

Figure	Credit
13-1	Image by Daisyree Baker

Chapter 14

Figure	Credit
14-1	Image by Jim Mosquera
14-2	Image by Jim Mosquera

Chapter 15

Figure	Credit
15-1	Image of Canadian Maple Leaf & U.S. Gold Eagle by Alice Mosquera. Other images in figure in the public domain.
15-2	Image by Alice Mosquera

Chapter 16

Figure	Credit
16-1	Image by Jim Mosquera

Chapter 17

Figure	Credit
17-1	Image by Mike Switzerland
17-2	Image by Jim Mosquera

Additional Credits

Cover design by Jim Mosquera. Images from the collage on the front cover by Alice Mosquera, The Truth About, others already credited in the chapters, along with images from the public domain.

Wizard of Oz images are in the public domain originally created by W.W. Denslow.

Economic & Investment Law graphics by Jim Mosquera

All other images from Wikimedia Commons and placed in public domain with attribution given where required.

References

References

Introduction

Budget of the United States Government, FY 2009, *gpoaccess.gov*

Buckler, William. *The Privateer,* Issue #656

Pisani, Joseph. "More Upper-Income Workers Living Paycheck to Paycheck", *CNBC*, September 16, 2009

Sutton, Chavon. "43% Have Less Than $10k for Retirement", *CnnMoney.com*, March 9, 2010

Bankruptcy stats, *Bankruptcyaction.com* w/data from Administrative Office of U.S. Courts

Bureau of Labor Statistics

U.S Department of Agriculture

Chapter 1

"Money", *Wikipedia.org*

"Money", *Websters.com*

"Money", *Webster's New World Dictionary of the American Language*

Smith, Adam. *The Wealth of Nations*

Mosquera, Jim. *The Sentinel Economic and Financial Newsletter, Volume 1 Issue 1*

Ministry of Culture, P.R. China

Table of Continental Currency Inflation, *The New York Herald.* January 26, 1863

Central Bank Museum, Costa Rica

REFERENCES

Trask, H.A. Scott. "Inflation and The American Revolution", Ludwig Von Mises Institute

United States Constitution. Cornell University Law School

United States Congress. Act of February 25, 1862, Chapter XXXIII, Washington, D.C.

Text of the Federal Reserve Act. Cornell University Law School

United States Department of the Treasury

Goodman, Jordan Elliot & Downes, John. *The Dictionary of Finance and Investment Terms*

31 USC TITLE 31, Section 405a-1

Dictionary.com

Economic Research. Federal Reserve Bank of St. Louis

Treasurydirect.gov

Board of Governors of Federal Reserve System. Mortgage Debt Outstanding

Mayer, Trace. "The Debt Pyramid"

Investopedia. Definition of Derivative

European Network on Debt and Development. "Dangerous Derivatives at Heart of Financial Crisis", October 22, 2008.

U.S. Treasury Fact Sheets. Currency & Coins

Visualeconomics.com

Jenkins, Merrill. *Money The Greatest Hoax on Earth*

Chapter 2

Prechter Jr., Robert R. *Conquer the Crash*

Mosquera, Jim. *The Sentinel Economic and Financial Newsletter – Inflation Supplement*

Lawrence of Arabia, Columbia Pictures, 1962

Chapter 3

Prechter Jr., Robert R. *Conquer the Crash*

Mises, Ludwig von. *Human Action*

Mosquera, Jim. *The Sentinel Economic and Financial Newsletter, Volume 1 Issues 5 & 6*

Mosquera, Jim. "Barter networks help in tough economic times", *Examiner.com*, November 23, 2009.

Goodman, Jordan Elliot & Downes, John. *The Dictionary of Finance and Investment Terms*

Evans-Pritchard, Ambrose. "US money supply plunges at 1930s pace as Obama eyes fresh stimulus", *London Telegraph*

Kendall & Hochberg. *Elliott Wave Financial Forecast*, October 1, 2010

Chapter 4

Strauss, William & Howe, Neil. *The Fourth Turning*

Baseball-Reference.com

Cheung, Edward. "Baby Boomers, Generation X and Social Cycles Volume 1: North American Long-waves"

Bernstein, Jake. *The New Prosperity*

Von Baranov, Eric. *Kondratyev Theory Letters*

Frost, A.J., & Prechter, Robert. *Elliott Wave Principle*

King, John L. *Chaos in America*

Carolan, Christopher. *The Spiral Calendar*

REFERENCES

Mosquera, Jim. *The Sentinel Economic and Financial Newsletter - Stock Market Supplement*

Aizenman, N.C. "New High in Prison Numbers", *Washington Post*, February 29, 2008

"The Marihuana Problem in the City of New York", *The La Guardia Committee Report*, Mayor's Committee on Marihuana, by the New York Academy of Medicine, City of New York, 1944

Wilson, Euan. "The Coming Collapse of a Modern Prohibition", *The Socionomist*, July 2009

Marihuana Tax Act of 1937

Committee on Finance, US Senate, 75c 2s. HR6906. Library of Congress transcript, July 12, 1937

Schlesinger Jr., Arthur. "The Cycles of American Politics"

Murray, Charles. "Losing Ground: American Social Policy 1950-1980"

Prechter Jr., Robert R. *The Wave Principle of Human Social Behavior and the New Science of Socionomics*

Prechter Jr., Robert R. *Conquer the Crash*

"Jim Cramer On Daily Show": Jon Stewart Hits Hard (VIDEO), *Huffington Post*, March 12, 2009

McInnis, Doug. "Survivor GMAC making changes after mortgage crisis", *Crain's Detroit Business*

"The Man Who Figured Out Madoff's Scheme", *CBS News, 60 Minutes*

Kerber, Ross. "The Whistleblower", *Boston Globe*, January 8, 2009

Fhi.gov

Phillips, Nicholas. "Martin Sigillito is accused of fleecing regular Joes and Racquet Club jet setters alike out of $45 million", *Riverfront Times*, August 4, 2010

Woolfolk & Webby. "Medical marijuana for the masses", *Daily Democrat*, Woodland, CA, October 18, 2010

Chapter 5

"Paulson Warns Of 'Fragile' Economy", Treasury Secretary Talks To Scott Pelley About The Controversial $700 Billion Bailout, CBS News, *60 Minutes*

Maybury, Richard. *The Clipper Ship Strategy*

Mosquera, Jim. *The Sentinel Economic and Financial Newsletter - Volume 1 Issue 3*

Naisbitt, John & Abordene, Patricia. *Megatrends 2000*

Goodman, Jordan Elliot & Downes, John. *The Dictionary of Finance and Investment Terms*

Holmes, Steven A. "Fannie Mae Eases Credit to Aid Mortgage Lending", *New York Times*, September 30, 1999

Investopedia, "Liars Loans"

MyFoxPhoenix.com

Chapter 6

Buckler, William. *The Privateer*, June 2010

Walker, David M. *Comeback America*

U.S. Census Bureau. Government Employment and Payroll Historical data

U.S. Census Bureau. All Races by Median and Mean Income

Lone Star College – Kingwood. "American Cultural History - The Twentieth Century"

Bureau of Labor Statistics. International Comparisons of Annual Labor Force Statistics, 10 Countries, 1960–2007

REFERENCES

"Cash for golf carts – Cash for Clubbers", *Wall Street Journal*, October 17, 2009

Mosquera, Jim. "Cash for clunkers", *Examiner.com*, August 8, 2009

Mosquera, Jim. "Cash for clunkers economic analysis", *Examiner.com*, September 16, 2009

Chapter 7

Creditscoring.com

Capone, Jr. Ph.D, Charles A. "Research Into Mortgage Default and Affordable Housing: A Primer", Microeconomic and Financial Studies Division U.S. Congressional Budget Office Washington, DC

Walker, David M. *Comeback America*

Historical Tables, Budget of U.S. Government, Office of Management and Budget

Borrus, Amy, McNamee, Mike, Timmons, Heather. "The Credit-Raters: How They Work And How They Might Work Better", *Business Week*, April 8, 2002

"Ratings for a country - Will Financial Reform Negatively Bias U.S. Sovereign Credit Ratings", *Thoughtsworththinking.net*, May 21, 2010

FCIC web site, FCIC opening remarks, June 2, 2010

CSPAN, Warren Buffett testifies before Financial Crisis Inquiry Commission, June 2, 2010

"The Federal Government's Financial Health A Citizen's Guide to the Financial Report of the United States Government", *Whitehouse.gov*

Crawshaw, Julie. "Rogoff: U.S. Has Defaulted Before, May Do So Again", *Moneynews.com*, March 5, 2010

Reinhart & Rogoff. *This Time is Different*

Standard & Poors, Sovereign ratings

"The World's Biggest Debtor Nations", *CNBC presentation*

Chapter 8

Mulligan, Thomas S. "Beanie Babies" *Los Angeles Times* as printed in *Seattle Times*, August 31, 2004

"South Sea Bubble", *Wikipedia.org*

Mosquera, Jim. "Economy and speculative bubbles", *Examiner.com*, August 4, 2009

Mackay, Charles. *Extraordinary Popular Delusions and the Madness of Crowds*

"Highlighting Recent FBI Ponzi Scheme Investigations", Federal Bureau of Investigation, April 1, 2009

Goodman, Jordan Elliot & Downes, John. *The Dictionary of Finance and Investment Terms*

Reinhart & Rogoff. *This Time is Different*

Desmond, Robert. "Newspaper Reference Methods", University of Minnesota

Chapter 9

U.S. Census Bureau, Census of Housing, Census figures showing home ownership in US

U.S. Census Bureau, 2010 Statistical Abstract

Mosquera, Jim. *The Sentinel Economic and Financial Newsletter, Volume 1 Issue 2*

Federal Deposit Insurance Corporation for deposit insurance

REFERENCES

Parker & Prechter. "The Financial/Economic Dichotomy in Social Behavioral Dynamics: The Socionomic Perspective", *Journal of Behavioral Finance*, Volume 8 Issue 2

Mosquera, Jim. "Stock market fall predictable", *Examiner.com*, May 6, 2010

Chapter 10

Emergency Banking Relief Act of 1933

Reinhart & Rogoff. *This Time is Different*

Watts, C.M. "FDIC: Banks Operating at 79% Loan-to-Deposit Ratio", *Mortgage News Daily*

Federal Deposit Insurance Corporation, "Section 109 Host State Loan-to-Deposit Ratios"

Prechter Jr., Robert R. *Conquer the Crash*

"Farming in the 1930s – Bank Failures", Wessels Living History Farm

Prechter Jr. , Robert R. *Elliott Wave Theorist*, November 2009

Federal Deposit Insurance Corporation, "Bank failures in brief"

Federal Deposit Insurance Corporation, "Failed bank list"

Federal Deposit Insurance Corporation, "Riegle-Neal Interstate Banking and Branching Efficiency Act of 1994"

Federal Deposit Insurance Corporation / Office of Thrift Supervision, 2004 Summary of Deposits

Federal Reserve Bank of St. Louis (FRED)

Streitfeld, David. "Some not worrying about paying mortgage", *New York Times*

Veribanc Blue Bank Report, September 2008

Kendall & Hochberg. *Elliott Wave Financial Forecast*, August 2010.

Chapter 11

Metropolitan Life, "The 2010 MetLife Study on the American Dream"

Simon, Ruth & Hagerty, James. "One in Four Borrowers is Under Water", *Wall Street Journal*, November 24, 2009

Ritholtz, Barry. "Alone in 32 Story Condo: How Did This Mortgage Close?", *Ritholtz.com*

Donsky, Paul. "Volume of 'subdivision' vacant lots overwhelms banks", *The Atlanta Journal-Constitution*

T2 Partners presentation on the mortgage crisis, "An Overview of the Housing/Credit Crisis and Why There is More Pain to Come", April 3, 2009

Mosquera, Jim. *The Sentinel Economic and Financial Newsletter, Volume 1 Issue 12*

Jona, Ilaina. "US shopping center vacancies hit records – report", Reuters, Jan 6, 2010, Securities Industry and Financial Markets Association

Shenn, Jody. "Housing Crash to Resume on 7 Million Foreclosures, Amherst Says", *Bloomberg*, September 23, 2009

Weaver, Karen & Shen, Ying. "Drowning in Debt – A Look at Underwater Homeowners", Deutsche Bank, Securitization Reports, August 2009

Agencies. "Burj Khalifa flats' rent crashes", *MSN India*, October 25, 2010

Ch 12

Economic Research, Federal Reserve Bank of St. Louis

Boyd, Donald & Dadayan, Lucy. "State Tax Decline in Early 2009 Was the Sharpest on Record", Nelson A. Rockefeller Institute on Government

REFERENCES

Mosquera, Jim. "Latest job report an illusion", *Examiner.com*, June 8, 2010

Lubin, Gus. "10 States Where an Absurd Percentage of Population Works for Government", *Business Insider*

Rosenberg, Stan. "Controller Says Harrisburg, Penn., May Default", *Wall Street Journal*

Varghese, Romy. "Harrisburg Defaults as Localities Struggle", *Wall Street Journal*

Lisanti, Joseph. "Build America Bonds", *NY Daily News*, November 22, 2009

Goodman, Jordan Elliot & Downes, John. *The Dictionary of Finance and Investment Terms*

Ch 13

Investment Company Institute 2010 Fact Book

Smith, Ted. "The Vanishing Economy: TV Coverage of Economic Affairs 1982-1987", VCU

Precther Jr., Robert R. *Elliott Wave Theorist*, July 2009

Precther Jr., Robert R. *Elliott Wave Theorist*, April 2010

Arnott, Robert & Asness, Clifford. "Does Dividend Policy Foretell Earnings Growth?", Social Science Research Network

Eaton Vance Investment Managers, "The Dividend Story"

Goodman, Jordan Elliot & Downes, John. *The Dictionary of Finance and Investment Terms*

Indexarb.com (dividend yields)

Prechter, Robert. *Conquer the Crash*

Smallinvestors.com, Cash holdings by stock mutual funds

Standard & Poors Index Services

Arends, Brett. "The biggest lie about U.S. companies", *Marketwatch*, August 3, 2010.

Ch 14

Investment Company Institute 2010 Fact Book

Prechter, Robert. *Conquer the Crash*

Ch 15

Mosquera, Jim. *The Sentinel Economic and Financial Newsletter, Volume 1 Issue 1*

Goldmoney.com

Ch 16

Yahoo Finance

Ch 17

Taleb, Nassim. *Black Swan*

Goodman, Jordan Elliot & Downes, John. *The Dictionary of Finance and Investment Terms*

Appendix A

Mosquera, Jim. *The Sentinel Economic and Financial Newsletter - Inflation Supplement*

Appendix B

Mosquera, Jim. "Economy and speculative bubbles", *Examiner.com*, August 4, 2009

Appendix C

Mosquera, Jim. *The Sentinel Economic and Financial Newsletter, Volume 1 Issue 2*

Appendix D

Mosquera, Jim. *The Sentinel Economic and Financial Newsletter, various*

Acknowledgements

Writing this book was difficult if for no other reason than I had never written one. Compounding the difficulty was the "other" job I have that pays the bills. Given these realities, undoubtedly those close to me had to make some sacrifices. I would like to thank my wife, Alice, for her editing work and photography. I would also like to thank my son, Jared for having the patience to deal with a father so absorbed in his "manuscript".

I sincerely hope this book provides readers the knowledge necessary to right their own finances. Perhaps more importantly, getting your own financial house in order will allow you to see what needs to be done at a national level. The problems outlined in this book will only get worse without proper action.

About the Author

Jim Mosquera has degrees in Industrial Engineering with a Master's emphasis on Operations Research. His collegiate research involved the computer simulation of real-world systems such as vehicular traffic flows and surgical scheduling environments. After college, he entered the field of voice and data communications where over the last twenty years he has had responsibilities in engineering, sales support, training delivery and product development. In 2002, Mr. Mosquera was awarded a patent for a business application that provided labor quotation for the installation of telecommunications projects. Mr. Mosquera has also developed software for commodity futures and options trading.

Mr. Mosquera operates the economic and financial web site called The Sentinel (www.TheSentinel.biz). He may be contacted through the email address, jim@thesentinel.biz. He is also a contributor to various online publications.

During his leisure time, he likes to exercise and support his local sports teams like the St. Louis Cardinals.

6733140R0

Made in the USA
Charleston, SC
01 December 2010